A BRIEF HIS
ANCIENT

BY

JAMES HENRY BREASTED, Ph.D., LL.D.
PROFESSOR OF ORIENTAL HISTORY AND EGYPTOLOGY
IN THE UNIVERSITY OF CHICAGO

ABRIDGED AND EDITED FROM THE
AUTHOR'S "ANCIENT TIMES"

BY

W. HUGHES JONES
EDUCATION OFFICER, ROYAL AIR FORCE

WITH A FOREWORD

BY

F. S. MARVIN

Published 2003
Lost Arts Media
Long Beach, CA

GINN AND COMPANY LTD.,

All rights reserved

1927

Printed on Acid-Free Paper

**A Brief History of Ancient Times
by James Henry Breasted
ISBN 1-59016-083-5**

©2003
LOST ARTS MEDIA
All Rights Reserved

Published by
LOST ARTS MEDIA
P.O. Box 15026
Long Beach, CA
VISIT WWW.LOSTARTSMEDIA.COM OR CALL
1 (800) 952-LOST FOR OUR FREE CATALOG

LOST ARTS MEDIA publishes, markets and distributes a variety of products and services. Our mission it to provide fascinating and educational books, videos and mutlimedia products to help inform, enlighten and inspire humanity at large. We specialize in bringing rare and classic books back into print. We are also involved in document research, video production, e-books, DVD authoring, broadcasting, screenwriting, conference promotion, online services, amongst many other creative endeavors. We carry Books, Booklets, Audio, CD, Video, DVD, Music, Multimedia and other products on Acting and Cinematography, Alchemy, Alternative Medicine, American History, Ancient America, Ancient Astronauts, Ancient Civilizations, Ancient History, Ancient Mysteries, Ancient Religion and Worship, Angels, Anthropology, Anti-Gravity, Archaeology, Apocrypha, Area 51, Astrology, Astronomy, Astro-Physics, Atlantis, Biblical Studies, Biology, Books on Books, Townsend Brown, Buddhism, Children's Books, Cold Fusion, Colloidal Silver, Comparative Religions, Cooking and Household, Coursework and Study Guides, Craftwork and Hobbies, Crop Circles, Dictionaries and Reference, Early History, Education and Schooling, Electromagnetics, Electro-Gravity, Egyptian History, Electromagnetic Smog, Entertainment, European History, Famous People, Michael Faraday, FBI Files Revealed, The Federal Reserve, Fluoride, Folklore and Mythology, the Freedom of Information Act, Free Energy, Freemasonry, Furniture and Decorating, Games, General History, Geology and Minerals, Ghosts, Global Manipulation, Gnosticism, Gravity and Gravity Waves, Greek History, Gyroscopic Anti-Gravity, Healing Electromagnetics, Health and Nutrition, Health Issues, Hermetic Studies, the Hidden History of Holidays, History of the Americas, HIV, Human Origins, Humor, John Keely, Knights Templar, Lost Cities, Lost Continents, Medieval History, Mercury Poisoning, Mesopotamian History, Mesopotamian Religion, Metaphysics, Mithraic Studies, Money and Business, Music Studies, Natural History, Novelty Books, Occultism, Oriental Philosophy, Painting and Drawing, Paganism, Paleontology and Prehistoric World, Paradigm Politics, the Paranormal, Pesticide Pollution, Personal Growth, Phallicism, The Philadelphia Experiment, Philosophy, Physics, Powerlines, Prophecy, Psychic Phenomena, Pyramids, Questions and Answers, Quotations, Rare Books, Religion, Remote Viewing, Roman History, Roswell, Walter Russell, Sasquatch, Scalar Waves, Science and Technology, SDI, John Searle, Secret Societies, Sex Worship, Short Stories, Sitchin Studies, Smart Cards, Solar Power, Song Books, Sovereignty, Space Travel, Spiritualism, Spirituality, Sports and Athletics, Stage Magic and Tricks, Stonehenge, Story of Language, Sumeria, Sun Myths, Symbolism, Tachyon Fields, Nikola Tesla, Theater and Drama, Theology, Time Travel, Translations from the Past, Travel and Adventure, The Treasury, UFOs, Underground Bases, Vedic Philosophy, World Control, The World Grid, World History, Writing and Authorship, Yoga, Zero Point Energy and so much more. Call 1 (800) 952-LOST or 1 (562) 596-ARTS or write for our free catalog.

INTRODUCTION

From the smallest of atoms to the grandest of galaxies, everything in the universe has its history. The known history of civilized peoples on this planet is no different, and yet each of us can touch no more than the smallest part of it. It is through books such as this one, which cover a comprehensive span of our history, that we are able to acquaint ourselves with the great, and some not so great, civilizations that preceded our own. From the early stone age, the great civilizations of Babylonia and Sumeria, the era of pyramid building, and the Hebrew and Persian empires, to the better-known republics of the Greeks and Romans, these advanced cultures helped to provide a basic understanding of who we are as a species.

The varied ways in which these previous cultures have influenced successive descendants is nearly unlimited. The earliest of civilized man brought us an understanding of fire and manufactured tools. From these early beginnings, the more advanced cultures, which began our recorded history, have contributed greatly to our society. For example, the first recorded civilization on earth, the Sumerians, provided the basis for our modern-day writing, agriculture, astronomy, mathematics, calendar, numeral system, time reckoning, educational institutions, our code of laws, construction trades, metallurgy, art, and religion. They were the masters of invention, science, industry, and exploration, which is important because all that we have, and are, came from these sources.

Our predecessors have helped us become a master of nature and to extend our physical abilities beyond the norm. We can only hope that the achievements and advancement of knowledge will be duly recorded for future generations and for the future of mankind. As a professor of Oriental History and Egyptology at the University of Chicago in the 1920s, Professor James Henry Breasted provides a qualified historical perspective and a sound account of the achievements of Western civilization. This book was skillfully written from the author's vast wisdom and scholarship of the nations of the world. In the past, the teaching of history has often lacked both the scope and comprehensiveness that this small volume offers. For this reason, this book will make a fine addition to any library on ancient history.

Tédd St. Rain

FOREWORD

We are now all agreed as to the necessity of studying History, and the growing stream of historical books, the increasing number of students at the universities, the provision of specialist teachers at all large schools, show that the agreement is taking practical shape.

But when we come to the question, "What sort of History should be studied?", agreement is more difficult, seeing that everything in the Universe has its history, and that no living student, least of all young people at school, can touch more than the smallest part of it. Yet even here the right lines of limitation are becoming clearer, by considering what is the dominant purpose which we should have in view in undertaking the study either for ourselves or for the education of others. It must be to understand our position in the civilized community to which we belong, what has led up to it, what use it is to us or we to it, what hopes it offers for the future, based on the past.

In short, civilization as a whole must be the master-thought, but to say this by no means relegates to the background the political side of History which has figured so largely in the teaching of the past. The community, whether it be the nation, or the Empire, or Western Europe, or even the confederation of peoples in the League of Nations, has a political framework which it is imperative to realize. No view of History, especially for educational ends, can avoid putting the State—its growth and functions—in a leading place. But other sides of man's activity must find their place also, for we live a social life and enjoy our powers through a host of other things that our forefathers have done for us besides founding an orderly and legal government.

They developed speech and the means of handing on the records of their thought to their successors. They learnt how to make and conquer fire, and elaborated the endless range of tools from the first wheel to the aeroplane, from the flint-axe to the steam-hammer, which have extended man's physical powers and made him the growing master of Nature. They expressed their ideal in forms of beauty with all the varied material which Nature could supply. Art, Science, Industry, Invention, and Exploration must therefore all find some recognition, side by side with State-building, or politics, in the story of mankind.

This *Brief History of Ancient Times* aims at supplying the indispensable foundation of this knowledge for Western peoples who have derived their culture from the Middle East,—from Egypt and Babylonia, through Greece and Rome. It is indispensable, because all we have, or are, comes from these sources and from further back, and Western Civilization, which has thus been made, and to which we belong, has been now for many generations the dominating force in the world. In spite of the internal conflicts which it is now overcoming, in spite, too, of the external animosity and jealousy which are at the moment unusually active, it shows no serious sign of yielding ground. Accommodated, as it doubtless will be, to other cultures and other climes, it will pursue its way, and we may well feel confident, and serious, that by the process of History we have had transmitted to us in the West the best hopes for the future of mankind.

There is probably no man living who is better qualified to give a sound account of this historical preparation for Western Civilization than Professor Breasted. He is a profound and original student of a large and most important part of it, and he approaches the whole in the spirit of progress, based on solid achievements in the past. The book has been clearly and skilfully condensed from Professor Breasted's larger works, and contains what is both possible and necessary for scholars to master before they go on to the more detailed study of their own and other nations in the modern world.

It is matter of common knowledge and regret that History teaching in the past has so often lacked both the background and the breadth of view that such a work as this is exactly calculated to supply.

F. S. MARVIN.

CONTENTS

PART I

EARLY MANKIND IN EUROPE

CHAP.		PAGE
I.	THE EARLY AND MIDDLE STONE AGES	9
II.	THE LATE STONE AGE	20

PART II

EGYPT

III.	BEFORE THE PYRAMIDS	31
IV.	THE PYRAMID AGE	45
V.	THE FEUDAL AGE AND THE EMPIRE	61

PART III

BABYLONIA AND ASSYRIA

VI.	THE SUMERIANS	75
VII.	BABYLONIA	91
VIII.	ASSYRIA	102

PART IV

PERSIA: PALESTINE

IX.	THE PERSIANS AND THE HEBREWS	115

PART V
GREECE

CHAP.		PAGE
X.	The Civilization of Crete	142
XI.	The Greeks	153
XII.	The Age of the Tyrants	170
XIII.	Fifth-Century Athens	187
XIV.	The Hellenistic Age	216

PART VI
ROME

XV.	The Kingdom of Rome	235
XVI.	The Republic of Rome	244
XVII.	The Roman Empire	279

A BRIEF HISTORY OF
ANCIENT TIMES

COLUMNS IN THE GREAT HALL OF KARNAK

A BRIEF HISTORY OF ANCIENT TIMES

PART I

EARLY MANKIND IN EUROPE

CHAPTER I

THE EARLY AND MIDDLE STONE AGES

1. FIRE

IF we go back far enough in the story of man, we reach a time when he had nothing whatever but his hands with which to protect himself, satisfy his hunger, and meet all his other needs. He must have been without speech and unable even to build a fire. There was no one to teach him anything. The earliest men had to learn everything for themselves by slow experience, and every tool, however simple, had to be invented. After several hundred thousand years the earliest men of Europe made certain discoveries that enable us to learn something about them. We find that early in this progress man could kindle a fire, and later we find that he could make useful weapons and tools out of stone. When man learned to shape stone to suit his needs and thus to make a rough tool or weapon, he entered into what we now call the Stone Ages. The Stone Ages began in Europe at least fifty thousand years ago, and probably earlier.

We learn about the Stone Ages in two ways: (1) by searching for things made by the Stone Age people, such as tools, weapons, and other articles shaped by their hands; (2) by studying the customs and habits of modern savage races, such as the native Tasmanians (now extinct), Australians, and New Zealanders, who, when they were first discovered by us, were still living

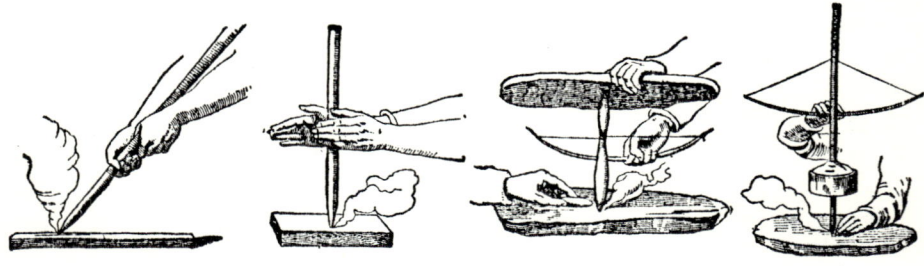

METHODS OF FIRE LIGHTING

a Stone Age kind of life and using Stone Age weapons and tools. By using these two methods of study together we can reach conclusions concerning early man and his mode of life in the Stone Ages many thousands of years ago.

The first thing we find is that man had very early learned to control one of the most powerful forces in nature, namely *fire*. How do we know this? First, on examining the places where Stone Age man had lived, we find clear traces of fire having been used. Secondly, by studying the modern backward races we find not a single people without the use of fire. How, then, did the Stone Age men light their fires? The answer is that without doubt they used similar methods

The Early and Middle Stone Ages

to those of modern backward people. The preceding diagram shows some of these methods.

In the sketch on the left of the picture we see fire being produced by holding a stick firmly in the hands and by moving the point of it back and forth in a groove shaped in a larger piece of wood. The second sketch shows a better way. A round stick is twirled round by moving the hands to and fro, and after a time the point of the stick causes enough heat at the pointed tip to make a spark. The third sketch shows a still better way, invented very much later. The stick that twirls round is held firmly in position by means of a piece of wood pressing on it from above. The thong of

Modern Australian Native lighting a Fire

the bow is made to pass round the middle of the stick, and the turning movement is produced by moving the bow forward and backward with the right hand. The cleverest method of all is shown in the fourth sketch. It is the drill-borer, the idea of which is in use in workshops of the present day. Two thongs are attached to the bow. The ends are fastened to the top of the stick and the thongs are wound round the stick. It is necessary only to move the bow up and down to make the stick turn backward and forward.

The illustration on page 11 gives us a view of one of the more simple methods of fire-making. Man having made this discovery of the control of fire could then cook his food, warm his body, and harden the tip of a wooden stick in the fire, thus making a useful spear.

2. FLINT-WORKING

The Stone Ages are divided into three parts: the Early Stone Age, the Middle Stone Age, and the Late Stone Age. These divisions are made because each age shows some marked progress, especially in the way the Stone Age men prepared flints for use as weapons and tools. Let us look at the picture of North American Indians making flint weapons. The farthest Indian is loosening a large flint stone in the ground. This is taken by the middle Indian, who crashes it down upon a rock and breaks it into small pieces. One of these pieces is then taken by the nearest Indian, who holds it

A GROUP OF NORTH AMERICAN INDIANS MAKING FLINT WEAPONS (After Holmes)

The Early and Middle Stone Ages

in his left hand while he strikes it with a stone in his right hand. These blows chip off pieces of flint, and the Indian is so skilful that he can thus shape a flint hatchet. This process of shaping flint *by blows* was the earliest method used by man, and produced the roughest stone tools. In the course of thousands of years two improvements followed: chipping the edge by *pressure*, and sharpening the edge by *grinding*. It is this difference in making a sharp edge on the stone tools that helps us to divide the Stone Ages into the three parts given above. The Early Stone men used the blow method to produce an edged tool. The Middle Stone men used the pressure method, and the Late Stone men made their axe edges sharp by means of the grindstone.

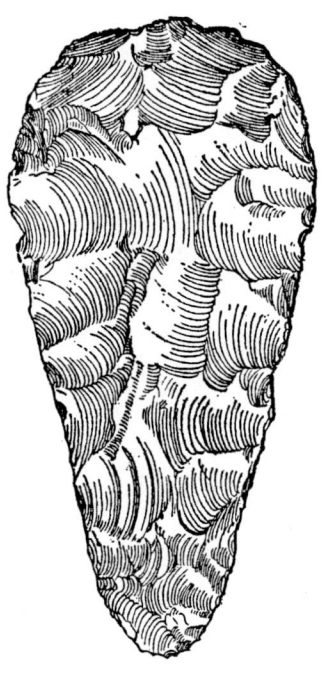

A Flint Fist-hatchet of the Early Stone Age

3. The Fist Hatchet

The fist hatchet is the earliest well-finished type of tool made by man, though rough flint flakes older than the fist hatchet have been found which show us man's earliest efforts at shaping stone.

The men of the Early Stone Age used the fist hatchet for almost everything. Either end might be used as a cutting edge, but it was usually held in the fist by the narrower part, and had no handle. It was from eight to ten inches long, and sharp enough for man to cut the roots and branches he wanted for food, to shape his fire-making tools, and to hew out his heavy wooden club. These fist hatchets have been found in many places in Europe as well as in other parts of the world.

We do not know much about the Early Stone Age man, but he must have slowly improved his rough stone hatchet, and he probably learned to make other tools of wood, though these have of course rotted away and perished, so that we know nothing of them. Single-handed he made war upon all animals. There was not a beast that was not his foe. There was as yet no dog, no sheep or fowl, to which he might stretch out a kindly hand. The ancestor of the modern dog was then either the jackal or the fierce wolf. The beasts which were the ancestors of our modern domestic animals were either not yet in existence in Europe or, like the horse, wandered in the forests in a wild state.

4. The Middle Stone Age

Towards the end of the Early Stone Age the climate in Europe became colder, and as time passed, the ice, which all the year round still overlies the region of the North Pole and the summits of the Alps, began to descend. The northern ice crept farther and farther southward until it covered England as far south as the Thames, and Europe almost to Switzerland. The glaciers of the Alps moved down the Rhone Valley as far as the spot where Lyons now stands. This great change ended the Early Stone Age. The map shows us how far the ice stretched over Europe.

The coming of the ice brought with it a new period

The Early and Middle Stone Ages

of progress, that of the Middle Stone Age. Unable to build himself a shelter from the cold of the Ice Age, the hunter took refuge in the limestone caves, where he and his descendants continued to live for thousands of years. We can imagine him at the door of his cave, carefully chipping off the edge of his flint tools. He has left the rude old flint hatchet far behind, for the

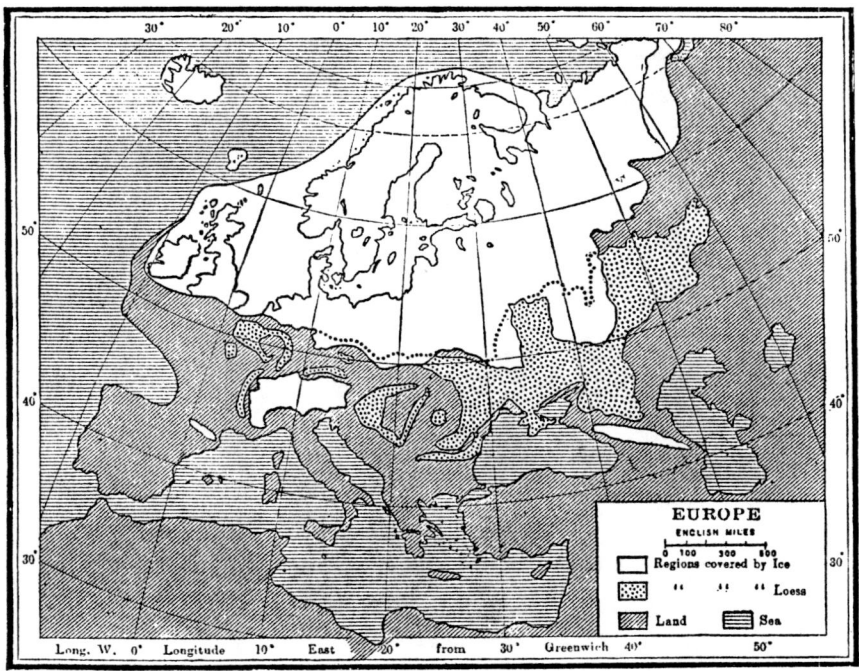

hunter has now found a way of making a much sharper cutting edge than by chipping with blows as was formerly done. The discovery enabled him to produce a great variety of flint tools, many of which can be seen in the diagram overleaf. From right to left they include knives, spear and arrow points, scrapers, drills, and various edged tools.

These tools show great skill in the making. The fine edges have been produced by chipping off a line of flakes along the margin, seen especially in the long piece on the right of the picture. This chipping was done by *pressure*. Flint is so brittle that if a hard piece of bone is pressed firmly against a flint edge, a flake of flint, often reaching far back from the edge, will snap off. This was a great improvement over the earlier method of producing an edge by the process of striking.

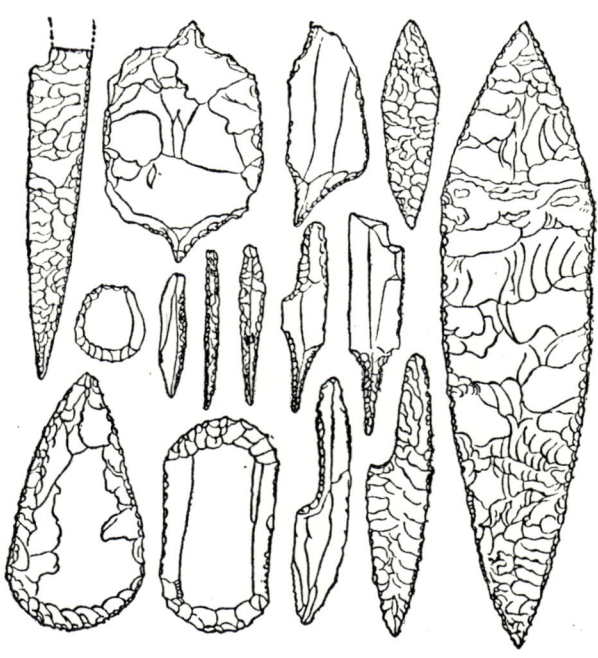

FLINT TOOLS AND WEAPONS OF THE MIDDLE STONE AGE

With these new and better weapons the hunter of the Middle Stone Age was a much more dangerous foe of the wild creatures than were his ancestors of the Early Stone Age.

In a single cavern in Sicily there have been dug up the bones of no less than two thousand hippopotamuses which these Middle Stone Age hunters killed. In France one group of such men slew so many wild

The Early and Middle Stone Ages

horses for food that the bones which they tossed about their camp fires gathered in masses, forming a layer in some places six feet thick and covering a space of fifty by two hundred feet.

5. BONE, IVORY, AND ART

The new pressure-chipped tools made by the Middle Stone Age men were sharp enough to cut and shape bone, ivory, and especially reindeer horn. With his new and sharper tools the hunter made barbed ivory

MODERN ESKIMO NATIVE HURLING A SPEAR WITH A THROWING-STICK

spear-points, which he mounted on long wooden shafts. He also discovered how to make and use the bow and arrow, and he carried at his girdle a sharp flint dagger. For straightening his wooden spear-shafts and arrows he invented a shaft-straightener of reindeer horn. Another clever device of horn or ivory was his new throwing-stick, by means of which he could throw his long spear much farther and with greater power than he could before. This device is used to-day by the Eskimo.

The spear lies in a groove in the throwing-stick (*a*), which the hunter grasps at one end. At the outer end (*b*) of the throwing-stick is a hook against which the butt of the spear lies, and as the hunter throws forward his arm, holding on to the throwing-stick in his hand and allowing the spear to go, the throwing-stick acts as though the arm were stretched out to a greater length, giving great sweep and power as the spear is thrown. Modern schoolboys would not find it hard to make and use such a throwing-stick.

Some of the most interesting discoveries of this time are the fine ivory needles which are found still surviving in the rubbish in the French caverns where the wives of the prehistoric hunters lost them and failed to find them twenty thousand years ago. Their

IVORY NEEDLE OF THE MIDDLE STONE AGE

great importance to us is that they show that these women were already sewing together the skins of wild animals as clothing.

It is surprising to find that these Middle Stone Age hunters could carve, draw, and even paint with great skill. A Spanish nobleman exploring a cavern on his estate in northern Spain was at the time digging among the heap of rubbish on the floor of the cave, where he found flint and bone tools, when his little daughter, who was playing about in the gloom of the cavern, suddenly shouted, " Toros ! Toros ! " (" Bulls ! Bulls ! "). At the same time she pointed to the ceiling. The startled father, looking up, saw a wonderful sight. In a long line stretching far across the ceiling of the cavern was a huge procession of bison bulls painted in bright colours on the rock. For at least

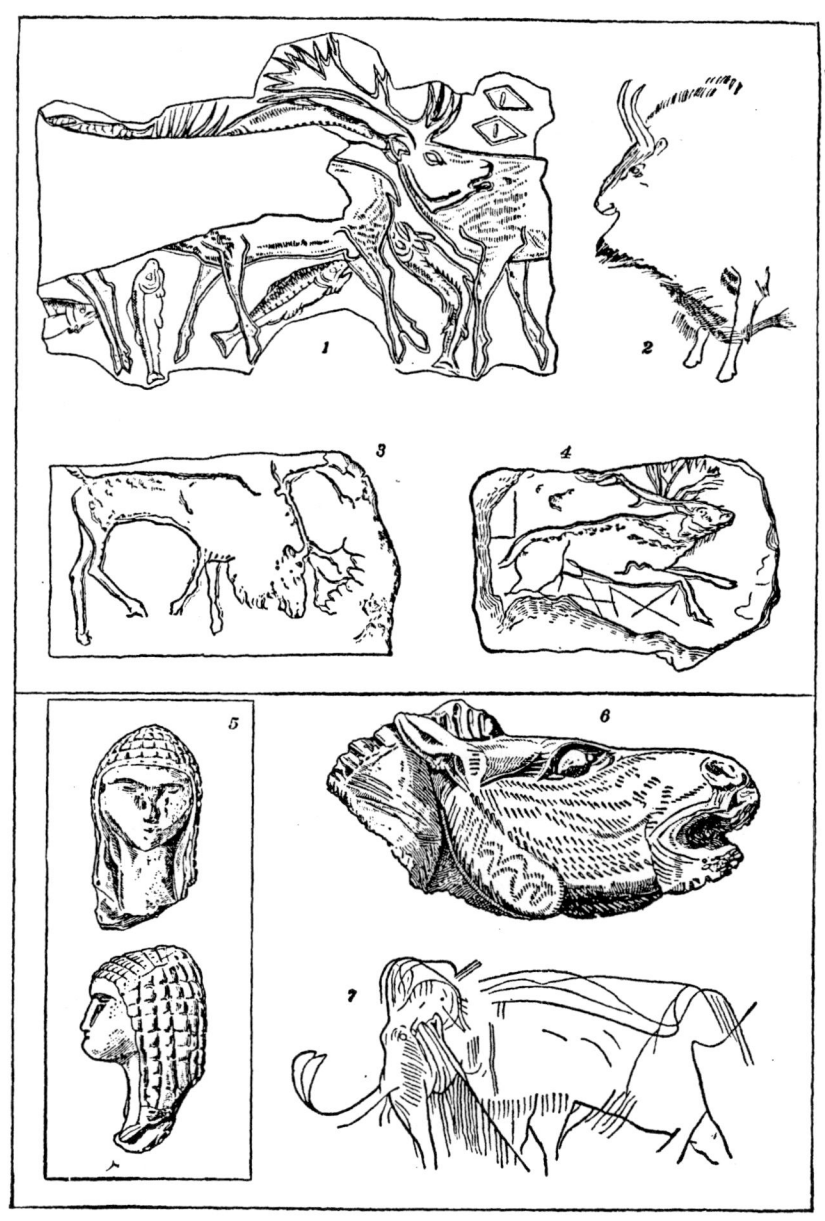

CARVINGS IN IVORY (1 AND 3-7) AND IN STONE OF CAVERN WALLS (2), MADE BY THE HUNTERS OF THE MIDDLE STONE AGE

ten thousand years no human eye had seen these cave paintings of a vanished race of prehistoric men, till the eye of a child rediscovered them.

The preceding diagram shows some examples of this art of the caves. Note how vigorously well done is the bison bull at bay and facing his enemy (No. 2). Note also the difference in action between the grazing deer (No. 3) and the running deer (No. 4). See also how the artist has caught the tense expression of the wild horse's head as he neighs (No. 6), and how the long hair of the mammoth is suggested by means of a few clever lines (No. 7).

CHAPTER II

THE LATE STONE AGE

6. GRINDING AND POLISHING

WE now come to the Late Stone Age. The men of this period made the great discovery that the edge of a stone tool could be ground upon a whetstone just as we grind a steel tool at the present day. In certain old shell heaps of Denmark we find the earliest heavy stone axes with a ground edge. They made the man of the Late Stone Age much better able to control the world about him. His list of tools as he went about his work was almost as large as that of the modern carpenter. Besides the axe, he had chisels, knives, drills, saws, and whetstones, made mostly of flint, but sometimes of other hard stones. Our ancient worker has now learned to attach a wooden handle by lashings around the axe head, or even to bore a hole in the axe head and insert a handle. These tools as found to-day often show a polish due to the wear which they have had in the hands of the user.

It is a mistake to suppose that such stone tools were not very useful to man. A recent experiment in Denmark has shown that a modern worker with a stone axe was able in ten working hours to cut down and make into logs twenty-six pine trees eight inches thick.

LAKE VILLAGE (Restoration)

Indeed the entire work of getting out the timber and building a house was done by one workman with stone tools in eighty-one days. It was therefore quite possible for the men of the Late Stone Age to build houses and to live a life much more comfortable than that of savages.

Many traces of the earliest wooden houses are to be found in Switzerland. Here the house-building people of the Late Stone Age, wishing to make themselves safer from attack from man and beast, built their villages out over the Swiss lakes. These lake-dwellers cut down trees with their stone axes and made them into piles some twenty feet long, sharpened at the lower end. These they drove several feet into the bottom of the lake in water eight or ten feet deep. On a platform supported by these piles they built their houses. The platform was connected with the shore by a bridge. A part of it could be removed at night for protection. The fish nets drying on the rail, the

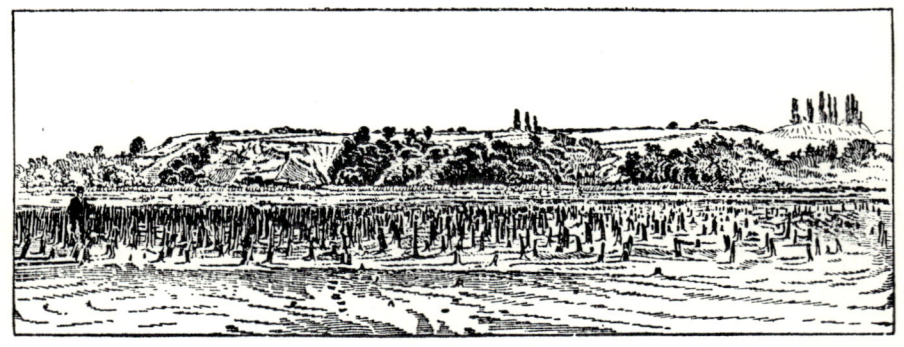

SURVIVING REMAINS OF A SWISS LAKE VILLAGE

"dug-out" boat of the hunters who bring in the deer, and many other things have been found on the lake bottom in recent times in Switzerland.

At Wangen, in Switzerland, as many as fifty thousand piles were driven by the Late Stone Age builders into the bottom of the lake for the support of the village. The above illustration shows these remains, which were found after a very dry season when the Swiss lakes fell to a low level in 1854.

The Late Stone Age

7. Pottery and Spinning

These lake-dwellers seem to have lived a life of peace and prosperity. Their houses were comfortable shelters, and they were furnished with wooden furniture and implements, and with wooden pitchers and spoons. And they had some new things, such as dishes, bowls, and jars made of pottery. Although roughly made without the use of the potter's wheel, and unevenly

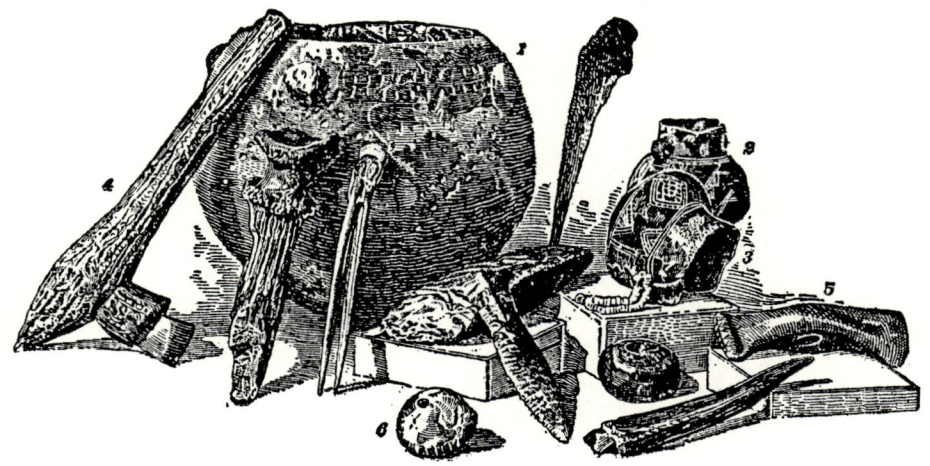

LATE STONE AGE PROSPERITY

baked without an oven, these pottery vessels were very useful, and such vessels have been used by man ever since.

The picture on this page shows how much better things were made by the Late Stone Age men than was the rude stone hatchet of the Early Stone Age people. This group shows three important inventions made or received by the men of the Late Stone Age: (1) Pottery jars, like Nos. 2 and 3, with rough decorations, the oldest baked clay in Europe, and (No. 1) a large kettle in which the lake-dwellers' food was cooked. (2) *Ground*-edged tools, like No. 4, a stone chisel with a ground edge mounted in a deer-horn handle like a hatchet. Also No. 5, a stone axe with a ground edge, and pierced with a hole for the axe handle. The lake houses were built with such tools. (3) Weaving, as shown by No. 6, a spinning-whorl of baked clay, the earliest spinning-wheel. When hung by a rough thread of flax eighteen to twenty inches long it was given a whirl which made it spin in the air like a top, thus rapidly twisting the thread by which it was hanging. The thread when twisted enough was wound up, and another length of eighteen to twenty inches was drawn out of the unspun flax to be twisted in the same way. One of these earliest spinning-wheels has been found in the Swiss lakes with a reel of flaxen thread still attached.

8. Seeds and Animals

While not ceasing to be a hunter and a fisherman, the lake-dweller now discovered other ways of getting food. For thousands of years, while the men hunted, the women of these early ages had gathered the seeds of wild grasses to be crushed between two stones and made into rough cakes. They now gradually learned that they themselves could plant and grow these grasses on the margins of the forest and along the shores of the lake. When they had learned to do this, the women of these lake-dwellers were already farmers. The grains they planted were barley, wheat, and some millet. Oats and rye were still unknown and came into Europe much later. They had no trouble in growing plenty of these new foods; more than a

The Late Stone Age

hundred bushels of grain were found on the lake bottom under the vanished village of Wangen in Switzerland. And up the hill-side there stretched the lake-dwellers' little field of flax beside the growing grain.

Another important thing that the men of the Late Stone Age did was to tame some of the wild animals, especially the dog, the goat, the sheep, cattle, and, later on, the horse. This taming of animals, like the beginnings of farming, made a great difference in the way men lived and the things they did. The hunter had to spend more and more of his time as a farmer and a shepherd. Thus by the end of the Late Stone Age, though they had not completely given up their hunting, men had become either settlers with their fields, farms, and villages, or they had become shepherds and wanderers who followed a roving life, leading their flocks about and pasturing them where the grasslands were too poor for farming. Such shepherd people we call nomads, and they still exist to-day. Without any fixed dwelling-places, accompanied by their wives and children, they led a wandering life, driving their flocks from pasture to pasture. The nomad life always remained more rude and less civilized than that of the settlers, the farmers, and the villagers.

9. Buildings and Towns

The settlers of the Late Stone Age in time began to leave behind them bigger things than pottery and stone tools. In all Europe before this there had existed only frail houses and huts. But towards the close of the Late Stone Age the more powerful leaders of the people learned to erect great tombs, built of enormous blocks of stone. These tombs fringe the western coast of Europe from Spain to the south of Scandinavia. There are to-day no less than 3400 stone tombs of this age on the Danish island of Seeland alone. There are also very many in France and England.

It was in such tombs as this that the dead chiefs

LATE STONE AGE TOMB IN FRANCE

were buried. The stones, weighing even as much as forty tons each, were sometimes dragged many miles from the nearest quarry, but much heavier ones were also used. These blocks were not smoothed but left rough as they came from the mountain side.

Stonehenge is, perhaps, the greatest monument of the Late Stone Age that still exists. It is a large stone circle enclosing a tomb or group of tombs of the Late Stone Age chiefs. The circle is about one hundred feet

The Late Stone Age

STONEHENGE

across, and we can still trace a long avenue connecting it with a Stone Age town. Not far away is a Late Stone Age race-course nearly two miles long. Western Europe produced nothing more than this crude architecture in stone until the coming of the Romans.

Near every group of stone tombs there must have been a town where the people lived who built the tombs. The remains of some of these towns have been discovered, and they have been dug out from the earth covering them. Almost all traces of these have disappeared, but enough remains to show that they had been surrounded by walls of earth, with a ditch on the one side and probably with a wooden stockade along the top of the earth wall. They show us that men were learning to live together in considerable numbers and to work together on a large scale. It required a large number of men working under leaders to raise the earth walls of such a town, to drive down the 50,000 piles supporting the lake settlement at Wangen (Switzerland), or to move the enormous blocks of stone for building the chieftain's tomb.

The memorial stone shown opposite is to be seen in northern France. The vast block once stood upright in one piece, having been erected by the men of the Late Stone Age as a tombstone. It is almost sixty-five feet long, and weighs some three hundred tons.

These towns and these works could not have been built unless men worked together under governors and had some kind of rules or laws. Many little states, each consisting of a fortified town with its surrounding fields and each under a chieftain, must have grown up in Late Stone Age Europe. Out of such beginnings nations were yet to grow.

The Late Stone Age

10. The Next Stage

After fifty thousand years or more of such progress carried on by their own efforts, the men of Stone Age Europe seemed, about 3000 B.C., to have reached a point where they could advance no farther. They were still without *writing* for making records of business, government, and other important matters;

. Fallen Memorial Stone of the Late Stone Age in Northern France

they were still without *metals* with which to make tools and develop trade; and they had no *sailing-ships* in which to carry on commerce. Without these things they could go no farther. All these and many other possessions of civilization came to early Europe from the nearer Orient.

The word Orient is used to-day to include Japan, China, and India. These lands make up a *farther* Orient. There is also a *nearer* Orient, consisting of the lands around the eastern end of the Mediterranean, that is, Egypt and Western Asia, including Asia Minor. We shall use the word " Orient " in this book as the name for the nearer Orient. In order to understand the further course of European history we must turn to the Orient, whence came these most necessary things —writing, metals, and sailing-ships—which made it possible for our European ancestors to gain the civilization *which has come down to us.*

Civilization as we know it in its higher form thus began in the Orient, and it is between five and six thousand years old. There it long flourished and produced great nations, while the men of Late Stone Age Europe continued to live without metals or writing. As they gradually gained these things, leadership in peace and war shifted slowly from the Orient to Europe.

PART II

EGYPT

CHAPTER III

BEFORE THE PYRAMIDS

11. THE николе VALLEY

We are to begin our story of the early Orient in Egypt. The traveller who visits Egypt at the present day lands in a very modern-looking harbour at Alexandria. He is presently seated in a comfortable railway carriage, in which we may accompany him across a low flat country stretching far away to the sunlit horizon. The wide expanse is dotted with little villages of dark mud-brick huts, and here and there rise groves of graceful date palms. The landscape is carpeted with stretches of bright and vivid green as far as the eye can see, and wandering through this growth is a network of irrigation canals. Brown-skinned men of slender build, with dark hair, are seen from time to time along the banks of the canals, swaying up and down as they lift an irrigation bucket attached to a simple device called a *shadoof*.

In this picture of a shadoof the man below stands in the water holding his leather bucket (*A*). The pole (*B*) of the sweep is above him, with a large ball of dried Nile mud on its lower end (*C*) as a lifting weight, seen just behind the supporting post (*D*). This man lifts the water into a mud basin (*E*). A second man (in the middle) lifts it from its first basin (*E*) to a second basin (*F*), into which he is just emptying his bucket; while a third man (*G*) lifts the water from the middle basin (*F*) to the top basin (*H*) on the bank, where it runs off to the left into trenches spreading over the fields. The low water makes necessary three lifts (to *E*, to *F*, to *H*) without ceasing night and day for one hundred days. The irrigation trenches are thus kept full of water until the grain ripens. All this work must be done because Egypt has no rain.

AN EGYPTIAN SHADOOF, THE OLDEST OF WELL SWEEPS, IRRIGATING THE FIELDS

The black soil we see from the train is very fertile, and is made richer each year by the overflow of the river, whose waters rise above its banks in the summer,

Before the Pyramids

spread far over the flats and stand there long enough to deposit a very thin layer of rich earth. This earth has built up the Nile Delta which we are now crossing.

This picture shows the Nile flood as seen from the road to the Pyramids of Gizeh, which lie near the southern end of the Delta. As our train approaches this point we begin to see the heights on either side

THE INUNDATION SEEN FROM THE ROAD TO THE PYRAMIDS OF GIZEH

of the valley into which the narrow end of the Delta merges. These heights are the plateau of the Sahara Desert, through which the Nile has cut a vast deep trench as it winds northward from inner Africa. This trench or valley is seldom more than thirty miles wide, while the strip of soil on each side of the river rarely exceeds ten miles in width. On either edge of the soil strip one steps out of the green fields into the sand of

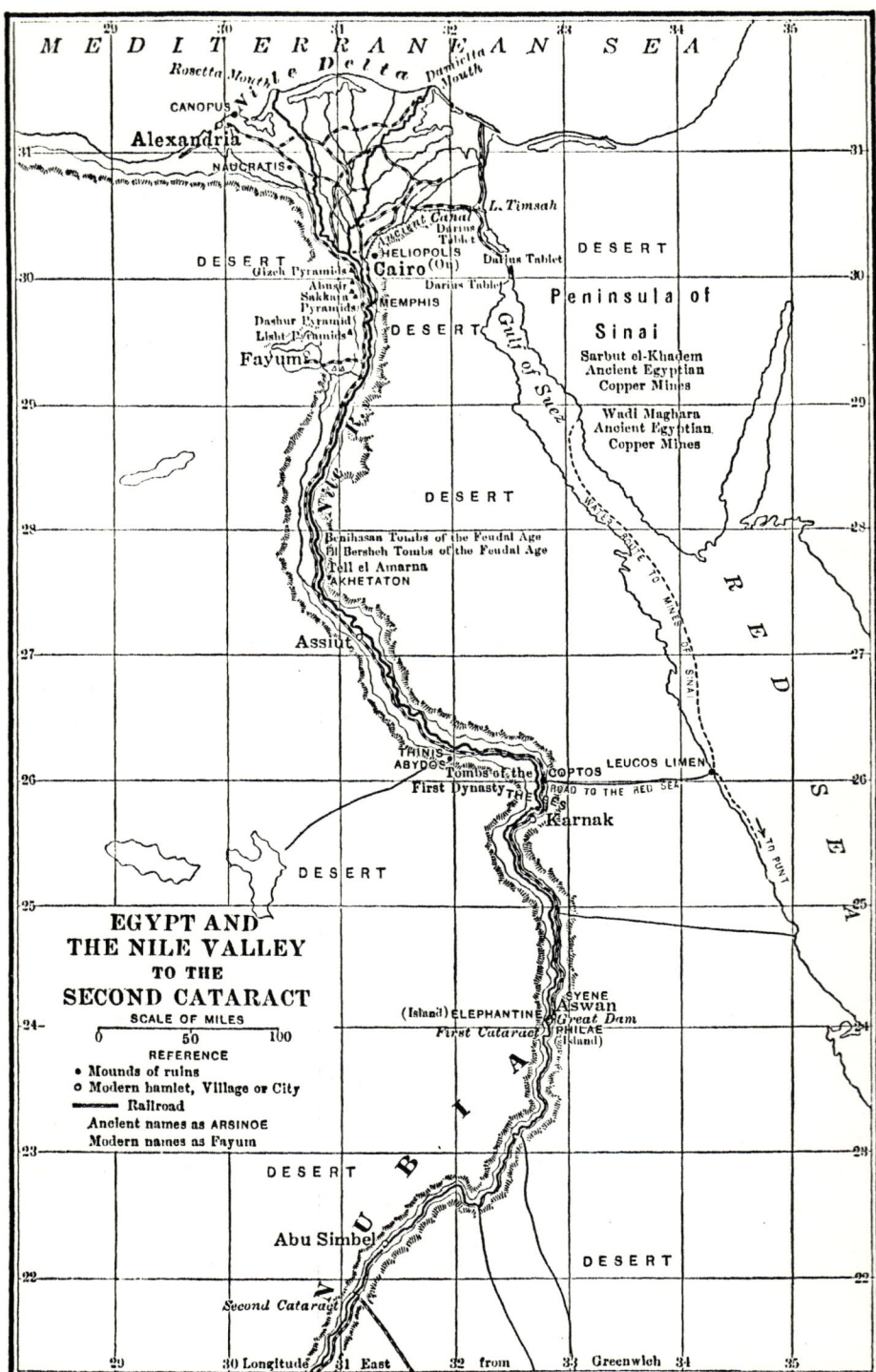

Before the Pyramids

the desert which has drifted down into the trench. Or, if one climbs the cliffs forming the walls of the trench, he stands looking out over a vast waste of rocky hills and stretches of sand trembling in the heat of the blazing sunshine.

As we journey on, let us realize that this valley can tell us an unbroken story of human progress such as we can find nowhere else. We look out upon the sandy margin of the desert, where there are thousands of low mounds covering the graves of the earliest ancestors of the brown men we see in the Delta fields. When we have dug out such a grave to the bottom, we find lying there the ancient Nile peasant, surrounded by pottery jars and stone implements.

LOOKING DOWN INTO THE GRAVE OF A LATE STONE AGE EGYPTIAN

In the grave shown in this picture the Egyptian has been lying for over six thousand years, and the *stone* tools which we find there and which he used so long ago tell us of the generations of Nile-dwellers who, like the Late Stone Age men of Europe, lived without the use of metal. Barley and split wheat are sometimes found in the jars around the body, for the dead were supplied with food by those who buried them. These and fragments of linen found in such graves show us from what country the first grain and flax probably came into Europe. Such ancient Nile peasants were therefore watering their fields of flax and grain over six thousand years ago, just as the brown men whom the traveller sees from the carriage windows to-day are still doing.

12. Picture Signs

These ancient peasants lived in villages of low, mud-brick huts. In each village, six or seven thousand years ago, lived a chief man who controlled the irrigation trenches of the district. To him the peasants were obliged to carry every season a share of the grain and flax which they gathered from their fields, otherwise the supply of water for their crops would be stopped. These payments were the first taxes that we know of in history.

When the peasant had paid his tax a note of it was made on the wall of his hut. The note consisted of a rough picture of a basket grain-measure scratched on the mud wall. Near the picture was scratched a number of strokes, which showed the number of measures of grain he had paid. This kind of picture sign is the earliest type of writing in the world. It is the first stage in the process of learning to write. There are uncivilized peoples to-day who have not gone any further than this stage. Thus the modern Alaskan natives in North America still send messages in the form of pictures scratched on a piece of wood.

Pictorial Message scratched on Wood by Alaskan Indians

In this picture the figure of a man with empty hands hanging down helplessly, palms down, as an Indian sign for emptiness or nothing, means "no". The figure with the hand on its mouth

Before the Pyramids

means "eating" or "food". It points to the tent, and this means "in the tent". The *exact words* of the message are not represented, but the idea, or meaning, of the picture is clear. It means "there is no food in the tent", or "there is a lack of meat in the tepee". As the message does not use the words, we can translate it into our own words.

Here is another example of Indian picture-writing. It should be noted again that the exact words are not indicated by this record, but the adventure is so suggested that it might be put into words in a number of different ways. This Dakota Indian prepared the story of his life in a series of eleven drawings, of which the above is but one. It records how he slew five enemy braves in a single day. The hero, with rifle in hand, is mounted upon a horse. The figure of an antelope below the horse shows that the chief is called Running Antelope. His shield bears a falcon, the animal emblem of his family. We see the trail of the horse as he swept round the copse at the left, in which were concealed the five enemy braves whom he slew. Of these, one figure bearing a rifle represents all five, while four other rifles in the act of being discharged show the number of braves in the copse.

PICTORIAL RECORD OF THE VICTORY OF A DAKOTA CHIEF NAMED RUNNING ANTELOPE

The early Egyptian kings of six thousand years

ago prepared strikingly similar picture records. The meaning of this Egyptian picture is as follows: Above is the falcon (compare the falcon on the shield of the Dakota Indian in the previous picture). The falcon is the *sign* for a king, and it leads the head of a man by a cord. Behind the head are six lotus leaves (each the sign for 1000) growing out of the ground to which the head is attached. Below is a single-barbed harpoon and a little rectangle, which is the sign for a lake. The whole tells the picture-story that " the Falcon King led captive 6000 men from the land of the Harpoon Lake ".

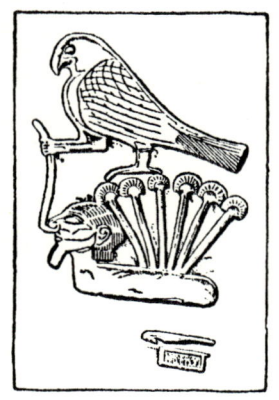

EXAMPLE OF EGYPTIAN WRITING IN THE PICTORIAL STAGE

13. SOUND SIGNS

Picture signs do not form real writing. In the diagram describing the hungry Alaskan Indians the last sign in the drawing can mean either tent or tepee. Nowadays when we write the word " tent " we mean tent, and when we write " tepee " we mean tepee. When the early Egyptians had progressed as far as making any particular drawing always mean the same word, they were then beginning to write in the true sense. Thus it would become a habit that the drawing of a loaf would always be read " loaf " and not " bread "; and the sign for " leaf " would always mean " leaf " and not " foliage "; and the sign for " bee " would always be " bee " and not " wasp ".

Before the Pyramids

You can see what the next stage is. If you draw this picture 🐝, it means the insect " bee ". But it also has the sound " be ". It would not be very easy to make a drawing of the verb " to be ", so you would use the drawing having the *sound* " be ", which you know is the same as the sound " bee ", and the drawing of this is 🐝, therefore this will also do for "be".

This new idea in writing became very useful. Suppose you wanted to write the word " belief ". It is very difficult to make a drawing or picture of " belief ", but it is not difficult to make a drawing for the sound " be ". It is 🐝. Again it is not difficult to make a drawing for the sound " lief ", which is just the same as the sound of " leaf ". It is 🍃. Having thus a means of writing " bee " and " leaf ", the next step would be to put them together, thus 🐝 🍃, and they would then represent the word " belief ".

When a large number of pictures had become *sound signs*, it was possible for the Egyptian to write any word he knew, whether the word meant a thing of which he could draw a picture or not. This possession of *sound signs* was what made real writing possible. It probably arose among these Nile-dwellers earlier than anywhere else in the ancient world.

Egyptian writing contained at last over six hundred signs, and the art of writing meant the use of a large number of sign-groups, each group being a word, and a series of such groups formed a sentence.

14. A Picture Alphabet

The Egyptian invented a further stage in the art of writing. As we have seen, he had at first used pictures in a vague way to express the idea or meaning of a sentence. Then he used pictures for actual words, and always the same picture for the same word. Then he used pictures for syllables, and always the same picture for the same syllable sound. Finally he used a picture for a letter, and always the same picture for

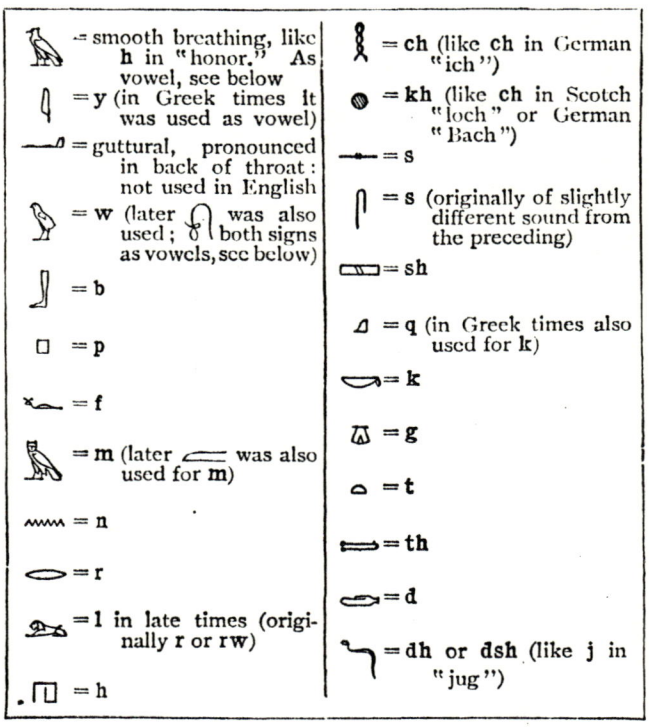

THE EGYPTIAN ALPHABET

the same letter. He had, in fact, invented an alphabet. The above diagram shows the Egyptian picture alphabet. Let us see how they used this alphabet. Examine the following Egyptian word: There are five signs in this word, but only the first three are letters. The last two figures are signs that help us to know the meaning of the word. The figure on the right is a man. This tells us that the word denotes a person. The next figure is that of a man with his hand on his mouth. This tells us that the word has something to do with the mouth. The remaining three pictures can be found in the alphabet, and they represent *ch-q-r*. No vowels appear in the Egyptian alphabet, and therefore no vowels appear in *written* Egyptian words. The whole picture means a poor man or pauper (literally " hungry ").

Let us now write two English words in hieroglyphic (which is the correct name for picture-writing).

The three wavy lines on the right are a sign or hint to us that the word has something to do with water. By looking at the alphabet we find that the three remaining pictures are *p-n-d*. The word, then, is " pond ".

This is another English word in hieroglyphic. The  first three signs indicate the letters *f-m-n*, and the last sign means " hunger " ; hence *f-m-n* spells " famine ".

You can now practise putting other English words in hieroglyphics ; for example, " man " (*m-n* and the sign for kneeling man) ; " drink " (*d-r-n-k* and the sign for kneeling man with hand on mouth) ; " speak " (*s-p-k* and the sign for kneeling man with hand on mouth) ; "brook" (*b-r-k* and the sign for "water", as in "pond").

15. PEN, INK, AND PAPER

The Egyptian soon discovered good writing materials. He found out that he could make an excellent paint or ink by thickening water with a little vegetable gum and then mixing in soot from the blackened pots over his fire. Dipping a pointed reed into this mixture, he found he could write very well. He also learned that he could split a kind of river reed, called *papyrus*, into thin strips, and that he could write on them better than on bits of pottery, bone, or wood. Desiring a larger sheet, he hit upon the idea of pasting his papyrus strips together with overlapping edges. This gave him a very

A Papyrus Page (one-third of size of original)

thin sheet, but by pasting two such sheets together, back to back, with the grain crossing at right angles, he produced a smooth, tough, pale-yellow paper.

The above picture is a photograph of a small portion of a papyrus book. In form such a book was a single strip of papyrus paper five or six to ten or twelve inches wide and often fifteen to thirty or forty feet long. When not in use this strip was kept rolled up, and thus the earliest books were rolls, looking when small like a rolled-up certificate or, when large, like a roll of wallpaper.

Before the Pyramids

The writing in the preceding picture is a page from the story of a shipwrecked sailor, the earliest Sindbad, as read by boys and girls of Egypt four thousand years ago.

In this way arose pen, ink, and paper. All three of these devices have come down to us from the Egyptians, and paper still bears its ancient name " papyrus ", but slightly changed. If you want to see the Egyptians using these inventions, look closely at this picture of the tax-collectors.

On the left are the village officials who have not paid the village taxes to the treasury. On the right

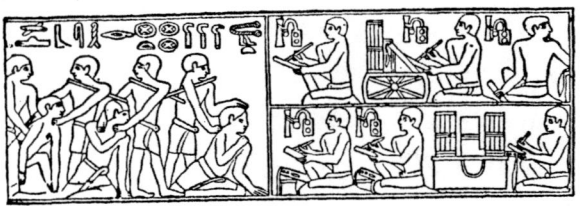

TAX-COLLECTORS

are the clerks making the accounts. They are squatting in two rows, and they write with the papyrus resting on the right knee, except the two who have desks. The left hand holds a sheet of papyrus, the right the pen.

It is of the greatest importance for us to remember that the invention of writing and the use of pen, ink, and paper has had a greater influence in uplifting the human race than any other intellectual achievement in the career of man. It is more important than all the battles ever fought and all the methods of government ever devised.

16. Metals

Meantime the Egyptians were making progress in other matters. It was probably in the peninsula of Sinai (see map on p. 34) that some Egyptian, wandering thither, once happened to bank his camp fire with pieces of copper ore lying on the ground about the camp. The charcoal of his wood fire mingled with the hot fragments of ore piled around to shield the fire, and thus the ore was "reduced", as the miner says; that is, the copper in metallic form was released from the lumps of ore. Next morning as the Egyptian stirred the embers he discovered a few glittering globules, now hardened into beads of metal. He drew them forth, and turned them admiringly as they glittered in the morning sunshine. Before long, as the experience was repeated, he discovered whence these strange shining beads came. He produced more of them, at first only to be worn as ornaments by women. Then he learned to cast the metal into a blade to replace the flint knife which he carried at his girdle.

Without knowing it, this man stood at the dawning of a new era in the history of the world, the Age of Metal; and the little bead of shining copper which he drew forth from the ashes, if this Egyptian wanderer could have seen it, might have reflected to him a vision of steel buildings, Forth bridges, huge factories roaring with the noise of thousands of machines of metal, and vast stretches of steel roads along which thunder rushing locomotives.

For these things of our modern world, and all they signify, would never have come to pass but for the little bead of metal which the wandering Egyptian held in his hand for the first time on that eventful day so long ago. Since the discovery of the use of fire over fifty thousand years earlier, man had made no conquest of the things of the earth which could compare in importance with this discovery of metal.

At this point we realize that we have followed early man out of the Stone Age (where we left him in Europe) into a civilization possessed of metal, writing, and government. It was the discovery of metal that made possible the building of the Pyramids. They tell us better than any printed page what the Egyptian builder with a *copper* chisel in his hands could do.

CHAPTER IV

THE PYRAMID AGE

17. THE PYRAMIDS

No traveller ever forgets the first drive from Cairo to the pyramids of Gizeh, as he sees their giant forms rising higher and higher above the crest of the western desert. A thousand questions arise in the visitor's mind. He has read that these vast buildings he is approaching are tombs, in which the kings of Egypt were buried. Such mighty buildings reveal many things about the men who built them. In the first place, these tombs show that the Egyptians believed in a life after death, and that to obtain such a life they thought it was necessary to preserve the body from destruction. They built these tombs to shelter and protect the body after death. From this belief came also the practice of embalming, by which the body was preserved as a mummy. It was then placed in the great tomb, in a small room deep down in the pyramid masonry. Other tombs of masonry much smaller in size clustered about the pyramids in great numbers.

The Great Pyramid itself covers an area of thirteen acres. It is a solid mass of masonry containing 2,300,000 blocks of limestone, each weighing on an average two and a half tons; that is, each block is as heavy as a large waggon-load of coal. The sides of the pyramid at the base are seven hundred and fifty-five feet long, and the building is nearly five hundred feet high. An ancient story tells us that a hundred thousand men were working on this building for twenty years.

An examination of the picture opposite of the ancient cemetery at Gizeh will help us to understand the meaning of the pyramids. These royal tombs belonged to the leading kings of the early part of the Pyramid Age (about 3000 to 2500 B.C.). The Great Pyramid, the tomb of King Khufu, is on the right. Next in size is that of King Khafre on the left. On the east side (front) of each pyramid is a temple where the dead kings received food, drink, and clothing for the life hereafter. These temples, like the pyramids, were built on the desert plateau above, while the royal town was in the valley below, on the far right. For convenience, therefore, the temple was connected with the town below by a covered gallery or causeway of stone. This causeway may be seen descending in a straight line from the pyramid and temple of King Khafre, and the ending below, just beside the Sphinx, is a large oblong building of stone, called a valley temple, to distinguish it from the pyramid temple on

The Pyramid Age

the plateau above. It was a splendid structure of granite, serving not only as a temple, but also as the entrance to the causeway from the royal city. Here beside his valley temple we see a great statue of King Khafre, which he had had carved as a colossal portrait of himself, with the body of a lion. It is commonly

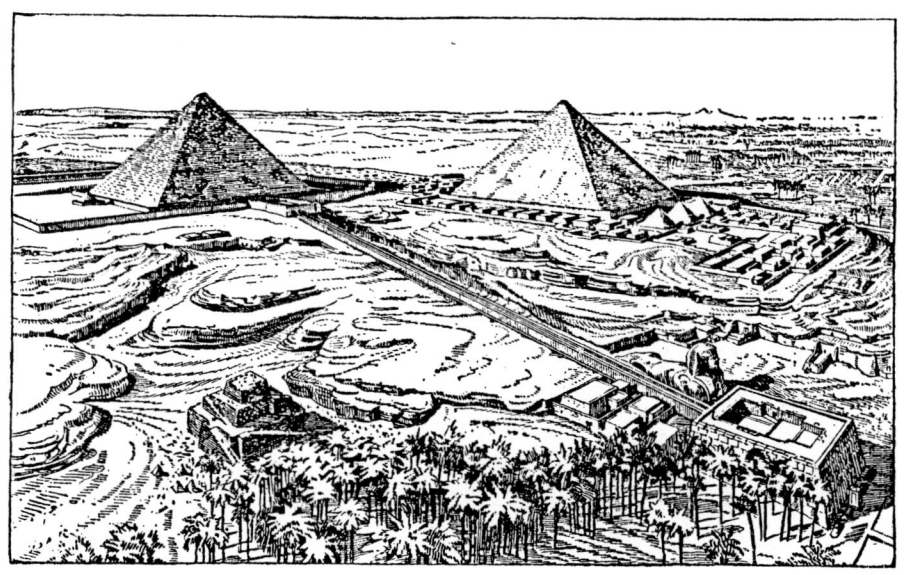

Restoration of the Great Pyramids and Other Tomb-Monuments in the Ancient Cemetery of Gizeh, Egypt. (After Hoelscher)

called the Great Sphinx. It is the largest portrait figure ever made; the head is sixty-five feet high, the body is about one hundred and eighty-seven feet long, and the face is about fourteen feet across. At the lower left-hand corner of the picture is an unfinished pyramid showing the inclined ascents up which the stone blocks were dragged. These ascents were built of sun-baked brick, and were removed after the pyramid was finished.

18. The Gods

The Egyptians had many gods, but there were two whom they worshipped above all others. The sun which shines so gloriously in the cloudless Egyptian sky was their greatest god, and their most splendid temples were erected for his worship. Indeed, the pyramid is a symbol sacred to the Sun-god. They called him Re (pronounced *ray*). We find another symbol of the Sun-god in this picture.

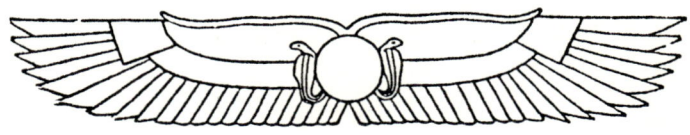

WINGED SUN-DISK, A SYMBOL OF THE SUN-GOD

In this form the Sun-god was believed to be a falcon flying across the sky.

The other great power which the Egyptians worshipped was the shining Nile. The great river and the fertile soil he refreshed and the green life which he brought forth—all these the Egyptians thought of together as a single god, Osiris, the everlasting life of the earth which revives and fades every year with the changes of the seasons.

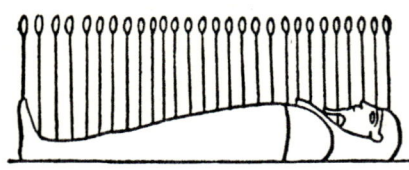

THE DEAD OSIRIS EMBALMED

We show here an Egyptian picture of the dead Osiris. From the body of the god stalks of grain have sprouted, a symbol suggesting the eternal life of the god, by means of which he survived death. It was a beautiful thought to the Egyptians that this same life-giving

The Pyramid Age

power of the Nile which furnished him his food in *this* world would also care for him in the *next* world when his body lay out yonder in the great cemetery of Gizeh.

There were many other Egyptian gods whose symbols were animals, but the animal worship usually attributed to Egypt was a weakness belonging to the latest age. The animals were not gods in this early time, but only symbols of the gods.

THE BALANCE OF JUDGMENT

There was a good sense of judgment and justice in the religion of Egypt, as we can see by studying the picture above. It shows us the judgment after death of a man named Ani. At the left we see entering, in white robes, the deceased man, Ani, and his wife. Before them are the balances of judgment for weighing the human heart, to determine whether it is just or not. A jackal-headed god manages the scales, while an ibis-headed god stands behind him, ready to record the verdict of the balances. Behind him is a monster ready to devour the unjust soul, as his heart (looking like a tiny jar) is weighed over against right and truth (symbolized by a feather) in the right-hand scale pan.

19. The Tomb Pictures

The pyramids were surrounded by the tombs of the queens and the great lords of the age. The tombs are sometimes of vast size. The opening in the top of each is a shaft leading down to the burial chamber in the native rock far below the tomb structure. This structure is of stone, surrounding a heap of sand and

Tombs of Egyptian Nobles

gravel inside. The door of the chapel room can be seen in front of each tomb. A stroll among the tombs crowded around the pyramids of Gizeh is almost like a walk among the busy people who lived in this populous valley in the days of the pyramid builders. We find the door of every tomb standing open, and there is nothing to prevent our entrance. We stand in an oblong room with walls of stone masonry. This is a chapel chamber to which the Egyptians believed the dead man buried beneath the tomb might return every day. Here he would find food and drink left for him daily by his relatives. He would also find the stone walls of this room covered from floor to ceiling with carved scenes, beautifully painted, picturing the daily life on a great estate. The place is now silent and deserted, or if we hear the voices of the donkey boys talking outside, they are speaking Arabic, for the ancient Egyptian language of the men who built the tombs so many thousand years ago is no longer spoken. But everywhere in bright and charming colours we see pictures of the life—the days of toil and pleasure—which these men of nearly five thousand years ago actually lived. We shall get glimpses of this varied life in the pictures and sections that follow.

20. Farming

The following scenes of agricultural life in early Egypt are copied from the pictures drawn on the walls of a nobleman's tomb.

In the first picture the tall figure of the nobleman stands at the right. He is inspecting three lines of cattle and a line of fowl brought before him. Note the two scribes who head the two middle rows. Each is writing with a pen on a sheet of papyrus, and one carries two pens behind his ear. Such reliefs after being carved were coloured in bright hues by the painter.

The next scene shows us the Egyptians ploughing and sowing in the Pyramid Age. Here you see that there are two ploughmen, one driving the oxen and one holding the plough. This wooden plough is derived from such a wooden hoe as we see in use in front of the oxen. The handle of the hoe here grasped by the user was lengthened so that oxen might be

NOBLEMAN ON HIS ESTATE

yoked to it. The hoe handle thus became the beam of the plough. Two short handles were then attached by which the ploughman behind could guide it. The man with the hoe breaks up the clods left by the

PLOUGHING AND SOWING IN THE PYRAMID AGE

plough, and in front of him is the sower scattering the seed from the curious sack he carries before him. At

The Pyramid Age

the left is a scribe of the estate. The picture-writing above the figure explains what is going on.

A touch of life is given to this milking-time picture by the fact that the ancient cowherd has tied up the hind-legs of the cow because she is unruly. Behind her another man

MILKING-TIME

is holding her calf, which rears and plunges in an effort to reach the milk just as a calf might do to-day.

Note that we find no horses in these tomb pictures of the Pyramid Age, for the horse was still unknown to the Egyptians. The donkey, however, is everywhere, and it would be impossible to harvest the grain without him. Here you see a donkey carrying a load of grain sheaves. The foal accompanies its mother while at work.

HARVESTING WITH DONKEY

21. THE COPPERSMITH AND CABINET-MAKER

The tomb pictures give us detailed examples of the Egyptian craftsmen and their work. On the wall next the one on which the farming scenes are drawn we find again the tall figure of the nobleman inspecting the booths and yards where the men of his estate are working. Yonder is the smith. He has never heard of his ancestor who picked up the first bead of copper over a thousand years earlier. Much progress has been made since that day. This man can make excellent copper tools of all sorts, but the tool which demanded the greatest skill was the long flat rip-saw, which the smith knew how to hammer into shape out of a broad strip of copper five or six feet long. Such a saw may be seen in use in the next illustration. Besides this, he knew how to make one that would saw great blocks of stone for the pyramids. Moreover, this coppersmith

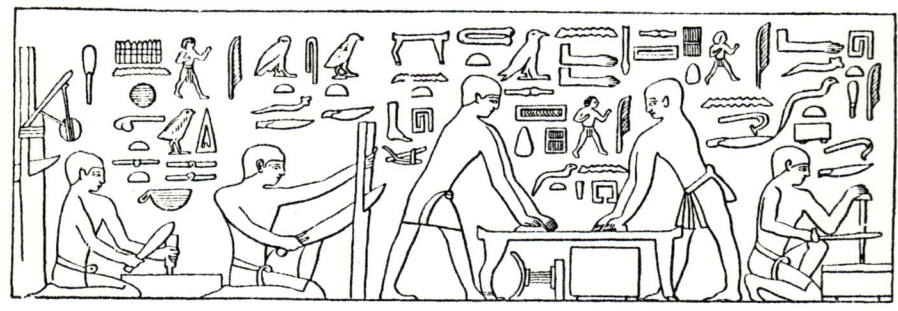

CABINET-MAKERS

was already able to deliver orders of considerable size. We know that he could furnish thirteen hundred feet (about a quarter of a mile) of copper drain-piping for a pyramid temple, the earliest plumbing known to us.

The above picture is one of a cabinet-maker's workshop, and it shows us what men could do when they were provided with good metal tools by the coppersmith. At the left of the picture a man is cutting with a chisel, which he taps with a mallet; the next man " rips " a board with a copper saw; next two men are finishing off a couch; and at the right a man is drilling a hole with a bow-drill. These Egyptian cabinet-makers became very skilful artists, and the next illustration shows an arm-chair of Egyptian work which was placed in the tomb of a nobleman about 1300 years B.C. and was discovered in excellent condition in his tomb in 1905.

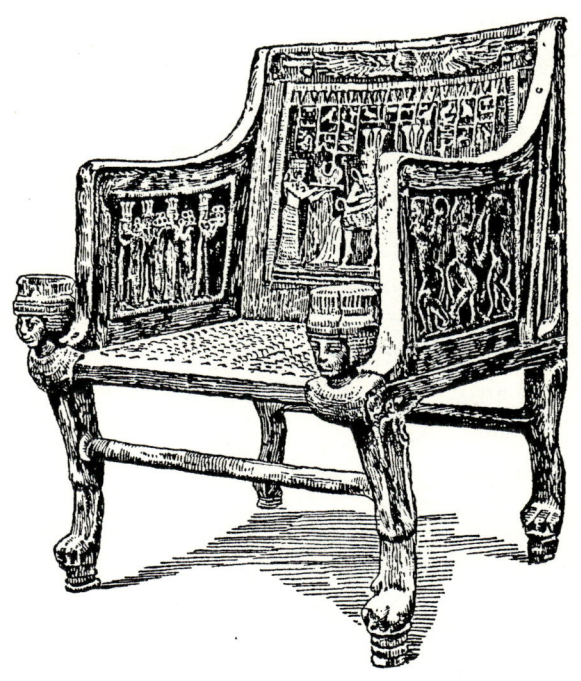

Egyptian Arm-chair

22. The Goldsmith and the Potter

The booth of the goldsmith (see overleaf) is filled with workmen and apprentices. The workmen hammer and cast, solder and fit together richly wrought jewellery, which is hardly equalled in beauty by the work of the best goldsmiths and jewellers of to-day. On the left of the upper row in the diagram the chief goldsmith weighs precious stones and a scribe records them. Next, six men with blowpipes blow the fire in a small clay furnace. Then a workman pours out molten metal or paste, and at the right end four men are beating gold leaf. In the middle row are shown pieces of finished jewellery, and a jewel box in the centre. On the lower

GOLDSMITH'S BOOTH

row workmen seated at low benches are putting together and engraving pieces of jewellery. Several of these men are dwarfs.

In the next space on the tomb wall we find the potter. No longer is he building up his jars and bowls with his fingers alone as in the Stone Age. The man sits before a horizontal wheel, upon which he shapes the

EGYPTIAN POTTERS

whirling vessel. When the soft clay vessels are ready, they are no longer burned in an *open* fire, as among the Late Stone Age potters in the Swiss lake villages; but here in the Egyptian potter's yard are long rows of closed furnaces of clay as tall as a man. When the pottery is packed in these furnaces it is burned evenly, because it is protected from the wind.

In the picture you see the potter crouching before his horizontal wheel, which is like a flat round plate, on which rests the jar that is being shaped. The potter keeps the wheel whirling with one hand, and with the other he shapes the soft clay as it turns on the wheel. This wheel is the ancestor of our lathe. Two men (at the right end) are just filling a tall furnace with bowls and jars, and another furnace (at the left) is already very hot, for the man stirring the fire is holding up his hand to shield his face from the heat.

23. A Nobleman's Home

We shall find the Egyptians' sense of beauty very evident if we examine the home life of the nobles of the Pyramid Age.

Here is a picture of the chapel wall again. We see the nobleman sitting in his palanquin, a comfortable wheel-less carriage borne upon the shoulders of slaves, as he returns from the inspection of his estate. His bearers carry him into the shady garden before his house, where they set down the palanquin and cease their song. His wife advances at once to greet him. Her place is always at his side; she is his sole wife, held in all honour, and enjoys every right that belongs to her husband. This garden is the nobleman's paradise. Here he may recline for an hour with his family and friends, playing at draughts, listening to the music of harp, pipe, and lute, watching his women in the slow and stately dances of the time, while his children are sporting among the arbours, splashing in the pool as

VILLA OF AN EGYPTIAN NOBLE

they chase the fish, playing with ball, doll, and jumping-jack, or teasing the tame monkey which takes refuge under their father's ivory-legged stool.

The garden is enclosed with a high wall. There are pools on either side as one enters, and a long arbour extends down the middle. The house, which is at the rear, is a large one built of sun-dried brick and wood.

It is light and airy, as suits the climate, and we find that it has many latticed windows on all sides. The walls of the living rooms are scarcely more than a frame to support gaily coloured hangings, which can be let down as a protection against winds and sandstorms when necessary. These give the house a very bright and cheerful aspect. The house is a work of art, and we see in it how naturally the Egyptian demanded beauty in his surroundings. This he secured by making all his *useful* things *beautiful*.

24. END OF THE PYRAMID AGE

The pyramid cemeteries have shown us something of the splendid civilization gained by the Egyptians of the Pyramid Age. We should notice particularly how many more things these men of the Nile could now make than the Stone Age men, who were still living in the lake villages and other towns of Europe at the very time these tomb chapels were being built. If space permitted, we might find other records here showing how the nobles of the Pyramid Age (just such nobles as the one whose estate and home we have in imagination visited) gained more and more power until the Pharaohs, as the great kings of Egypt were called, could no longer control them. Then in struggles among themselves they destroyed the Pharaohs' government, and the last king of the Pyramid Age fell soon after 2500 B.C. It had lasted some five hundred years.

But the end of the Pyramid Age was not the end of civilization on the Nile; other great periods were to follow. The monuments which these later ages left lie farther up the river, and we must make the voyage up the Nile in order to visit them, and to recover the wonderful story which they still tell us.

As we begin our voyage up the Nile, and our steamer moves away from the Cairo dock, we see stretching far along the western horizon the long line of the pyramids,

CLIFF TOMB OF AN EGYPTIAN NOBLE OF THE FEUDAL AGE

reminding us again of the splendour and progress of the Pyramid Age, which we are now leaving behind. At length they drop down and disappear behind the fringe of palm groves. Other great monuments are before us. Along the palm-fringed shores, far away to the south, we shall find the buildings, tombs, and monuments which will tell us of two more great ages on the Nile—the Feudal Age and the Empire.

We steam steadily southward, and soon the river begins to wind from side to side of the deep valley, carrying the steamer at times close under the weather-worn cliffs. As we scan the rocks we look up to many a tomb door in the face of the cliff, and leading to a tomb chapel cut in the rock.

These cliff tombs looking down upon the river belonged to the Feudal Age of Egyptian history. The men buried in these cliff tombs succeeded in gaining greater power than their noble ancestors who lived five centuries before them in the Pyramid Age. They were granted lands by the king under a scheme which in later Europe we call *feudal*, because " feud " means a holding of land. They were thus powerful barons, living like little kings on their broad estates, made up of the fertile fields upon which these tomb doors now look down.

The Feudal Age lasted several centuries, and was flourishing by 2000 B.C. There were of course Pharaohs in this Feudal Age as in the Pyramid Age, but they had less power and the nobles had more power than in the earlier time.

CHAPTER V

THE FEUDAL AGE AND THE EMPIRE

25. MEDICINE AND DECIMALS

THE civilization, the arts and crafts, the farming, the pottery, the cabinet-making, and all the things we know of in the Pyramid Age were carried on into the Feudal Age and developed. It is not necessary to give a further description of them, and we shall but note some of the special qualities of this Feudal Age.

Many written records have been found in the cliff tombs, and they show us that the nobles of this period were very eager to be known as men who loved justice and kindness as well as beauty and splendour. In the rock chapel shown in the last picture we can read how the nobleman buried there was proud of his kind treatment of his people. He says: "There was no citizen's daughter whom I misused; there was no widow whom I oppressed; there was no peasant whom I evicted; there was no shepherd whom I expelled; there was none wretched in my community; there was none hungry in my time".

There are also written records on science to be found in these tombs, though very few papyrus rolls were needed to deal with the science of the time. The largest and most valuable of all contained what they had learned about medicine, surgery, and the human body. This oldest medical book, when unrolled, is to-day sixty-six feet long, and has recipes for all sorts of ailments. Some of them are still good, and call for remedies which, like castor oil, are still in common use.

There are also rolls containing simple rules of arithmetic based on the decimal system which we still use. Even observations of the stars with simple instruments were made.

26. AN EARLY SUEZ CANAL

Along with this higher progress the Pharaohs of the Feudal Age improved the condition of the country. They erected huge earthen dykes and made vast basins to store up the Nile water for irrigation, thus greatly increasing the yield of the lands and estates. They measured the height of the river from year to year, and their marks of the Nile levels are still to be found on the rocks at the Second Cataract.

At the same time, these Pharaohs were reaching out by sea for the wealth of other lands. Their fleets sailed over towards Greece, and probably controlled the large island of Crete. They dug a canal from the north end of the Red Sea westward to the nearest

An Early Sea-going Ship

branch of the Nile in the eastern Delta, where the river divides into a number of mouths. The Pharaohs' Mediterranean ships could sail up the eastern mouth of the Nile, then enter the canal and, passing eastward through it, reach the Red Sea. Thus the Mediterranean and the Red Sea were first connected by this predecessor of the Suez Canal four thousand years ago.

This scene is carved on the wall of a temple. It gives us the earliest picture of a sea-going ship. The people on board are all bowing to the king whose figure stood on shore. The big double mast is unshipped and lies on supports rising by the three steering oars in the stern. The models and ornaments of these earliest-known ships spread in later times to ships found in all waters from Italy to India.

In this age, too, the Pharaoh has organized a small standing army. He could now make his power felt both in north and south, in Palestine and in Nubia. But not long before 1800 B.C. the power of the Pharaohs of the Feudal Age suddenly declined and their line disappeared.

The monuments along the river banks have thus far told us something of the story of two of the three periods into which the career of this great Nile people falls. After we have left the tombs of the Feudal Age, and have continued our journey over four hundred miles southward from Cairo, all at once we catch glimpses of vast masses of stone masonry and lines of tall columns rising among the palms on the east side of the river. They are the ruins of the once great Thebes, which will tell us the story of the third period, the Empire. The dates of the three ages are:

(1) The Pyramid Age, about 3000–2500 B.C.
(2) The Feudal Age, about 2000 B.C.
(3) The Empire, about 1580–1150 B.C.

27. The Horse and the Chariot

The good rule of the Pharaohs of the Feudal Age did much to prepare the way for Egyptian leadership in the early world. Many wars were fought in Asia, and we find great sculptures being carved for the glory of the later fighting emperors.

In the next picture we see the giant figure of a Pharaoh as he stands in his war chariot, scattering the enemy before his plunging horses. The Pharaohs of the Pyramid Age had never seen a horse, and this is the first time we have met the horse in the ancient monuments. After the close of the Feudal Age the animal began to be imported from Asia; the chariot came

A Pharaoh of the Empire fighting in his Chariot

with him, and Egypt, having learnt warfare on a scale unknown before, became a military empire.

The Pharaohs now became great generals with a well-organized standing army made up chiefly of archers and heavy masses of chariots. With these forces the Pharaohs created an empire which extended from the Euphrates in Asia to the Fourth Cataract of the Nile in Africa. This world power of the Pharaohs lasted from the sixteenth century to the twelfth century B.C.—something over four hundred years.

28. KARNAK

The wealth which the Pharaohs captured in Asia and Nubia during the Empire period brought them power and magnificence unknown to the world before. Especially was this shown in their vast and splendid buildings. A new and important chapter in the history of art and architecture then began.

The Karnak Temple, which stood in the once vast city of Thebes, is like a great volume of history telling us much of the story of the Egyptian Empire. It contains the greatest colonnaded hall ever erected by man. The columns of the central aisle are sixty-nine feet high. The vast capital forming the summit of each column is large enough to contain a hundred men standing crowded upon it at the same time.

Behind the great hall of the temple of Karnak towers a huge obelisk, a shaft of granite in a single piece nearly a hundred feet high. It was erected early in the Empire by the first great woman in history, Queen Hatshepsut. It was no small task to cut out such blocks as these from the granite quarries at the First Cataract, transport them on a huge boat down the river, and erect them in this temple.

Two obelisks can be seen in this picture lying base to base on a large Nile barge some three hundred feet long. The obelisks are each $97\frac{1}{2}$ feet long, and weigh about 350 tons each, the two making a burden of some 700 tons in the barge. It is being towed by thirty tug-boats in three rows of ten each. Each tug-boat has thirty-two oarsmen, making nine hundred and sixty oarsmen in all. Under the guidance of the engineers in the other small boats, these men towed the obelisks down-stream from the granite quarries of the First Cataract to Thebes, a distance of about one hundred and fifty miles. Under each obelisk we can see the sledge on which it was dragged on shore to the place where they were both set up in the Karnak Temple.

TRANSPORTING THE 350-TON OBELISKS

Queen Hatshepsut also had enterprising sea-going ships, a fleet of which she sent through the Red Sea to Punt to bring back the luxuries of tropical Africa for a beautiful terraced temple which she was erecting against the western cliffs of Thebes. Such works show what an efficient and successful ruler this great woman was.

Only two of Hatshepsut's fleet of five ships are shown in the picture overleaf. The sails on the long spars are furled and the vessels are moored. The sailors are carrying the cargo up the gang-planks, and one of them is teasing an ape on the roof of the cabin. The inscriptions above the ship read:

" The loading of the ships very heavily with marvels

of the country of Punt; all goodly fragrant woods of God's Land (the East), heaps of myrrh-resin, with fresh myrrh trees, with ebony and pure ivory, with green gold of Emu, with cinnamon wood, khesyt wood, with two kinds of incense, eye-cosmetic, with apes, monkeys,

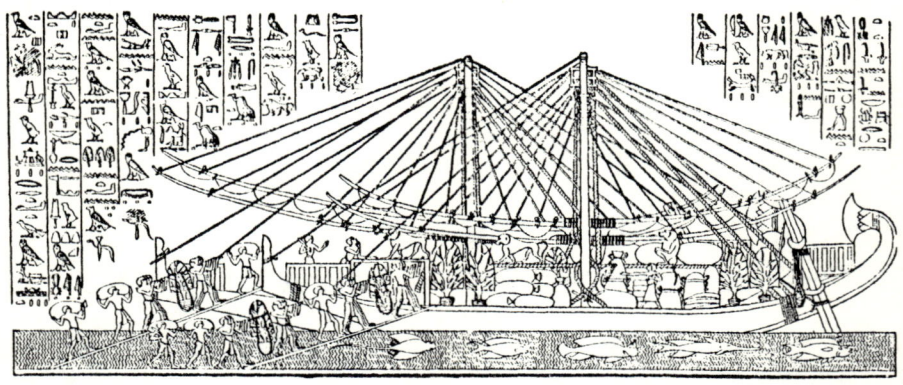

PART OF THE FLEET OF QUEEN HATSHEPSUT LOADING IN THE LAND OF PUNT

dogs, and with skins of the southern panther, with natives and their children. Never were brought the like of this for any king who has been since the beginning."

The scene is carved on the wall of the queen's temple at Thebes, in the garden of which she planted the myrrh trees.

29. THE FIRST GREAT GENERAL

As we examine the obelisk of Hatshepsut, we find around the base the remains of stone masonry with which it was once walled in almost to the top. This was done by the queen's half-brother, Thutmose III, in order to cover up the records which proclaimed to

OBELISKS AT KARNAK

the world the hated rule of a woman. Thus Thutmose III had the names of the queen and the men who aided her all cut out, including that of the skilful architect and engineer who erected this obelisk and its companion. But the masonry covering the obelisk has fallen down, and it still proclaims the fame of Hatshepsut.

Thutmose III was the first great general in history, the Napoleon of Egypt, the greatest of the Egyptian

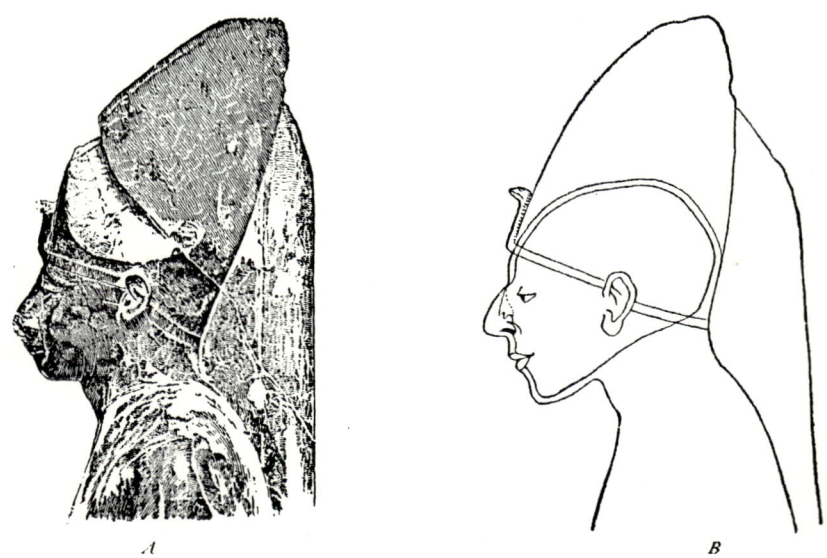

Portrait of Thutmose III, the Napoleon of Ancient Egypt (*A*), compared with his Mummy (*B*)

conquerors. The portrait (*A*) carved in granite can be compared with the actual face of the great conqueror as we have it in his mummy. Such a comparison is shown in (*B*), where the profile of this granite portrait (outside lines) is placed over the profile of Thutmose III's mummy (inside lines). The correspondence is very close, showing great accuracy in the portrait art of this age.

Thutmose ruled over fifty years, beginning about 1500 B.C. On the temple walls at Karnak we can read the story of nearly twenty years of warfare, during

The Feudal Age and the Empire

which Thutmose crushed the cities and kingdoms of Western Asia, and joined them together to form a great empire.

30. ONE GOD IN EGYPT

When the Empire was about two hundred years old a young man named Amenhotep IV became Pharaoh. He believed in only one god, the Sun-god, and he began a new and remarkable chapter in the religious history of Egypt by the attempt to destroy the old gods, and to persuade the people of Egypt to adopt only the worship of the Sun-god. He commanded that throughout the great Empire, including its people in both Africa and Asia, only the Sun-god whom he called Aton should be worshipped. The young Pharaoh changed his own name from Amenhotep (which contained the name of the god Amen whom he hated) to Ikh-naton, which means "Aton (the Sun-god) is satisfied".

Ikhnaton (whose wonderful face you should study closely in the following picture) finally left magnificent Thebes, where there were so many temples of the old gods, and built a new city farther down the river which he called "Horizon of Aton". It is now called Amarna. In the Amarna tomb chapels we may still read on the walls the hymns of praise to the Sun-god which Ikhnaton himself wrote. They show us the simplicity and beauty of the young king's faith in the sole God. He had gained the belief that one God created not only all the lower creatures but also all races of men, both Egyptians and foreigners. Moreover, the king saw in his God a kindly Father, who maintained all his creatures by his goodness, so that even the birds in the marshes were aware of his kindness, and uplifted their wings like arms to praise him, as a beautiful line in one of the hymns tells us. In all the progress of men which

REMARKABLE LIMESTONE PORTRAIT HEAD OF IKHNATON

we have followed through thousands of years, no one had ever before caught such a vision of the great Father of all.

31. THE VALLEY OF THE TOMBS

The new faith of Ikhnaton could not be understood by the common people of Egypt of the fourteenth century B.C. The old gods had too strong a hold on them, and the priests of the old gods, whose livelihood was threatened, did their utmost to preserve the old religions. Thus discontent spread in Egypt. The Pharaoh had much trouble in keeping the Empire together. Though it held together for another hundred years, there were many signs that the end was near,

VALLEY AT THEBES WHERE THE PHARAOHS OF THE EMPIRE WERE BURIED

and, indeed, by the middle of the twelfth century B.C. the Egyptian Empire was no more.

The great Pharaohs who maintained themselves for over four hundred years as emperors were buried near Thebes in a wild and desolate valley formed by a deep depression in the western desert. Here, in over forty vast rock-hewn galleries reaching hundreds of feet into the mountain, the bodies of the Egyptian emperors were laid to rest, only to suffer pillage and robbery after the fall of the Empire. Their weak successors as kings at Thebes hurried the royal bodies from one hiding-place to another, and finally concealed them in a secret chamber hewn for this purpose in the western cliffs. Here they lay undisturbed for nearly three thousand years, until, in 1881, they were discovered and removed to the National Museum at Cairo, where they still rest. Here also the tomb of King Tutenkhamen was discovered in 1922. Thus we are able to look into the very faces of these lords of Egypt and Western Asia who lived and ruled from thirty-one hundred to thirty-five hundred years ago.

Thebes, then, is the closing chapter in the story of the Empire. The pyramids, tombs, and temples along the Nile have told us briefly the story of early Egypt in three epochs. The pyramids of Gizeh and the neighbouring cemeteries of Memphis tell us about the Pyramid Age. The cliff tombs, which we found on the Nile voyage, reveal the history of the Feudal Age. And the temples and cliff-tombs of Thebes give us the story of the Empire. The Nile has become for us a great volume of history. Let us remember, however, that preceding these three great chapters of civilization on the Nile, we also found here at the beginning the earlier story of how man passed from Stone Age barbarism to a civilization in which he had acquired metal, writing, and government.

In the same way, as we look forward, the monuments discovered along the Tigris and Euphrates can be made to tell their story of life in the early Orient in Asia. To that story we must now turn.

PART III
BABYLONIA AND ASSYRIA

CHAPTER VI

THE SUMERIANS

32. SCHOLARS AND DIGGERS

WE have seen how the monuments of the Nile have told us their story of the way in which men gradually gained civilization. In a similar way, the monuments discovered along the Tigris and Euphrates rivers in Asia show us that, following the Egyptians, the peoples of Mesopotamia (as this district of Western Asia is generally called) likewise gained industries, learned the use of metals, worked out a system of writing, and finally rose to the leading position of power in the ancient world.

Expeditions led by scholars are busy at the present day digging into the mounds of Mesopotamia, searching the ruins of the wonderful cities, about some of which, such as Babylon and Nineveh, we read in the Old Testament. The picture on p. 77 shows us what these mounds look like. The bare ground in front of us, now showing a scanty growth of desert shrubs, once formed a court or open square for public business and for the unloading of caravans. The great mound beyond contains the chief temple buildings, in which lived the scribes (clerks) and officials who carried on

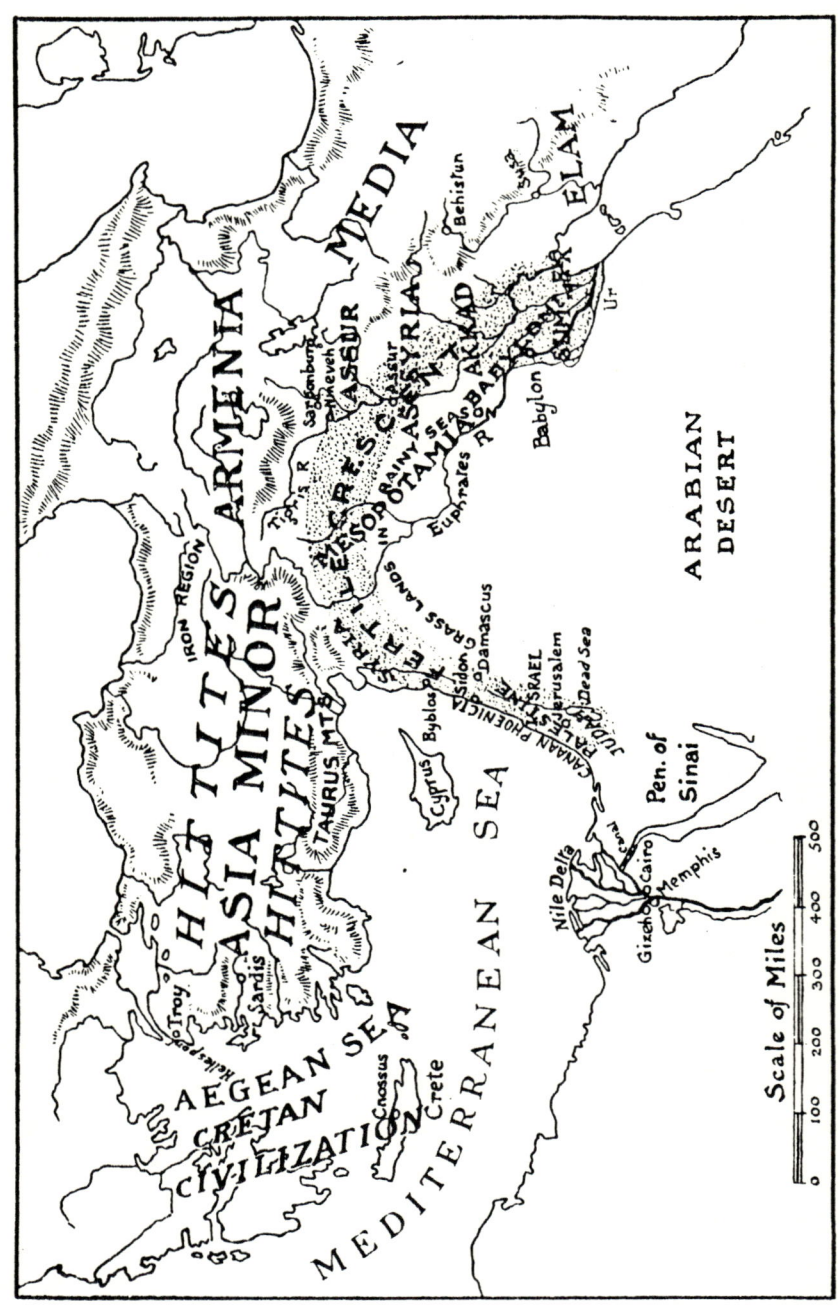

The Ancient Oriental World and Neighbouring Europe before the Rise of the Greeks

The Sumerians

the temple and government business of this town of Nippur nearly five thousand years ago.

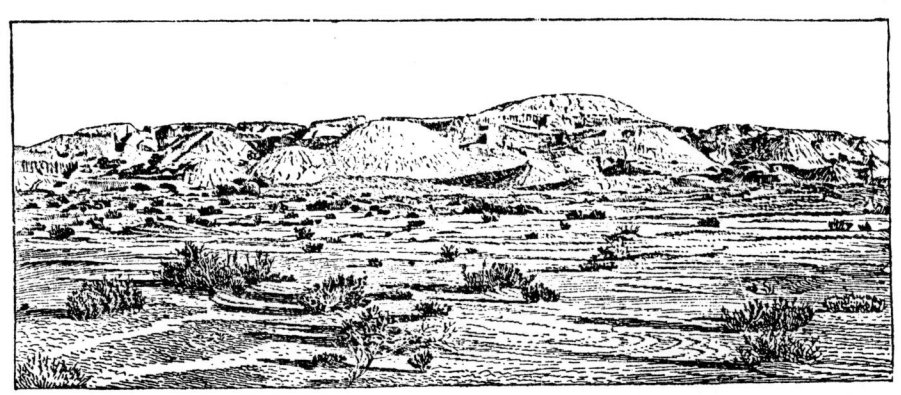

MOUND COVERING A PORTION OF THE ANCIENT BABYLONIAN CITY OF NIPPUR

The next picture gives us a view of Nippur as it now appears from the top of the temple mount. These ruins were dug out between 1889 and 1900. This view shows the work of digging going on. The earth (once sun-dried brick) is taken out in baskets and carried away by a long line of native labourers who empty their baskets at the far end of an ever-growing bank of earth.

As the excavators penetrate the ruins of the town, they find among them clay tablets or objects of pottery, stone, or metal. Thus are discovered the records, buildings, and household property once used by the people of ancient Babylonia. They lie at different levels, the oldest things nearer the bottom and the later ones higher up. Note in the picture that, beyond the labourers, the view of the horizon gives a good idea of the flat Babylonian plain.

The "Two Rivers", the Tigris and the Euphrates, rise in the mountains of Asia Minor and flow down through Mesopotamia to the Persian Gulf. On their banks arose the earliest civilization known in Western Asia.

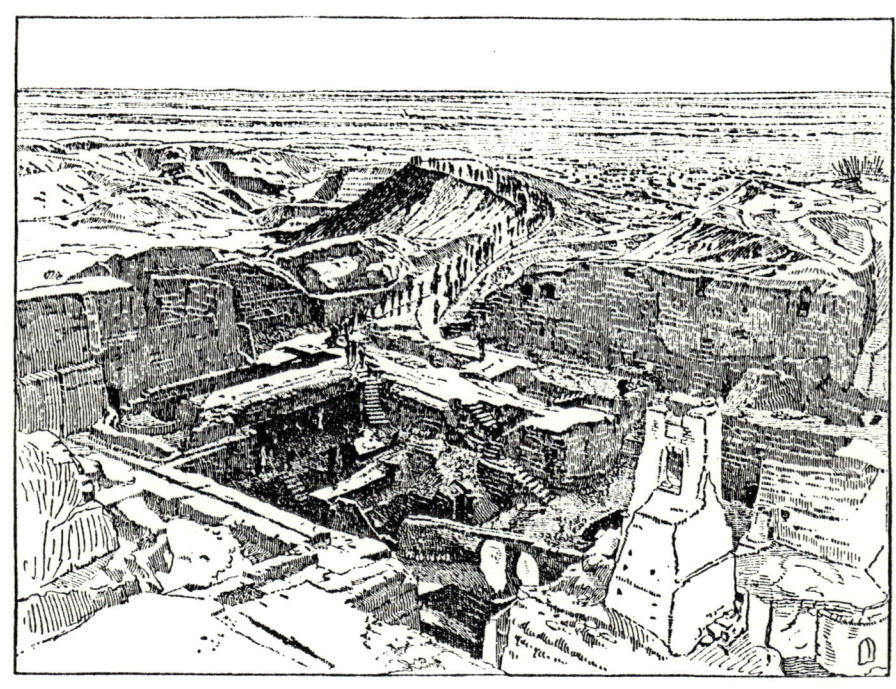

EXCAVATION OF THE RUINS OF ANCIENT NIPPUR

33. THE SUMERIANS

If you look at the map of the Near East on p. 79, you will see that the Tigris and the Euphrates join before they reach the sea. In the old days this was not so, for they entered the sea apart. Between the "Two Rivers" as they approached their mouths lay the plain of Shinar. The northern portion was called Akkad, and the remainder in the south formed the land of Sumer. The first important people that we have to consider were the inhabitants of the extreme south, the Sumerians.

Long before 3000 B.C. these people had drained

The Sumerians

some of the marshes around the mouths of the Two Rivers. Their villages of low mud-brick huts grew up gradually along the banks of the Euphrates. By means of hard work on the part of the people, civilization developed early among these Sumerians. They learned to control the flood of the rivers with dykes, to lead the waters across their fields in trenches, and to

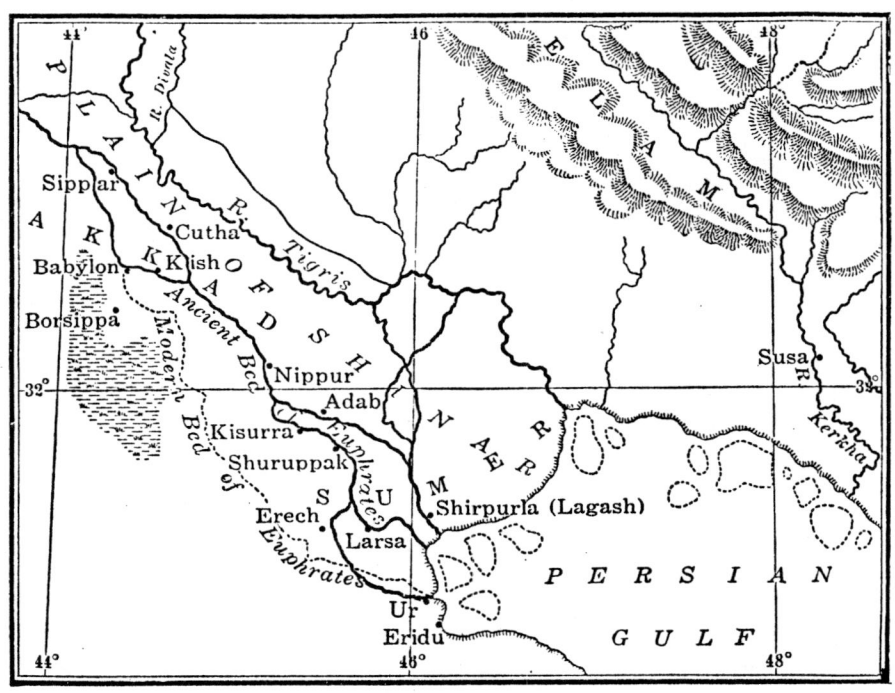

SKETCH MAP OF SUMER AND AKKAD

reap large harvests of grain. They grew barley and split wheat, and they had cattle, sheep, and goats. Oxen drew the plough, and donkeys pulled *wheeled* carts and chariots. The wheel as a device for moving things along appeared here for the first time. But horses were still unknown to them. Trade with the upper river brought them metal, probably from the

Nile Valley, and the smith learned to make utensils of copper, but he had not yet learned to harden the copper into bronze by mixing it with tin.

The next illustration shows us that the Sumerians were clever and patient workers, for such a machine for planting seed as you see here was quite unknown in England until late in its history. The seeder is drawn by oxen with their driver beside them. Behind the seeder follows a man holding it by two handles.

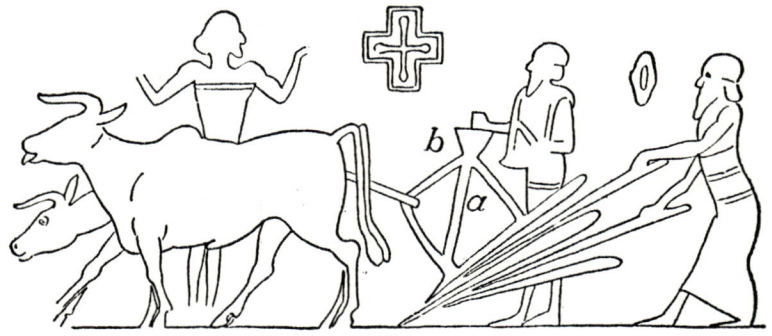

ANCIENT BABYLONIAN SEEDER, OR MACHINE PLANTER
(After Clay)

It is very pointed, and evidently makes a shallow trench in the soil as it moves. Rising from the frame of the seeder is a tube (*a*), on the top of which is a funnel (*b*). A third man walking beside the seeder is shown dropping the grain into this funnel with one hand, while with the other he holds what is probably a sack of seed-grain hung from his shoulders. The grain drops down through the tube and falls into the trench made by the seeder.

34. WRITING ON CLAY

The needs of trade and government taught the Sumerians to make records scratched in rude pictures

The Sumerians

with the tip of a reed on a flat disc of soft clay. When dried in the sun such a record became very hard, and if well baked in an oven it became a pottery tablet that would last a very long time. On the earliest of these tablets we can still see the original *pictures* which made

	1	2	3
Foot; turned around in 2			
Donkey			
Bird; turned over with feet to the right			
Fish			
Star			
Ox; turned over in 2			
Sun or Day			
Grain; top of stalk turned over			

EARLY BABYLONIAN SIGNS SHOWING THEIR PICTORIAL ORIGIN
(Chiefly from Barton)

up the writing, as it did in Egypt. In the later tablets the pictures had become signs for words or syllables. The above diagram shows how the early pictures became the signs that were used later.

The signs used for writing are given in column 3. The oldest form, which was the picture, is given in column 1, and column 2 shows the change appearing.

The reed with which the pictures and signs were made usually had a blunt, square-tipped end. The writer did not scratch the lines of his signs on the clay, but, to make a mark, he pressed one corner of the square

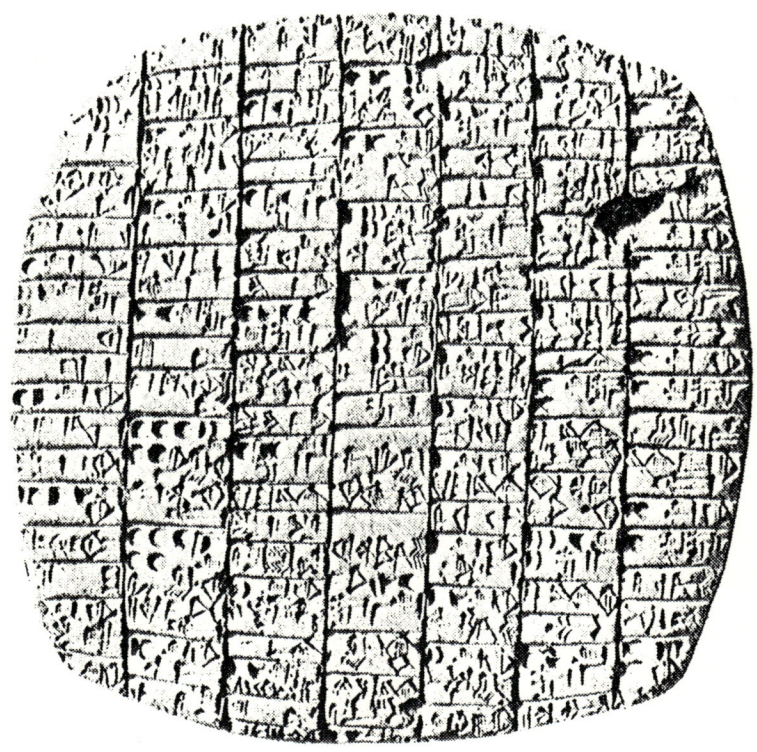

EARLY SUMERIAN CLAY TABLET WITH CUNEIFORM WRITING
(TWENTY-EIGHTH CENTURY B.C.)

tip of the reed into the soft clay, and then raised it again to press another mark in the same way. Each mark thus made was wider at one end than at the other, and hence it appeared triangular or wedge-shaped, thus ⌐ or ▎. In this way every picture or sign came to be made up of a group of wedge-shaped marks like ⋈, which was once a star. We therefore call the system *cuneiform* (Latin, *cuneus*, meaning wedge) or wedge-form writing.

The tablet shown on page 82 contains business accounts. The numbers can be recognized as circles and other curved signs, which were made with the circular *upper* end of the scribe's *stylus* (the name given to the reed with which he wrote). Note that the signs are not pictures, but that they are the signs which developed from the pictures as shown in the last illustration but one.

35. Temple Towers

Religion played an important part in the lives of the Sumerians, and of this there are many proofs to be found among the ruins. Almost in the centre of the plain of Shinar rose a great tower. It was of baked brick, for there was no stone in the district. This tower was the sacred mount of the Sumerian god of the air, at the ancient town of Nippur, the holy place of the Sumerians. In shape the building was almost a cube, though slightly narrower at the top. In front were three lofty flights of stairs rising nearly a hundred and fifty feet and coming together at a door almost half-way up the front of the building. In the upper part of the tower was a square temple, with a court open to the sky, and behind it a holy place.

The Sumerians erected such a tower at Nippur to give their god a house on a mountain top, such as we suppose he had once occupied before they left their former mountain home to dwell on the Babylonian plain. Other towns copied the idea, and the temple tower of Babylon itself in later ages gave rise to the tale of the Tower of Babel (or Babylon) as given us by the Hebrews.

It is interesting to know that the church spires of England to-day have sprung out of these Sumerian towers. The illustrations opposite show us the development. Fig. 1 is the square, tapering tower at Nippur.

TEMPLE TOWERS

In the ancient lighthouse tower of Alexandria (Fig. 2) this square, tapering tower of Babylonia has the stairway thrown to the inside, and the architect added a six-sided part above it, with a round part on top. This idea was copied in the Moslem mosques, as shown in Figs. 3 and 4, and there are many church spires in Europe to-day with a square part below, six sides above, and a round section above that. In Fig. 5, the

The Sumerians

spire of the church of St. John at Parma, Italy, we see such a tower. Out of these have developed the spires of our own churches.

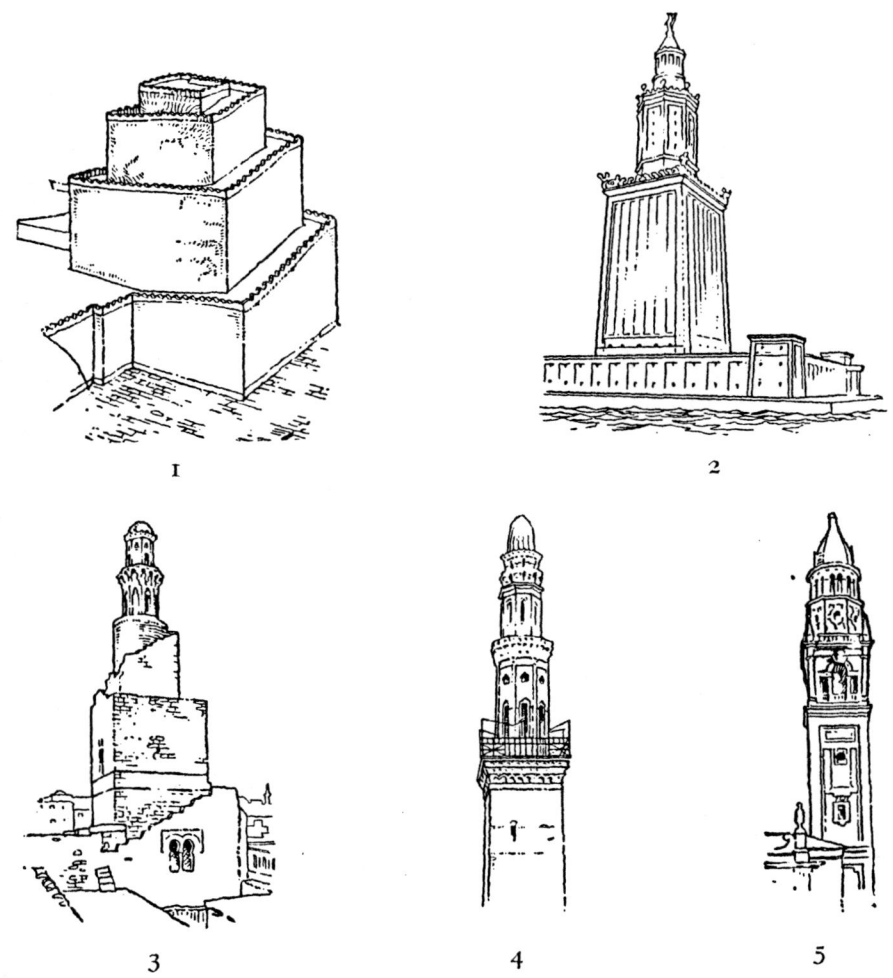

THE CHRISTIAN CHURCH SPIRE AND ITS ORIENTAL ANCESTRY

36. TEMPLE AND TOWN

The tower was not itself the only temple of the god, although we have seen that he had a shrine at the top. Alongside the tower there was a small low temple building serving as the temple proper. Approaching from the outside, the visitor saw only bare walls of sun-dried brick. These enclosed a court behind which was the sacred chamber. Indeed it is clear that this lower dwelling of the god was simply a dwelling-house like those of the townsmen. Around the temple enclosure stretched the houses of the townsfolk—bare, rectangular structures of sun-dried brick, each with a court to the north side, and on the south side of the

RESTORATION OF AN EARLY BABYLONIAN HOUSE
(After Koldewey)

court a main chamber from which the other rooms were entered.

The ordinary building material of the entire ancient world was sun-baked brick. The houses of the common people in the Orient even at the present day are still built of such brick. The walls of such houses in course of time are slowly eaten away by the rains, till after a heavy rain an old house falls down. We recall Jesus' parable of the man whose house fell down. When this happens at the present day, the rubbish is levelled off and the house is rebuilt on top of it. This practice has been going on for thousands of years.

The Sumerians

As this process went on for many centuries, it produced a high mound of rubbish on which the town stood. Babylonia to-day is full of such great mounds long since forsaken and deserted, but every city mound is a rich storehouse of ancient civilization, for the clay tablets containing the household letters, bills, receipts, notes, and accounts which were in the houses when they fell were often covered by the falling walls, and they still lie in the mound.

37. Vases and Seals

The Sumerian craftsman was an artist of great merit. He did skilful work in metal, sometimes with beautiful decorations. This vase, the finest piece of metal-work from early Babylonia, is adorned with two bands of engraving extending entirely round it. They furnish an excellent example of early Sumerian art. In the broader band we see a lion-headed eagle clutching the backs of two lions, which in their turn are biting two ibexes. This balanced arrangement of animal figures was a discovery of Sumerian art about 3000 B.C. or possibly a little earlier. Animal figures balanced in pairs like the lion and unicorn and used as symbols or

Silver Vase of a Sumerian City-king

arms of kings and nations have passed into the European life of to-day. The eagle still appears in the arms of Russia, Austria, Prussia, and other nations of Europe, and has reached America as the " American " eagle.

The same beautiful arrangement of figures is seen in a later Babylonian work shown in the following illustrations. At the extreme left of the first picture a

ANIMAL SCULPTURE

hero, Gilgamesh, is slaying a wild bull. He is aided by the hero Engidu, half man, half bull. Next, Gilgamesh alone is slaying a lion. In the second picture a lion is twice shown slaying a wild bull.

Instead of signing his name to a clay tablet, letter, or bill, the Babylonian rolled over the soft clay a little stone roller or cylinder engraved with pictures, of which an example is shown opposite. Sometimes they bore the owner's name as well. The picture mark left by the roller in the soft clay served as a signature. These seals have been found in great numbers in the ruins of Babylonia. Such a seal is shown in the next picture. The demand for these personal seals developed the beautiful art of engraving tiny figures on a hard stone surface. We call a craftsman who can do such work on stone a lapidary. The early Sumerian lapidaries soon became the finest craftsmen of the kind in the ancient world.

38. Drill and Discipline

We found on the Nile the earliest arts of peace; we find here among the Sumerians the earliest arts of war in the history of man. When the people of one city heard that a neighbouring city-kingdom was trying to take possession of a strip of their land, they were glad to follow their king in order to drive out the invaders. In the picture on page 90 we see a Sumerian city-king leading out his troops (about 2900 B.C.).

An Early Sumerian Cylinder Seal

The king himself, whose face is broken off from the stone, marches at the right, heading his troops, who follow in a closely packed group. This is the earliest example of grouping men together in a mass, forming a single unit called a *phalanx*. This must have required long drill and discipline after many centuries of loose, irregular, scattered fighting. This was the first chapter in the long history of the art of war, and it took place in Asia. Such discipline was unknown at this time in Egypt. These Sumerian troops have their spears set for the charge, but they carry no bows. Tall shields cover their entire bodies, and they wear close-fitting helmets, probably of leather. The scene is

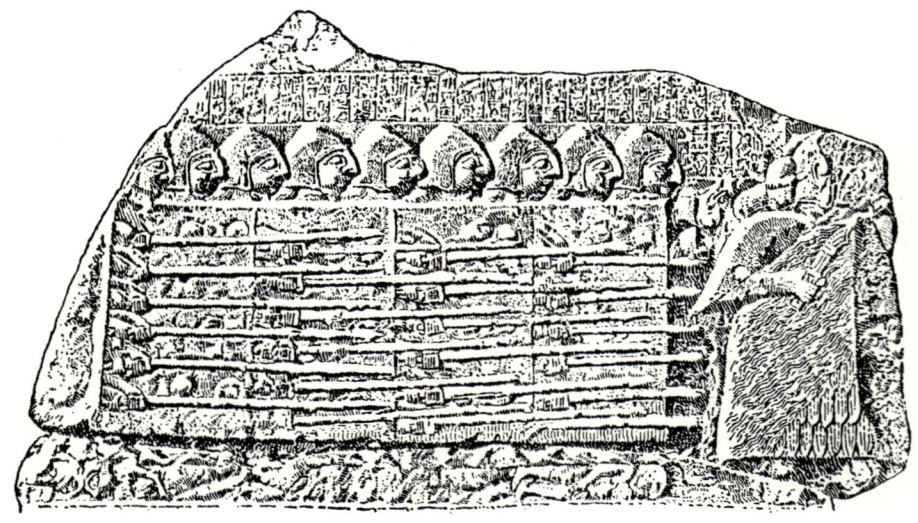

SUMERIAN TROOPS IN CLOSE ORDER

carved in stone, and is a good example of the rude Sumerian sculpture in Babylonia in the days when more beautiful carvings were being made in Egypt in the time of the Great Pyramids.

In the next chapter we shall see a new people called the Semites settling in the river valleys and developing the civilization of the Sumerians.

CHAPTER VII

BABYLONIA

39. Men of the Desert

WHILE the city-kingdoms of Sumer were thus fighting among themselves, they were also called upon to meet an enemy from the outside. These were the men of

SEMITIC NOMADS NEAR SEA OF GALILEE

the Arabian desert. Arabia is totally lacking in rivers, and enjoys but a few weeks of rain in mid-winter; hence it is a desert very little of which can support life. Its people are, and have been from the earliest ages, a great white race called Semites. The Semites have always been divided into many tribes and groups. With two of these we are familiar, the Arabs and the

Hebrews. For ages they have moved up and down the grass-grown portions of the Arabian world, seeking pastures for their flocks and herds.

Such wandering shepherds are called nomads. They do not always keep to the desert or this roving life. When they drift in from the desert and reach the more fertile places, they sometimes slowly give up the wandering life of the desert for the settled life of the

SEMITIC BOWMEN OF EARLY BABYLONIA FIGHTING IN OPEN ORDER

farming peasant. Among such movements we are familiar with that of the Hebrews from the desert into Palestine as described in the Bible.

There were similar movements of the nomads from the desert towards the mouths of the Tigris and Euphrates, and we find Semitic groups beginning early to settle down in the district to the north of the Sumerians. Some of them were perhaps there before the Sumerians came in the country. These desert wanderers had never learned discipline and drill in war like the Sumerians. This illustration shows us the Semitic bowmen of early Babylonia fighting in open

Babylonia

order. They had no plans; each man leaped about in the fray as he pleased, and the fight was a loose series of single combats between two enemies. This loose, rough-and-tumble fighting was the earliest method of warfare, before men learned to train and drill themselves in groups or masses. The Sumerians, as we have seen, were the earliest men who took this step. Thus two races faced each other on the plain of Shinar: in the north the half-settled and rough Semitic nomads of Akkad, and in the south the well-trained and civilized Sumerians, who were for a long time superior to the new-comers both in war and peace.

40. SARGON

About 2750 B.C. there arose in Akkad a Semitic chieftian named Sargon. So skilful in war did he become that he succeeded in defeating the Sumerian spearmen and making himself lord of all the plain of Shinar. The old Sumerian city-kings were overcome, and the Sumerian towns down to the mouths of the Two Rivers submitted to him. Sargon was the first great leader in the history of the Semitic race, and he was the first ruler to build up a great nation in Western Asia. The important thing to be remembered about Sargon is that his conquests forced his own wandering tribesmen, the Akkadians, to make a complete change in their manner of life, and they did this under the influence of the Sumerians whom they had conquered. The once wandering Semitic shepherds were obliged to drop their unsettled life and to take up fixed abodes.

At first these new-comers did not even know how to write, and they had no industries. Some of them, however, now learned to write their Semitic tongue by using the Sumerian wedge-form signs for the purpose. It was then that a Semitic language began to be written for the first time. We can see this uniting of the Sumerian and the Semite in the following illustration, which is a copy of the seal impression of one of the men in the picture.

The third figure (wearing a cap) is that of a prince, Ubil-Ishtar, who is a brother of the king. He is a

A SEMITIC PRINCE AND HIS SUMERIAN SECRETARY
(TWENTY-SEVENTH CENTURY B.C.)

Semite, as his beard shows. Three of his four attendants are also Semites with beards and long hair, but one of them (just behind the prince) is beardless and shaven-headed, which shows he is a Sumerian. He is the prince's secretary, for being a Sumerian he is skilled in writing. His name, " Kalki ", we learn from the inscription in the corner, which is in the Semitic tongue, and illustrates how the Semites have learned the Sumerian signs for writing.

Thus the life of the desert Semite mingled with that of the non-Semitic mountaineer on the Babylonian plain, much as Norman and English mingled in England. On the streets and in the market-places of

Babylonia

the Euphrates towns, where once the bare feet, clean-shaven heads, and beardless faces of the Sumerian townsmen were the only ones to be seen, there were now the sandalled feet, the dark beards, and heavy locks of hair of the Semites of Akkad. The latter adopted the Sumerian calendar, weights and measures, system of numerals, and business methods. With the arts of peace they also gained those of war. They learned to make helmets of leather and copper weighing over two pounds. These are the earliest known examples of the use of metal as a protection in war.

In time, a united nation of "Sumer and Akkad" gradually developed. They have left us no great buildings or imposing monuments, but the two peoples prospered greatly and their united kingdom lasted for over three hundred years.

41. The Letters and Laws of Hammurapi

As the kings of "Sumer and Akkad" slowly weakened, a *new* tribe of Semites began descending the Euphrates, just as the men of Akkad had done under Sargon. A little after 2200 B.C. this new tribe seized Babylon, which was at that time a small unknown village on the Euphrates. The new kings of Babylon at once began to fight their way towards the leadership of Sumer and Akkad. After a century of warfare there appeared, about 2100 B.C., a Babylonian king called Hammurapi, who made his city of Babylon for the first time supreme throughout the land. He was the second great Semitic ruler, as Sargon had been the first. Only a few generations earlier his ancestors, like those of Sargon, had been drifting about the desert.

Hammurapi now put forth his strong hand upon the busy life of the Babylonian towns, and he created a system of government such as Babylonia had never seen before. Many letters written by Hammurapi have been discovered, and they show us the deeds and the character of this great king.

Hammurapi's letters give us for the first time in history a glimpse into the busy life of a powerful ruler in Asia. The letters disclose the king to us sitting in the office of his palace at Babylon with his secretary at his side. In short clear sentences the king begins dictating his brief letters, conveying his commands to the local governors of the old Sumerian cities which he now rules. The secretary draws a reed stylus from a leathern holder at his girdle and quickly covers the small clay tablet with its lines of wedge-groups. The writer then sprinkles over the soft wet tablet a handful of dry powdered clay. This is to prevent the clay envelope, which he now wraps about the letter, from sticking to the written surface. On this soft clay envelope he writes the address and sends the letter out to be put into the furnace and baked.

A LETTER WRITTEN BY HAMMURAPI, KING OF BABYLONIA (ABOUT 2100 B.C.)

Babylonia

Here is a summary of three of the letters received by the king and his replies to them:

The flood has obstructed the Euphrates and a long string of boats have been tied up and are waiting. The king's reply orders the governor of Larsa to clear the channel at the earliest moment.

The king is much interested in his vast flocks of sheep, as if the nomad instinct had not altogether vanished from the blood of his line. He orders the officials to appear in Babylon to celebrate the spring sheep-shearing as if it were a great feast.

The chief of the temple bakers finds that royal orders to look after a religious feast at Ur will call him away from the capital city when he has an important law-suit coming on. He easily obtains an order from the king postponing the law-suit.

Thus the letters show us this great king busy at his work of governing.

Hammurapi made a code of laws for his people. He first of all collected all the older written laws and customs of business and social life and arranged them into a system. He improved them and added new laws where he thought fit. He had these laws engraved on a stone nearly eight feet high.

Overleaf is a picture of the stone on which the laws were engraved, and they extend entirely round the shaft, occupying over three thousand six hundred lines. Above the laws is a fine relief showing King Hammurapi standing at the left receiving the laws from the Sun-god seated at the right. Hammurapi's shaven upper lip, showing him to be a man of the Syrian desert, is here in the shadow and cannot be seen. The flames rising from the god's shoulders show us who he is.

Hammurapi's laws insist on justice to the widow, the orphan, and the poor. Marriage was carefully regulated by these laws, and we see that the position of women in this early Babylonian world, as in Egypt, was a high one. Women engaged in business on their own account, and even became professional scribes.

42. A School in Babylon

To train men as priests and to furnish clerks for business and government in the days of Hammurapi, schools were necessary. These schools were usually attached to a temple. A school-house of Hammurapi's time has actually been uncovered, with the clay-tablet exercises of the boys and girls of four thousand years ago still lying on the floor. They show how the child began his long and difficult task of learning to understand and to write three or four hundred different signs. The pupil's

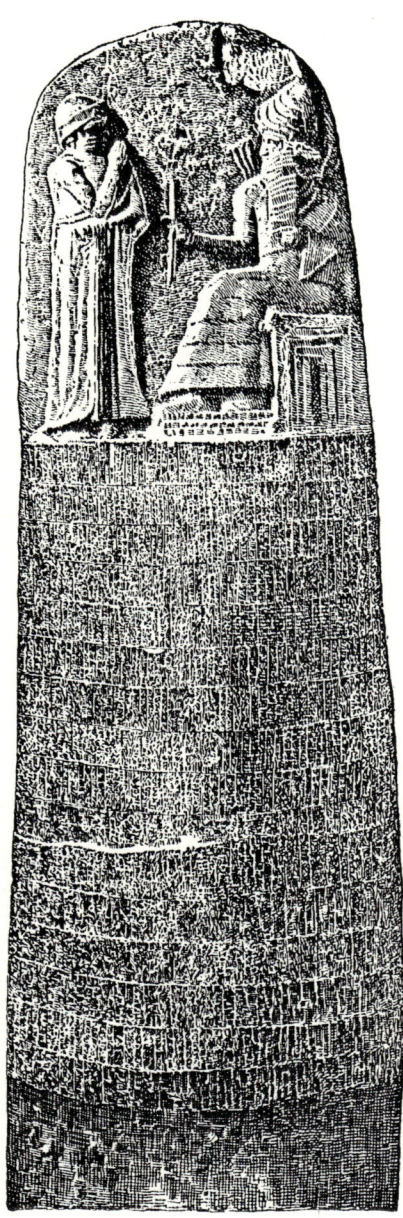

The Laws of Hammurapi, the Oldest Surviving Code of Laws (2100 B.C.)

Babylonia

slate was a soft clay tablet, on which he could rub out his exercises at any time by smoothing off the surface with a flat piece of wood or stone. With his reed stylus in his hand, he made long rows of single wedges. When he could make the single wedge neatly enough, the master set him at work on the wedge-groups forming the signs themselves. Lastly, he was able to undertake words and simple phrases leading up to sentences and quotations from old documents.

 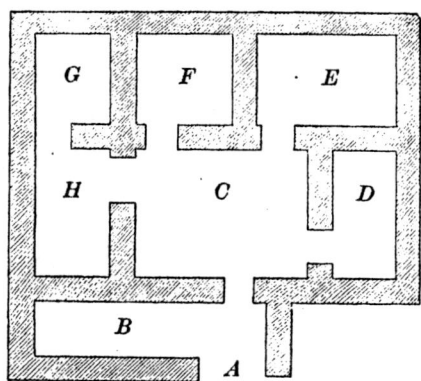

An Ancient Babylonian School-house in the Days of Hammurapi (about 2100 b.c.). (After Scheil)

On the right of the picture on this page is a diagram of the ground plan of a school-house, which was about fifty-five feet square. The children went in at the door (*A*) across the line of the long room (*B*), where the door-keeper sat and kept a list on a clay tablet of the boys that came late. Then the children entered a court (*C*) which was open to the sky, and we may suppose that they separated here, the big boys and girls going into their own rooms, while the little ones went into others. Somewhere in the school-house and probably in the court (*C*) was a pile or box of soft clay, where a boy who had already filled his clay-tablet slate with wedge-marks could quickly make himself a new slate by flattening a ball of soft clay.

On the left of the picture we see one of the doors of this oldest school-house in the world as it appeared on the day when it was uncovered by the French in 1894. The native Arab workmen who uncovered it stand in the doorway. The walls of sun-dried brick are still eight or nine feet high.

One of the tablets found in the school-house contains a proverb which shows how highly the Babylonians valued the art of writing. It reads: " He who shall excel in tablet-writing shall shine like the sun ". This was probably a copy-book exercise, and it may have encouraged many a painstaking boy.

43. THE DONKEY AND THE HORSE

Under the wise rule of such men as Hammurapi, the busy cities of Babylon prospered as never before. Their products were chiefly grain and dates ; but they also had flocks and herds, leather and wool. The weaving of wool was a great industry, for woollen clothing was commonly worn in Western Asia. A standing army kept the frontiers safe, and the slow donkey caravans of the Babylonian merchants plodding from town to town were able to go far into the surrounding districts.

We can look upon these donkey caravans as typical of the peaceful trading methods of these days in Babylon. Many a courtyard was piled high with bales, each bearing a clay seal with the impression of the merchant's name. These clay seals, broken away as the bales were opened, lie to-day in the rubbish of the Babylonian towns, where the modern excavator picks them up, still showing on one side the merchant's name and on the other the mark of the cord which bound the bale.

When Hammurapi died, this peaceful life and well-ordered commerce were interrupted by the arrival in the valleys of fresh groups of wild mountaineers, who swept away the successors of Hammurapi and triumphed over the Babylonians. These highlanders probably brought with them a new-comer even more important than themselves; for as they began to appear more and more often on the streets of the Babylonian towns, they seem to have led with them a strange animal, for which the Babylonians had no name. They called it "the animal of the mountains".

Thus it was that about four thousand years ago the tamed horse appeared for the first time in a civilized community, and began to play that important part in war and industry which he has held ever since. These mountaineers who brought the horse into Babylonia did not tame him themselves. They received him in trade from the north or from Asia Minor from tribes of the Indo-Europeans who had long before tamed the animal.

The repeated inroads of semi-civilized mountaineers from the north had such an important effect on the history of this part of Asia that we must now move northwards and study a new people—the Assyrians. They were Semites, but their story is different in many ways from that of the Babylonians.

CHAPTER VIII

Assyria

44. The Assyrians

THE next chapter of history along the Two Rivers carries us up-river from Babylonia to the north-west. Here, overlooking the Tigris on the east and the desert on the west and south, was an easily defended strip of high ground possessing a natural strength unknown to the towns on the flat plain of Shinar. The place was known as Assur, and it later gave its name to Assyria.

THE TIGRIS AND THE PROMONTORY OF ASSUR

The region about Assur was a highland enjoying a much more bracing climate than the hot plain of Babylon. It had many fertile valleys. Here were found rocks which furnished quarries of limestone, alabaster, and other and harder stone. Thus Assyria differed greatly from Babylonia, which was without stone that could be used for building, and had therefore developed architecture only in brick. These north-eastern valleys were green with rolling pastures and fields of barley and wheat. Herds of oxen and flocks of sheep and goats dotted the hill-side pastures. Donkeys served as the chief draft animals, and the horse was unknown in the beginning just as he was originally unknown in Babylonia. Here flourished a farming people, little given to other industries or commerce. In this respect Assyria was again different from Babylonia.

By 3000 B.C. a Semitic tribe of nomads from the desert had settled at Assur, forming a tiny city-kingdom. It is clear that they were in close contact with Sumerian towns, whose sculpture and writing they adopted. They also received the Sumerian calendar and most of the conveniences of Sumerian civilization. To these Assyrians civilization also came from the north and west, from the Hittites, the Arameans, the Phoenicians, and the Egyptians. Thus Assyria became a sort of meeting-place for the civilization of Egypt and of Sumer, and in many things we find the civilization of the former displacing the latter.

While benefiting in many ways from these neighbours to the north, west, and south, the Assyrians also found themselves open to attack from these directions, and in order to protect themselves they were compelled to become a military nation. In the end they created a great Assyrian Empire that stretched from the Persian Gulf to the Nile. The following picture illustrates their success.

Here we see an Assyrian recording the plunder taken from a captured Asiatic city. The captive women and children ride by in ox-carts on their way to slavery in Assyria, and a shepherd drives off the captured flocks. At the left an Assyrian officer reads from a tablet his notes on the spoil taken in the city. Two scribes write as he reads. The first (in front) holds in his left hand a thick clay tablet from which he has just lifted the stylus grasped in the right hand, as he pauses in his writing. The other scribe holds, spread out in his left hand, a roll of papyrus, on which

AN ASSYRIAN AND AN ARAMEAN SCRIBE RECORDING THE PLUNDER TAKEN FROM A CAPTURED ASIATIC CITY (EIGHTH CENTURY B.C.)

he is busily writing with a pen held in his right hand. He is an Aramean, writing Aramaic with pen and ink. We see here, then, the two different methods of writing practised at this time in the ancient world, the Asiatic clay tablet and the Egyptian papyrus, pen, and ink. The Arameans had copied the Egyptian methods, which were easier and better to use than the old Sumerian clay tablet and stylus.

45. A Battering-ram

The Assyrians, obliged for over a thousand years to defend their frontiers against their neighbours in both north and south, were strong because they had always to be ready for war. They introduced the horse into their armies and also added chariots. Then the Assyrian kings began pushing westwards, and by 1300 B.C. they crossed the Euphrates and swept back a powerful people called the Hittites from the great

Assyrian Battering-ram

river. At the same time they began to descend the Tigris with such force that they even captured and ruled for a time their old conqueror Babylon. Here we see a picture of an Assyrian king attacking a fortified city. The Assyrians developed powerful weapons for destroying a city wall. The city at the right is protected by walls of sun-dried brick. The defending archers on the wall are trying to drive away a huge Assyrian battering-ram, mounted on six wheels, which has been rolled up to the wall from the left. It is an ancient " tank " with its front protected by metal armour-plate. It carries a tower as high as the city wall, and Assyrian archers in the top of the tower are shooting at the defenders on the wall. Within the "tank" unseen men work the heavy beam of the ram. It is capped with metal and is shown smashing a hole in the city wall, from which the bricks fall out. An observation tower with a metal-covered dome and holes for peeping out shields the officer in command as he directs the working of the machine. In the rear (at the left) is the Assyrian king shooting arrows into the hostile city. He uses a powerful bow, probably invented in Egypt, which will shoot an arrow with great force from a thousand to fourteen hundred feet, and hence he can stand at a safe distance.

This scene, carved on a slab of alabaster, is an example of flat sculpture not practised in Babylonia. As in sculpture, so in architecture, the possession of stone enabled the Assyrians to do what had been impossible in stoneless Babylonia. The builder could erect heavy foundations of stone under his buildings. Above the foundations, the Assyrian building itself continued to be made of sun-dried brick as in Babylonia.

46. Nineveh

Assyria grew stronger generation after generation, until the once obscure little city of Assur had gained the lordship over Western Asia as head of an empire, a great group of conquered and subject nations. This was done under the leadership of a series of famous emperors. Their names are:

Sargon II	722–705 B.C.
Sennacherib	705–681 B.C.
Esarhaddon	681–668 B.C.
Assurbanipal	668–626 B.C.

Assyria

Sargon II raised Assyria to the height of her power as a military empire. On the north-east of Nineveh he built a new royal residence on a vaster scale and more magnificent than any Asia had ever seen before. The enclosure was a mile square, large enough to shelter a town of eighty thousand people, and the palace building itself covered twenty-five acres. Babylonia in her

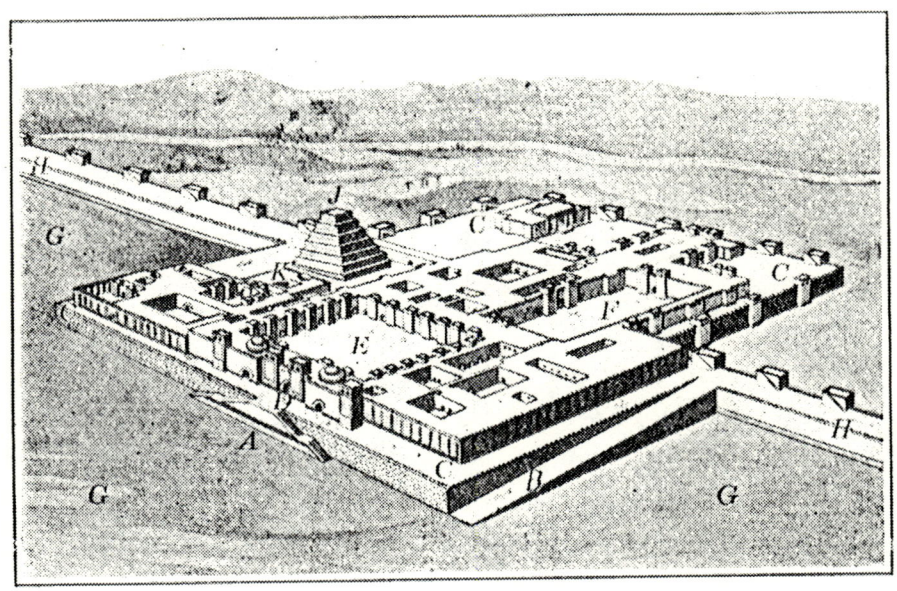

RESTORATION OF THE PALACE OF SARGON II

greatest days never possessed a seat of power like this. The palace stood partly inside and partly outside the city wall (*H H*) on a vast raised platform (*C C C C*) of brick masonry. Inclined roadways (*B*) and stairways (*A*) rose from the inside of the city wall. The king could thus drive up in his chariot from the streets of the city below (*G G G*) to the palace pavement above. The rooms and halls were grouped about a number of courts (*E F*). The main entrance (*D*) (with stairs before it leading down to the city) had massive towers and arched doorways built of richly coloured glazed brick, and adorned with huge human-headed bulls carved of alabaster. The streets and houses of the city filled the space below the palace within the city walls.

The emperors Sennacherib and Assurbanipal developed the work of Sargon II in the arts of war and peace. Sennacherib completely destroyed Babylon, the great city of Hammurapi, and even turned the waters of a canal over the desolate ruins.

To carry on such conquests Assyria had turned herself into a vast military machine more terrible than mankind had ever yet seen. An important new fact aided in bringing about this result. Through contact with the west, iron had been introduced among the Assyrians. The Assyrian forces were therefore the first large armies having weapons of iron. A single room in one palace was found to contain two hundred tons of iron implements. To a certain extent the rise and power of the Assyrian Empire were among the results of the use of iron. But it was the valour of such stalwart archers and spearmen as we see in this picture that had much to do in making Assyria mistress of the East for nearly two centuries. Sennacherib devoted himself to the city of Nineveh, north of Assur, and it became the far-famed capital of Assyria. Along the Tigris the vast palaces and temples of the Assyrian emperors arose. The lofty and massive walls of Nineveh which Sennacherib built stretched two miles and a half along the banks of the river. Here in his gorgeous palace he ruled the western Asiatic world. Nineveh became the centre of a wonderful scheme of government. The emperor had a system of royal

Assyria

ASSYRIAN SOLDIERS OF THE EMPIRE
(From the Palace Reliefs of Assurbanipal)

messengers, and in each of the more important places on the main roads he appointed an official to attend to all royal business. In this manner all clay-tablet letters or goods belonging to the royal house were sure of being forwarded. This plan formed the beginning of a post-office system which continued for many centuries in the Orient.

47. LIBRARIES OF CLAY

It must not be forgotten that the arts of peace also flourished in Assyria. Most of the crafts and industries we have referred to in connection with Sumer and Babylon were carried on with zeal in Nineveh. Literature in particular flourished. Assurbanipal, grandson of Sennacherib, boasts that his father instructed him not only in riding and shooting with bow and arrow, but also in writing on clay tablets and in all the wisdom of the time. A great collection of twenty-two thousand clay tablets was discovered in Assurbanipal's library rooms at Nineveh, where they had been lying on the floor for twenty-five hundred years. They are now in the British Museum. In this library the religious, scientific, and literary works of past ages had been carefully collected by the emperor's orders. They formed the earliest library known in Asia, and show us that the Assyrians were far more advanced in these matters than the Babylonians.

The next illustration is a copy of a portion of an old Babylonian story of the Flood from the library at Nineveh. It is a large flat tablet which was part of an Assyrian book consisting of a series of such tablets. This flood story tells us how the hero, Ut-napishtim, built a great ship and thus survived a terrible flood, in which all his countrymen perished. Each of these clay-tablet books, collected in fresh copies by Assurbanipal for his library, bore his "bookmark", just like

PORTION OF OLD BABYLONIAN STORY OF THE FLOOD FROM ASSURBANIPAL'S LIBRARY AT NINEVEH

a book in a modern library. To prevent anyone else from taking the book or writing his name in it, the Assyrian king's bookmark contained the following warning: "Whosoever shall carry off this tablet, or shall inscribe his name upon it side by side with my own, may Assur and Belit overthrow him in wrath and anger, and may they destroy his name and posterity in the land ". Assur and Belit were Assyrian gods.

48. BABYLON AGAIN

In the year 606 B.C. Nineveh was destroyed by the Chaldeans from the south and the Medes from the north. Then a new Chaldean Empire arose with Babylon as its capital. This empire lasted from 606 B.C. to 539 B.C. The greatest name of this period is that of Nebuchadnezzar, a king whom the Bible has made very familiar to us. He was the greatest of all the Chaldean emperors, and in 604 B.C. he began a reign in Babylon of over forty years, a reign of such power and glory, especially as shown to us in the Old Testament, that he has become one of the greatest figures of Oriental history.

His power extended far from his capital, and he made a special point of conquering the peoples to the west of Babylon. The Bible has made us all familiar with his conquest of the little kingdom of Judah. He finally carried away many Hebrews as captives to Babylonia and destroyed Jerusalem, their capital. His own capital of Babylon Nebuchadnezzar made very large and beautiful. He copied much from Assyria, and was able to surpass the Assyrians in the splendour of the great buildings which he erected. The Ishtar Gate leading to the palace quarter of Babylon still remains for us to wonder at.

This gate is the most important ancient building still standing in Babylon. The towers rising on either side of the gate are adorned with the figures of animals in splendidly coloured glazed tile as was used also in the Assyrian palaces. Behind this gate rose the gorgeous palace of Nebuchadnezzar, known as the Hanging Gardens of Babylon, where in the cool shade of palms and ferns the great king might enjoy an idle hour with his court, and look down upon the splendours

THE ISHTAR GATE OF THE PALACE QUARTER OF BABYLON IN THE CHALDEAN EMPIRE (SIXTH CENTURY B.C.)

of the great city whose fame spread far into the west. The Greeks numbered the Hanging Gardens as one of the Seven Wonders of the World. And this is the Babylon that has become familiar to all Christian peoples as the great city of the Hebrew captivity. Of all the glories that made it world-famous in its time, little now remains.

The mounds shown in this picture are the rubbish covering the palace of Nebuchadnezzar. The palms in the background fringe the Euphrates. The Arab workmen in the foreground have just uncovered part of the pavement of Nebuchadnezzar's splendid Festival Street or avenue for processions which connected the palace and the Ishtar Gate with one of the great

BEGINNING OF THE EXCAVATION OF ANCIENT BABYLON IN 1899

temples. All these works of *Chaldean* Babylon lie above the remains of the old Babylon of Hammurapi's age which Sennacherib swept away.

The next great period in the regions of the Tigris and the Euphrates is the Persian age. The Persians came down from the mountains, occupied the plains, and adopted the Babylonian civilization in all its different branches. With the Persians we must consider Palestine and the Hebrews, for they also are of great importance in the story of the progress of Western civilization.

PART IV
PERSIA: PALESTINE

CHAPTER IX

THE PERSIANS AND THE HEBREWS

49. THE PERSIANS

AFTER the death of Nebuchadnezzar (561 B.C.), whose reign was the high-water mark of Chaldean civilization, the old civilized lands of the Orient seemed to have lost most of their former power to go forward and make fresh discoveries and new conquests in civilization such as they had been making during the three great ages on the Nile and three similar ages on the Two Rivers. Indeed the leadership of the Semitic peoples in the early world was drawing near its close, and they were about to give way before the advance of new peoples. The nomads of the southern desert were about to yield to the hardy peoples of the northern and eastern mountains and plains. These nomads from the north were from the earliest times a great white race, which we call Indo-Europeans.

The Indo-Europeans were the ancestors of the leading people of Europe at the present day. These nomads of the northern grasslands, our ancestors, began to migrate in very ancient times, moving out along different routes. At last they stretched in a long line from the frontiers of India in the east westward across all Europe to the Atlantic. They were:

(a) The Aryans of North India.
(b) The Persians.
(c) The Medes.
(d) The Hittites.
(e) The Greeks.
(f) The Romans.
(g) The Celts.

The Medes and Persians were the most important of the early Indo-Europeans to come into contact with the old civilizations of which we have read in the preceding pages. They lived in the mountains to the east of the Tigris. Here the Persians occupied a district some four hundred miles long. They were a rude mountain peasant folk, leading a settled, agricultural life, with simple institutions, no art, no writing or literature, but with stirring memories of their past.

There arose among these Persian peasants a great man named Cyrus. He made his people into a fighting nation. He led them in rebellion against their powerful kindred the Medes. He made himself master of the Median country. Led by Cyrus, the power of the little Persian kingdom swept across Asia Minor to the Mediterranean within five years, and became the leading state in the Oriental world. Cyrus was now a man upon whom all eyes in the west were fastened with wonder and alarm.

Cyrus then conquered Babylonia, where he had no trouble in defeating the Chaldean army led by the young prince Belshazzar, whose name in the Book of Daniel is a household word throughout the Christian

The Persians and the Hebrews

world. In spite of the vast walls erected by Nebuchadnezzar to protect Babylon, the Persians entered the great city in 539 B.C.

This picture of a barrel-shaped clay record of the capture of Babylon by Cyrus tells how " without battle and without fighting Marduk (god of Babylon) made

BARREL-SHAPED CLAY RECORD OF THE CAPTURE OF BABYLON BY CYRUS (539 B.C.)

him (Cyrus) enter into his city of Babylon ; he spared Babylon tribulation, and Nabonidus, the (Chaldean) king of Babylon who feared him not, he delivered into his hand ".

50. PERSIAN ARCHERS

The Persian peasants who had enabled Cyrus to carry out his great plans seem to have been remarkable archers. The mass of the Persian army was made up of bowmen, whose storm of arrows at long range overwhelmed the enemy long before the hand-to-hand fighting began. Bodies of the skilful Persian horsemen hovering on either wing then rode in and completed the destruction of the foe.

Note in the picture showing the Persian soldiers that, although carrying spears when doing duty as palace guards, these men were chiefly archers, as is shown by the size of the large quivers on their backs. The bow hangs on the left shoulder. Notice the splendid robes worn by these palace guards. This was of course after the Persians had settled down in their

PERSIAN SOLDIERS OF THE PALACE GUARD

new territories and had borrowed the luxurious ideas and manners of the people they had conquered.

51. DARIUS

The Persians had found Babylon a great and splendid city, with the vast fortifications of Nebuchadnezzar stretching from river to river and his buildings visible far across the Babylonian plain. The city was the centre of the commerce of Western Asia and the greatest market in the early Oriental world. Along the Nile the Persian emperors now ruled the splendid cities whose colossal monuments we have already visited. These things and the civilized life which the Persians found along the Nile and the Euphrates soon influenced them greatly.

The organization of such a vast empire, stretching from the Indus River to the Ægean Sea, and from the Indian Ocean to the Caspian, was a great task. It demanded government on a larger scale than any ruler had ever attempted before. It was much too great a work to be completed by Cyrus. Begun by him, it was carried through by Darius the Great (521–485 B.C.), and his well-ordered empire remains one of the greatest achievements in the history of the ancient Orient, if not of the world.

A Corner of the Court of the Palace of Darius I at Susa

The rule of Darius was just, kind, and wise, but the subject people had of course no voice in their government. All that the Great King decreed was law, and all the peoples bowed to his word. This picture shows us a corner of the court of the palace of Darius at Susa, and it gives us some idea of the splendour in which the Persians lived.

This is a picture of the most important historical monument surviving in Asia. It is cut on the face of a rock and is made up of four important parts: the sculptures (*A*) and the inscriptions (*B, C, D*). The great inscription (*B*), in columns some twelve feet high,

TRIUMPHAL MONUMENT OF DARIUS THE GREAT

records the triumph of Darius over all his enemies in the many revolts which followed his coronation. It is in the Persian language, written with the cuneiform alphabet of thirty-nine letters which the Persians devised. The other two inscriptions (*C* and *D*) are translations of the Persian (*B*). Therefore (*C*) contains the same record as the Persian (*B*), but it is in the Babylonian language and is written in Babylonian cuneiform with its several hundred wedge-signs. The third inscription (*D*) is also in cuneiform, in the language of the region of Susa, and hence is called Susian. Thus the Great King published his triumph in the three most important languages of this eastern region, and placed the record overlooking a main road at Behistun, where the men of the caravans passing between Babylon and the Iranian Plateau would look up three hundred feet and see the splendid monument twenty-five feet high and fifty feet wide.

To reach this monument requires a dangerous climb, and it was on this lofty cliff, at the risk of his life, that a modern scholar, Sir Henry Rawlinson, copied all three of these cuneiform inscriptions. By the use of these copies Rawlinson succeeded in working out the translation of the Persian inscription (*B*), which proved to be the key to the ancient Babylonian cuneiform writing; and this great monument of Darius, therefore, enabled modern historians to recover the lost language and history of Babylonia and Assyria.

We shall hear more of the Persians when we come to read about the Greeks.

52. PALESTINE

If you examine the map on p. 76, you will note that Palestine is a sort of connecting link between Africa and Eurasia (Asia and Europe). In the days of Egyptian and Babylonian prosperity, strange faces from many a foreign clime could be seen crowding the market-places of Palestine amid a babel of various dialects. Here the rich jewellery, bronze dishes, and ivory furniture of the Nile craftsmen mingled with the pottery of the Ægean Islands and the red earthenware of the Hittites or the gay woollens of Babylonia.

The donkeys which lifted their voices above the hubbub of the market had grazed along the shores of both Nile and Euphrates, and their masters had trafficked beneath the Babylonian temple towers as well as under the shadow of the Theban obelisks. Palestine was the entrance to the bridge between Asia and Africa—a middle ground where the civilizations of Egypt and Babylonia, of Phœnicia, the Ægean and Asia Minor, all represented by their wares, met and mixed as they did nowhere else in the Orient.

CARAVAN OF CANAANITES

This picture shows us a caravan of Canaanites from Palestine trading in Egypt about 1900 B.C. as they appeared on the estate of a feudal baron in Egypt. The Egyptian noble had this picture of them painted with others in his tomb, where it still is. Observe the shoes, sandals, and gay woollen clothing, the costume of the Palestinian towns, worn by these Canaanites; observe also the metal weapons which they carry. The manufacture of these things created industries which had begun to flourish among the towns in Syria and Palestine by this time.

Just as the merchandise of the surrounding nations met in the markets of Palestine, so the armies of these nations also met there in battle. The situation of Palestine, between its powerful neighbours on the Nile and on the Euphrates, made it the battle-ground where these great nations fought for many centuries. Over and over again unhappy Palestine went through the experiences of little Belgium in the conflict between Germany and the Allies in 1914. Egypt held Palestine for many centuries. Later Assyria conquered it. Chaldea also held it, and finally it fell under the rule of Persia.

53. THE HEBREWS

The Hebrews were all originally men of the Arabian desert wandering with their flocks and herds, and finally drifting into Palestine as their home. Their history is told us in the Old Testament, and we must remember that this belongs as much to ancient history as the story of Egypt or Babylon. The history of the Hebrews, as they themselves have written it in the Book of Genesis, begins with the journey of Abraham from Ur of the Chaldees, up the valley of the Euphrates and down into Palestine. He moved thus with his family and his large possessions. There is no need to tell his story here. For this part of history the Bible should become your text-book, and you should follow the careers there of Abraham and his nephew Lot, of Isaac and his sons Jacob and Esau, and of one group of Hebrew tribes who became slaves in Egypt, where they suffered much hardship under a cruel Pharaoh. They were led out of Egypt by their leader Moses, who was their lawgiver and a great national hero whose deeds they never forgot. You will read in the Bible of the Hebrews conquering Canaan under Joshua, the successor of Moses, and how the land was shared among the twelve tribes of Israel.

The Hebrew slaves working in the Egyptian brickyards (see Exodus i, iv, and v, 6-19) must have looked like those in this picture when Moses led them forth into Asia. At the left below, the soft clay is being mixed in two piles; one labourer helps to load a basket of clay on the shoulder of another, who carries it to the brick moulder, at the right above. Here a labourer empties the clay from his basket, while the moulder before him fills with clay an oblong box,

Ancient Egyptian Painting of a Brickyard with Asiatic Captives engaged in Brick-making

which is the mould. He has already finished three bricks. At the left above, a moulder spreads out the soft bricks with spaces between for circulation of air to make them dry quickly in the sun. The overseer, staff in hand, sits in the upper right-hand corner, and below him we see a workman carrying away the dried bricks hanging from a yoke on his shoulders. Thus were made the bricks used for thousands of years for the buildings that formed so large a part of the cities of the ancient world, from the Orient to Athens and Rome.

The Persians and the Hebrews

54. TOWNS IN PALESTINE

The first mention of the Hebrews outside the Bible appears on a clay tablet, of which this is an illustration.

LETTER OF THE EGYPTIAN GOVERNOR OF JERUSALEM TELLING OF THE INVASION OF PALESTINE BY THE HEBREWS (FOURTEENTH CENTURY B.C.)

This tablet is a letter written in Babylonian cuneiform by a terrified Egyptian governor in Palestine who begs the Pharaoh for help, saying: " The Khabiru (Hebrews) are taking the cities of the king. No ruler remains to the king, my lord; all are lost." The king of Egypt to whom he wrote was Ikhnaton, reigning at the time when the Egyptian Empire in Asia was falling to pieces. This letter is one of a group of three hundred such cuneiform letters found in one of the rooms of Ikhnaton's palace at Tell el-Amarna (or Amarna), and called the Amarna letters, the oldest body of international correspondence in the world.

On entering Palestine the Hebrews found the Canaanites already dwelling there in flourishing towns protected by massive walls. The Hebrews were able to capture only the weaker Canaanite towns, and Jerusalem in the Judean highlands for centuries kept out the Hebrew invaders. Let us remember that these unconquered Canaanite towns possessed a civilization fifteen hundred years old, with comfortable houses, government, industries, trade, writing, and religion —a civilization which the rude Hebrew shepherds were soon adopting, for they could not avoid mixing with the Canaanites, as trade and business threw them together.

This mingling with the Canaanites produced great changes in the life of the Hebrews. Most of them left their tents and began to build brick houses like those of the Canaanites; they put off the rough sheepskin they had worn in the desert, and they put on fine Canaanite raiment of gaily coloured woven wool. After a time, in appearance and manner of living, the Hebrews were not to be distinguished from the Canaanites among whom they now lived.

Jericho is one of the most famous of these Canaanite towns. This is a picture of the long mound that covers the ancient city. The walls of the city and the ruins of the houses are buried under the rubbish which makes up this mound. Many of the ancient cities of Palestine, some of them as old as 2500 B.C., are now

THE LONG MOUND OF THE ANCIENT CITY OF JERICHO

only such mounds as this. The next picture shows the ruins of the houses of ancient Jericho. Only the stone foundations of these houses are preserved. The walls were of sun-dried brick, and the rains of over

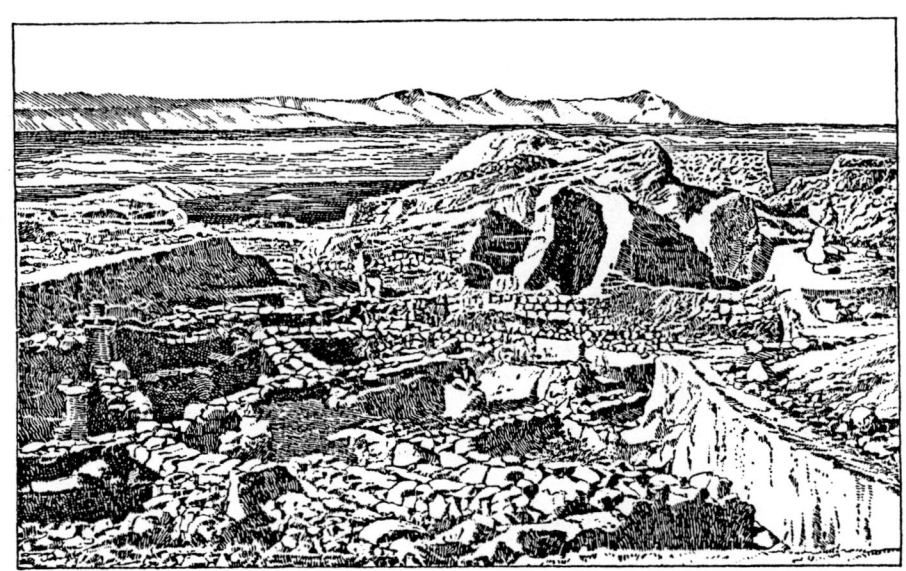

RUINS OF THE HOUSES OF ANCIENT JERICHO

three thousand years have washed them away. The houses in the picture date from about 1500 B.C., and in them lived the Canaanites whom the Hebrews found in Palestine. Here we find pottery jars, glass, and dishes of the household; also things carved in stone, like seals, amulets, and ornaments of metal. The industries of these people were clearly learned in Egypt. Cuneiform tablets of clay found in these ruins show the influence of Babylonian business.

GLIMPSE OF THE WALLS OF JERUSALEM FROM THE LOW VALLEY BELOW THE OLD CANAANITE FORTRESS

55. JERUSALEM

Even after the Hebrews had set up a king of their own, the old nomad customs were still strong, for Saul, the first king (about 1025 B.C.), still loved to live in a tent. His successor David saw the importance of a strong castle as the king's permanent home. He therefore seized the old Canaanite fortress of Jerusalem. From Jerusalem as his residence, David extended his power far and wide, and made the Hebrews a strong nation. His people never forgot his deeds as a warrior, and his skill as a poet and singer. Centuries later they revered him as the author of many of their religious songs or " psalms ".

In the picture of Jerusalem the houses on the right of the valley belong to the modern village of Siloam ; but on the left we see the high walls of Jerusalem where they pass round the ancient place of the temple. Here, above us at the left, looking down several hundred feet into this valley, was the Canaanite fortress captured by David, but it long ago fell into ruin and disappeared. The wall we see here is of a much later date.

56. Israel and Judah

David's son, Solomon, delighted in Oriental luxury and display. To provide himself with these he taxed the Hebrews heavily. The discontent was so great that when Solomon died the northern tribes withdrew from the nation and set up a king of their own. Thus the Hebrew nation was divided into two parts before it was a century old.

There was much hard feeling between the two Hebrew kingdoms, and sometimes fighting. Israel, as we call the northern kingdom, was rich and prosperous ; its market-places were filled with industry and commerce ; its fertile fields produced plenty of crops. Israel displayed wealth and a successful town life. On the other hand, Judah, the southern kingdom, was poor. Her land was meagre ; besides Jerusalem, she had no large towns, and many of the people still wandered around with their flocks.

These two methods of life came into conflict in many ways, but especially in religion. Every town in Palestine had for centuries its local town god, called its " baal " or " lord ". The Hebrew townsmen of the north found it very natural to worship these Canaanite town gods. They were thus unfaithful to their old Hebrew God Yahveh (Jehovah). To some good Hebrews, therefore, and especially those in the south, the Canaanite gods seemed to be the protectors of the wealthy class in the towns who were unjust to the poor, while Yahveh appeared as the guardian of the simple shepherd life of the desert, and the protector of the poor and needy.

You will remember the account in the Bible of Ahab, a king of the north, who had Naboth, one of his subjects, killed in order to seize a vineyard belonging to Naboth, and thus greedily to enlarge his palace gardens. Living in the desert east of the Jordan was a Hebrew of old nomad habits named Elijah. Reports of such wrongs as the murder of Naboth stirred him to anger. Still wearing his desert sheepskin, he suddenly appeared before Ahab in his stolen vineyard and blamed him for taking it. Thus this rough figure from the desert proclaimed war between Yahveh and the selfish greed of the town-dwellers. The followers of Elijah slew not only the royal family, but also the priests of the Canaanite " baals ". Such violent methods, however, could not produce lasting good. They were the methods of Hebrews who thought of Yahveh only as a war god.

57. THE UNKNOWN HISTORIAN

In addition to such violent leaders as Elijah, there were among the Hebrews more peaceful men who hated the town life and its luxury. They saw among the rich townsmen showy clothes, fine houses, beautiful furniture, and cruel hardness of heart towards the poor. These were things which had been unknown in the simple nomad life of the desert. Men who felt thus turned fondly back in their minds to the grand old days of their shepherd wanderings on the broad spaces of the desert where no man " ground the faces of the poor ".

It was a gifted Hebrew of this kind who now put together a simple history of the Hebrew forefathers—a glorified picture of their shepherd life. Unfortunately we do not know his name, for the Hebrews themselves early lost all knowledge of him, and finally associated what remained of his work with the name of Moses. He told the immortal tales of the Hebrew patriarchs, of Abraham and Isaac, of Jacob and Joseph. These tales, preserved to us in the Old Testament, are among the greatest literature that has come down to us from all the past. (See Genesis xxiv, xxvii, xxviii, xxxix-xlvii, 12.) They are the earliest example of historical writing in prose which we possess, and their nameless author, whom we might call the Unknown Historian, is the earliest historian known in the world.

58. THE FIRST SOCIAL REFORMER

About 750 B.C. another strange figure in sheepskin appeared in the streets of Bethel, where the northern kingdom had an important temple. It was Amos, a shepherd from the hills of Judah in the south. In the lonely places of his shepherd life Amos had learned to see in Yahveh far more than a war god of the desert. To him Yahveh seemed to be a God of fatherly kindness, not demanding vengeance and butchery like that practised by Elijah's followers, but nevertheless a God who would rebuke the selfish lives of the town-dwellers. The simple shepherd felt compelled to journey to the northern kingdom and to proclaim to the townsmen the evils of their manner of life.

We can imagine the surprise of the prosperous northern Hebrews as they suddenly met this rough shepherd figure clad in sheepskin standing at a street corner addressing a crowd of townsmen. He denounced their showy clothes, fine houses, beautiful furniture, and above all their sinful lives and hard-heartedness towards the poor, whose lands they seized for debt and whose labour they gained by making slaves of their fellow Hebrews. These things had been unknown in the desert.

By such addresses as these Amos became the first social reformer in Asia. We apply the term " prophet " to such great Hebrew leaders who pointed out the way towards unselfish living, brotherly kindness, and a higher type of religion. Fearing that his teachings might be lost if they remained merely spoken words, Amos finally sat down and put his sermons into writing, and thus they have survived.

59. ASSYRIAN CONQUESTS OF ISRAEL AND JUDAH

The two little kingdoms of the Hebrews were always in danger from attack by the great empires that surrounded them. Assyria (about 800 B.C.) was approaching the height of its power, and we see in the next

The Persians and the Hebrews

picture the relation between the greater and smaller countries. The picture shows the Hebrews paying tribute to the king of Assyria. The Assyrian king, Shalmaneser III, stands at the left, followed by two attendants. Before him hovers the winged sun-disk. His appearance in the middle of the ninth century B.C., campaigning in the west against Damascus, so frightened the Hebrews of the northern kingdom that their

HEBREWS PAYING TRIBUTE TO THE KING OF ASSYRIA

king (Jehu) sent gifts to the Assyrian king by an envoy, whom we see here bowing down at the king's feet. Behind the Hebrew envoy are two Assyrian officers who are leading up a line of thirteen Hebrews (not included here) bearing gifts of silver, gold, etc. Although it was over a century before the Assyrian kings succeeded in capturing Damascus, this incident showed the Hebrews what they might expect. The scene is carved on a black stone shaft set up by the Assyrian king in his palace on the Tigris, where modern excavators found it. It is now in the British Museum.

Later (in 732 B.C.) the Assyrian armies marched on Damascus and captured it. The kingdom of Israel was the next victim, and Samaria its capital was captured by the Assyrians in 722 B.C. Many of the unhappy Hebrews were carried away as captives, and the northern kingdom called Israel was destroyed, after having existed for a little over two centuries.

60. Isaiah

The national hopes of the Hebrews were now centred in the helpless little kingdom of Judah, which struggled on for more than another century and a quarter, in the midst of a great world conflict in which Assyria was the unchallenged champion.

In 700 B.C. a great effort was made by the Assyrian king Sennacherib to capture Jerusalem, but he failed. The next picture shows us an incident of this campaign in Palestine. The artist, in an attempt to sketch the stony hills of southern Palestine, has made the surface of the ground like scales. We see the Assyrian king seated on a throne, while advancing up the hill is a group of Assyrian soldiers headed by the Grand Vizier, who stands before the king, announcing the coming of the Hebrew captives. At the left, behind the soldiers, appear three of the captives kneeling on the ground and lifting up their hands to appeal for mercy. The inscription over the vizier's head reads: " Sennacherib, king of the world, king of Assyria, seated himself upon a throne, while the captives of Lachish passed before him". Lachish was a small town of southern Palestine. Sennacherib captured many such Hebrew towns and carried off over two hundred thousand captives, but even his own records make no claim that he captured Jerusalem.

The Persians and the Hebrews

Thus far thoughtful Hebrews had been accustomed to think of their God as dwelling and ruling in Palestine only. Did he have power also over the vast world stage where all the great nations were fighting? But

SENNACHERIB, KING OF ASSYRIA, RECEIVING CAPTIVE HEBREWS

if so, was not Assur, the great god of victorious Assyria, stronger than Yahveh, the God of the Hebrews? It was in the midst of black doubts like these, in the years before 700 B.C., that the princely prophet Isaiah, in one great oration after another, addressed the crowds which filled the streets of Jerusalem. The hosts of Sennacherib were at the gates, and the terrified throngs in the city were expecting at any moment to hear the thunder of the great Assyrian battering-rams beating down the crumbling walls of their city, as they had crushed the walls of Damascus and Samaria. Then the bold words of the brave Isaiah lifted them from despair like the triumphant call of a trumpet. He told them that Yahveh ruled a kingdom far larger than Palestine, that He controlled the great world stage, where *He* and not Assur was the triumphant champion. If the Assyrians had wasted and plundered Palestine, it was because they were but the lash in the hands of Yahveh, who was using them as a scourge to punish Judah for its wrongdoing. Isaiah made all this clear to the people by vivid Eastern illustrations, calling Assyria the " rod " of Yahveh's anger (Isaiah xi, 5-15).

Thus, while the people were expecting the destruction of Jerusalem, Isaiah bravely proclaimed a great and glorious future for the Hebrews and speedy disaster for the Assyrians. When at length a plague from the marshes of the eastern Nile swept away the army of Sennacherib and saved Jerusalem, it seemed to the Hebrews that it was the destroying angel of Yahveh who had smitten the Assyrian host (see 2 Kings xix, 32-37). Some of the Hebrews then began to see that they must think of Yahveh as ruling a larger world than Palestine.

About a century after the deliverance from Sennacherib, the Hebrews heard the good news of the destruction of Nineveh (606 B.C.), and they fondly hoped that the fall of Assyria meant final deliverance from foreign invasion. But they had only exchanged one foreign lord for another, and the Chaldeans followed the Assyrians in the control of Palestine. The Hebrews of Judah were unwilling to submit to the Chaldeans, and this brought upon them the same fate which their kindred of Israel had suffered. In 586 B.C. Nebuchadnezzar, the Chaldean king, destroyed Jerusalem and

The Persians and the Hebrews

carried away the people to exile in Babylonia.

The Hebrew nation both north and south was thus wiped out, after having existed about four and a half centuries since the crowning of Saul.

61. A Great Poet-preacher

After the destruction of Jerusalem some of the Hebrews fled to Egypt. Among them was the melancholy prophet Jeremiah, who had foreseen the coming destruction of Jerusalem with its temple of Yahveh. He strove to teach his people that each must regard his own heart as a temple of Yahveh, which would endure long after the temple in Jerusalem had crashed into ruin.

In the same way the Hebrew exiles in Babylonia were not yet certain of the truth of the teaching about God which they had heard from their great leaders the prophets. Their feelings are expressed in Psalm 137:

> How shall we sing Yahveh's song
> In a strange land?

Had they not left Yahveh behind in Palestine? And then arose a wonderful teacher among the Hebrew exiles, who gave them the answer. He was a great poet-preacher, a prophet of the exile, whose name we do not know, but whose addresses to his fellow-exiles are preserved in sixteen chapters attached to the Old Testament book of Isaiah (chapters xl-lv). In a series of triumphant speeches this greatest of the Hebrew prophets declares Yahveh to be the creator and sole God of the universe. He explained to his fellow-exiles that suffering and grief were the best possible training and discipline to prepare a people for service. He announced, therefore, that by bringing them into exile Yahveh was only preparing his suffering people for service to the world, and that He would yet restore them and enable them to fulfil a great mission to all men.

Thus had the Hebrew vision of Yahveh slowly grown from the days of their nomad life, when they had seen Him only as a fierce tribal war god, having no power beyond the corner of the desert where they lived, until now when they had come to see Him as the sole God of the world, a kindly father and a righteous ruler of all the earth. By this rich and wonderful experience of the Hebrews in religious progress the whole world was yet to profit.

62. The Old Testament

When, as we have seen, the victorious Cyrus, at the head of his Persian troops, entered Babylon and captured it, the Hebrew exiles in Babylon greeted him as their deliverer. His triumph gave the Hebrews a Persian ruler. With great humanity the Persian king allowed the exiles to return to their native land. Some had prospered in Babylonia and did not care to return. But at different times enough of them went back to Jerusalem to rebuild the city on a very modest scale and to restore the temples. There the Hebrew leaders devoted themselves to the study of the ancient writings of their race. A number of the old writings, some of them mentioned in the Old Testament, had been lost. But the leaders arranged and copied the orations and addresses of their prophets and all the old Hebrew writings they possessed. As time went on and the service of the restored temple developed, they arranged a remarkable book of one hundred and fifty religious songs—the hymn-book of the second temple, known to us as the Book of Psalms. For a long time, indeed for centuries, these various Hebrew books, such as the Law, the Prophets, the Psalms, and others, circulated in separate rolls, and it did not occur to anyone to put them together to form one book.

It was not until Christian times that the Jewish leaders put all these old writings of their fathers together to form one book. Printed in Hebrew, as they were originally written, they form the Bible of the Jews at the present day. These writings have also become a sacred book of the Christian nations. When translated into English it forms to-day the most precious legacy which we have inherited from the older Orient before the coming of Christ. It tells the story of how a rude shepherd folk issued from the wilds of the Arabian desert to live in Palestine and to go through experiences which made them the religious teachers of the civilized world. And we should further remember that, crowning all their history, there came forth from them in due time the Founder of the Christian religion. Thus one of the most important things that we owe to the Persians was their restoration of the Hebrews to Palestine.

63. Our Debt to the Orient

Persia was the last of the great Oriental powers, and, as its decline continued after 400 B.C., it gave way to the Greeks, another Indo-European people, who arose not in Asia but in Europe, to which we must now go. Before we do so, however, let us look back over Oriental civilization for a moment and review what it accomplished in over thirty-five hundred years. We recall how it passed from the discovery of metal and the invention of writing, through three great chapters of history on the Nile (about 3000 to 1150 B.C.), and three more on the Two Rivers (thirty-first century to 539 B.C.). When these six great chapters were ended, the East finally fell under the rule of the incoming Indo-Europeans, led by the Persians (from 539 B.C. on).

What did the Ancient Orient really accomplish for the human race in the course of this long career? It gave the world the first highly developed practical arts, like metal-work, weaving, glass-making, paper-making, and many other similar industries. To distribute the products of these industries among other peoples and carry on commerce, it built the earliest sea-going ships. It first was able to move great weights and undertake large building enterprises—large even for us to-day. The early Orient, therefore, brought forth a great group of inventions surpassed in importance only by those of the modern world. The Orient also gave us the earliest architecture in stone masonry. It produced the earliest refined sculpture, from the wonderful portrait figures and colossal statues of Egypt to the exquisite seals of early Babylonia. It gave us writing and the earliest alphabet. In literature it brought forth the earliest-known tales in narrative prose, poems, historical works, social discussions, and even a drama. It gave us the calendar we still use. It made a beginning in mathematics, astronomy, and medicine. It first produced government on a large scale, whether of a single great nation or of an empire made up of a group of nations.

The Persians and the Hebrews

Finally, in religion the Hebrews developed the earliest belief in a sole God and His fatherly care for all men, and laid the foundations of a religious life from which came forth the Founder of the leading religion of the civilized world to-day. For these things, accomplished—most of them—while Europe was still undeveloped, our debt to the Orient is enormous.

There were still boundless things for mankind to do in government, in thought about the natural world, in gaining deeper views of the wonders and beauties of nature, as well as in art, in literature, and in many other lines. This future progress was to be made in Europe—that Europe which we left at the end of our chapter on the Late Stone Age. To Europe, therefore, we must now return, to follow across the eastern Mediterranean the course of rising civilization as it passed from the Orient to our forefathers in early Europe some four to five thousand years ago.

PART V
GREECE

CHAPTER X

THE CIVILIZATION OF CRETE

64. METALS AND WRITING IN EUROPE

IN the first part of this book we traced briefly the story of Europe up to the end of the Late Stone Age. Then we moved to the Orient to watch the first appearance of civilization growing on the banks of the Nile, the Tigris, and the Euphrates. We now return to Europe because the good things of civilization began to spread there from the Orient from about 3000 B.C. Merchants from the East began to trade with the Stone Age people living on the islands in the Aegean Sea. They brought with them jars of decorated pottery and glittering blue glass beads. They also brought copper beads and copper neck-rings, and, most important of all, they showed the Stone Age people their copper daggers and axe heads. Such axe heads, though they were much thinner, did not break like stone axes, and they could be ground to a sharper edge than the stone axes. Thus Europe began to leave the Stone Age and to enter the Age of Metal. Many of the early metal weapons of Europe have been discovered, and they prove to us that Europe copied the ideas of the East.

The Civilization of Crete

The following picture shows us four early dagger blades of copper and bronze. We can easily see that the Egyptian dagger was copied by men in Italy, in the Jura Mountains, and in Denmark. We may note also that the later swords of Western Europe were simply the old Egyptian dagger made longer.

The island of Crete was the first part of Europe to develop a civilization on the lines of that of the Orient.

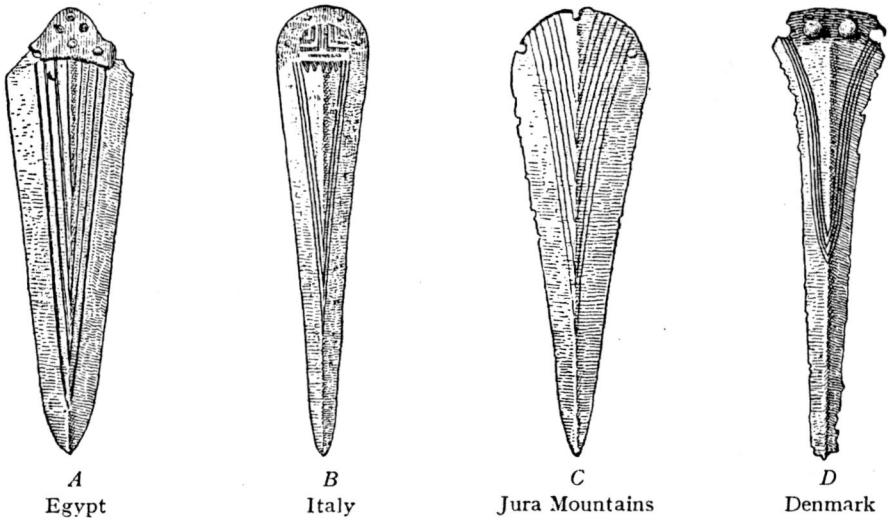

| *A* | *B* | *C* | *D* |
| Egypt | Italy | Jura Mountains | Denmark |

SERIES OF FOUR DAGGER BLADES OF COPPER AND BRONZE, SHOWING INFLUENCE FROM EGYPT TO DENMARK

Even in ancient ships sailors from the Nile could reach Crete in four or five days. Thus Crete became the link between Egypt and Europe. We can see the influence of Egypt on Crete in many ways. Compare the Egyptian and Cretan vases in the following picture. The earlier vases from Egypt (on the left), compared with those of Crete (on the right), show that the Cretan craftsmen copied the Egyptian forms in the latter part of the Pyramid Age (about 2700 B.C.). The Cretans also copied much from the Egyptian system of writing.

EARLY STONE VASES OF CRETE AND EGYPTIAN VASES FROM WHICH THEY WERE COPIED

The next picture shows us in the first column the Egyptian signs from which the Cretan signs shown in the second column were taken.

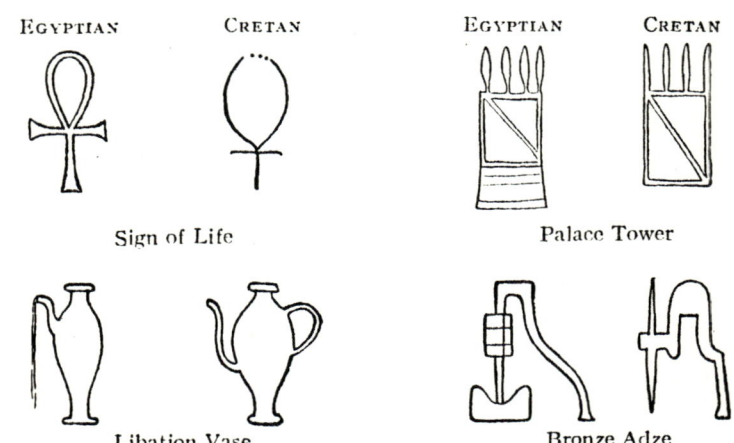

CRETAN HIEROGLYPHS AND THE EGYPTIAN SIGNS FROM WHICH THEY WERE TAKEN. (After Sir Arthur Evans)

65. THE SEA KINGS

By 2000 B.C. the Cretans had become a highly civilized people. Near the coast were manufacturing towns with industries in pottery and metal, enabling them to trade with other peoples. Farther inland the green valleys of the island must have been filled with villagers cultivating their fields of grain and pasturing their flocks. At Cnossus, not far from the middle of the northern coast, there grew up an important kingdom. The Late Stone Age town at Cnossus had long since fallen into ruin and been forgotten. Over a deep layer of its rubbish a line of splendid Cretan kings now built a fine palace arranged in the Egyptian manner, with a large cluster of rooms round a central court. Farther inland towards the southern shore arose another palace at Phaestus, perhaps another residence of the same royal family, or the capital of a second kingdom. These palaces were not fortified castles, for neither they nor the towns connected with them possessed any protecting walls. But the Cretan kings were not without means of defence. They already had their palace armouries, where armour and weapons of brass were stored. Hundreds of bronze arrowheads, with the charred shafts of the arrows, along with written lists of weapons and armour and chariots, have been found still lying in the ruins of the armoury rooms in the palace at Cnossus. Moreover, the Cretan kings were also learning to use ships in warfare, and for this reason they are called " The Sea Kings of Crete ".

Cretan business now required much greater speed in writing than was possible in using the old picture signs.

These pictures were often reduced to simpler forms, and each picture made to consist of only a few lines. This more rapid hand, called linear writing, was scratched on clay tablets. The chests of arms and weapons in the palace armoury had each a clay-tablet

CLAY TABLET BEARING A RECORD IN THE RAPID CRETAN HANDWRITING OFTEN CALLED LINEAR

label hanging in front of it. Great numbers of clay tablets stored in chests seem to have contained the records, invoices, and book-keeping lists necessary in conducting the affairs of a large royal household. Masses of these have been found covered by the ruins of the fallen palace. In spite of much study, scholars are not yet able to read these records, the earliest-known writing on the borders of the European world.

The Civilization of Crete

66. The Grand Age of Crete

A few centuries of such development as this carried Cretan civilization to its highest level, and the Cretans entered upon what we may call their Grand Age (1600–1500 B.C.). As the older palace of Cnossus gave way to a larger and more splendid building, the life of Crete began to unfold in all directions. The new palace itself, with its colonnaded hall, its fine stairways, and its large open areas, gives us the first real architecture in the northern Mediterranean. The palace walls were painted with fresh and beautiful scenes from daily life, all a-quiver with movement and action; for by learning the Egyptian art of glass-making the Cretans adorned them with glazed figures attached to the surface of the wall.

Noble vases were painted in grand designs drawn from plant life or often from the life of the sea, where the Cretans were now more and more at home. This wonderful pottery is considered to be among the finest work of decorative art ever produced by any people. The first vase (*A*) in the next illustration is an example of the early pottery, painted on a dark background with rich designs in white, orange, crimson, red, and yellow. The potters who made such vases were, together with the seal-cutters, the first really gifted decorative artists to arise in Crete. They flourished from 2000 B.C. onward, in the days of the first palace at Cnossus. We should notice that their designs do not picture carefully anything in nature, like flowers or animals (even though a hint of a lotus flower appears in the angle of the spiral); but the figures are almost purely imaginative and are

A Brief History of Ancient Times

drawn from Egyptian art. The second vase (*B*), however (some five hundred years later than the first), shows how the artists of the grand age had learned from Egyptian art to take their figures from the natural

A *B*
TWO CRETAN VASES SHOWING PROGRESS IN THE ART OF DECORATION

world, for we see that the design consists chiefly of Egyptian lotus flowers. The jar (*B*) is nearly four feet high and much larger than the first example (*A*).

67. A PROCESSION

The palace of Cnossus looked out upon a town of plain sun-dried brick. Here must have lived the Cretan

The Civilization of Crete

traders and merchants, the potters, metal-workers, painters, and other craftsmen, though many of these also lived and worked in the palace itself; while on the outskirts, or up the valley, dwelt the peasants who cultivated the fields. On one occasion we see the peasants marching in joyous procession, probably celebrating a harvest festival. The next picture shows

PROCESSION CARVED BY A CRETAN SCULPTOR

the upper part of a stone vase carved by a Cretan sculptor. The lower part is lost. The scene shows a procession of Cretan peasants with wooden pitchforks over their shoulders. Among them is a chorus of youths with wide-open mouths, singing a harvest song, doubtless in honour of the great Mother Earth, to whom the peasants believed they owed the fertility of the earth. The music is led by a priest with head shaven after the Egyptian manner, and he carries upraised before his face a sistrum, a musical rattle which came from Egypt. The work is so wonderfully carved that we seem to feel the forward motion of the procession.

68. Lords and Ladies

Upon such celebrations of the people there looked down from the palace a company of lords and ladies, who lived a very free and modern life. The ladies crowded the palace terraces and watched their champions struggling in fierce boxing matches, in which heavy metal helmets were worn. This scene is painted on the walls of the palace as part of the interior wall decoration. It has been restored somewhat, but

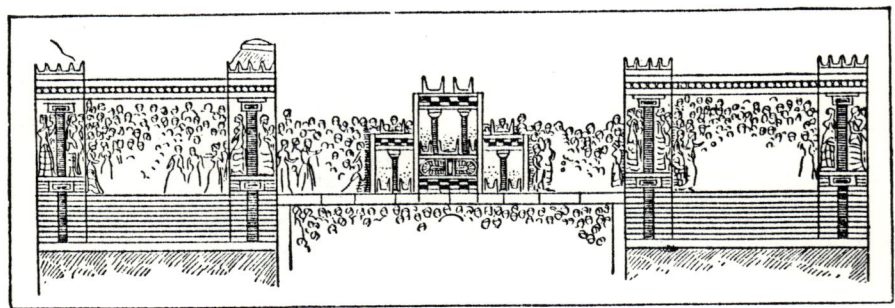

CRETAN LORDS AND LADIES OF THE GRAND AGE ON THE TERRACES OF THE PALACE AT CNOSSUS. (After Durm)

it forms a remarkable example of the Cretan artist's ability to produce the impression of a crowd of people seen from a distance.

Here is a delightful statuette of one of these Cretan ladies. The proud little figure stands with shoulders thrown far back and arms extended, each hand grasping a golden serpent which coils about her arms to the elbow. She wears a high tiara perched daintily on her carefully curled hair. Her dress consists of a flounced skirt and a tight bodice tapering to her slender waist. There is something quite modern about the costume.

The figure is carved in ivory, while the flounces are edged with bands of gold, and the belt about the waist is of the same metal. She represents either the great

IVORY AND GOLD STATUETTE OF A CRETAN LADY OF THE GRAND AGE

Cretan mother goddess or possibly a graceful snake-charmer of the court. In any case, the sculptor has given her the appearance of one of the noble ladies of the time.

69. Drain-Pipes

These nobles of Cnossus lived in comfortable quarters in the palace, where they even had bathrooms and sanitary drainage. These joints of pottery drain-pipe (two and a half feet long and four to six inches across) shown in the next sketch are part of the system of drainage in the palace, the oldest drainage system in the European world. The oldest-known system of drainage (copper) is in the pyramid temple of Abusir, Egypt, about a thousand years earlier than this system at Cnossus.

TILE DRAIN-PIPES FROM THE CRETAN PALACE OF CNOSSUS

Here, then, in the island of Crete, there had arisen a new world. The culture of the gifted Cretans under the influence of Egypt shook off the Late Stone Age lethargy of early Europe and sprang into a vigorous life all its own. Beside the two older centres of civilization on the Nile and the Two Rivers in this age, there thus grew up here in the eastern Mediterranean, as a *third* great civilization, this splendid world of Crete in the Aegean Sea. It is this third great civilization which forms the link between the civilization of the Orient and the later progress of man in Greece and Western Europe.

CHAPTER XI

THE GREEKS

70. The Greeks and the Phoenicians

INTO this civilized world of the eastern Mediterranean, with its arts, its industries, and its commerce, the uncivilized peoples of the north behind the Balkan Mountains and the Black Sea were now beginning to intrude. These uncivilized northerners were the Greeks. Driving their herds before them, with their families in rough carts drawn by horses, the rude Greek tribesmen must have looked out upon the fair pastures of Thessaly, the snowy summit of Mount Olympus, and the blue waters of the Aegean not long after 2000 B.C.

The Greek peninsula which they had entered contains about twenty-five thousand square miles. It is everywhere cut up into small plains and peninsulas, separated from each other by the sea or by mountain ridges. Five hundred islands are scattered along its eastern shores.

During the thousand years between 2000 and 1000 B.C. the Greeks took possession not only of the whole of the Greek peninsula, but likewise of the entire Aegean world—Greece, Crete, the sea-coasts of Asia Minor, and the many islands. The Greeks probably found that the old Aegean cities had kings to rule over them, and they followed this example. The old-time nomad leaders whom they had once followed in war and peace became rough shepherd-kings of the tribes. Each tribe settled down in a group of villages. In course of time the group of villages grew together and merged at last into

GREECE IN THE FIFTH CENTURY B.C.

a city. Such cities became the only " nation " which the Greeks ever knew. Each city-state had its own laws, its own army and gods, and each citizen felt a patriotic duty towards his own city and no other. Overlooking the city from the heights in its midst was the king's castle, which we call the " citadel " or the " acropolis ". Eventually the houses and the market below were protected by a wall. The king was the ruler of the city. He was assisted by a Council of elders who decided matters of importance. There was also an Assembly, composed of the weapon-bearing men. King and Council sat in the market-place and arranged the business and the disputes between the people. There were hundreds of such Greek city-states. Indeed the entire Aegean world came to be made up of such tiny nations.

It was while the Greeks were thus living in these little city-kingdoms that Greek civilization arose, especially during the last two and a half centuries of the rule of the kings (1000–750 B.C.). But even long after 1000 B.C. the life of the Greeks continued to be rough and even barbarous. Without any skill in craftsmanship the Greek shepherds and peasants were slow to take up building, industries, and manufacturing on their own account. For a long time even the dwellings of the Greek kings were usually but simple farmhouses of sun-dried brick, where the swine wandered into the court or slept in the sunshine beside the royal doorway.

But, like the Cretans before them, the Greeks were influenced by the traders from the East. For example, we find that they discarded the shaggy sheepskin of their former nomad life in favour of a shirt-like garment of woven wool. They had no name for it in Greek, but they heard the foreign merchants from whom they bought it calling it in their language a *kiton*.

To purchase articles like this garment, which they did not make themselves, the Greeks often went down to the seashore, where they and their women gathered about a ship drawn with its stern on the beach. Black bearded traders, who overlooked the crowd from the high stern of the ship, tempted the Greeks with glass or alabaster perfume bottles from Egypt and with rich blue porcelain dishes. If the women did not bid for these, they were quite unable to resist handsome ivory combs carved with lions in open-work and polished till they shone in the sun. Wealthy Greeks were attracted by magnificent large round plates of bronze or even of silver, richly engraved. Splendid purple robes hanging over the stern of the ship enriched the display of golden jewellery with flashes of brilliant colour. Here, too, were the *kitons*, as we would have heard these swarthy strangers from the sea calling them.

Phoenician Garment adopted by the Greeks

These strangers were Phoenicians, and the word for the new garment adopted by the Greeks was a Phoenician word. Ivory combs and other goods manufactured at Sidon and Tyre in Phoenicia were distributed by the Phoenician merchants through the

The Greeks

Mediterranean as far west as Spain, where combs like the one shown in this picture have been found in ancient graves. The Phoenicians learnt their methods of manufacturing from the Egyptians. In Egypt they learnt to make glass and porcelain, to weave linen and dye it, to cast and hammer and engrave metal. Thus they were the agents who brought the new peoples like the Greeks into touch with the older civilizations.

The most valuable thing the Greeks learnt from the Phoenicians was the art of writing, and especially the use of the alphabet. The Phoenicians had adopted a system of twenty-two alphabetic signs from certain Semites who lived near Egypt, and who had devised an alphabet drawn from Egyptian hieroglyphics. In this system each sign represented a consonant, and there were no signs for vowels. The immense importance of this alphabet is shown by the diagram on the next page, which is a table showing how the Phoenician letters passed through Greek and Latin forms to reach their present English forms. The Phoenician alphabet spread from Greece to Italy, and at last through Europe. Indeed, every alphabet of the civilized world has descended from the Phoenician alphabet.

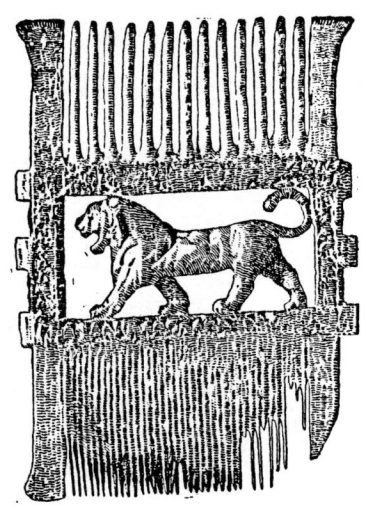

Ancient Phoenician Comb of Carved Ivory

Here the Greeks early displayed the mental superiority which, as we shall soon discover, they possessed.

A Brief History of Ancient Times

I	II	III	IV	V
PHOENICIAN	EARLY GREEK read from right to left	LATER GREEK read from left to right	LATIN	ENGLISH
∀	A	A	A	A
⅃	S ᛒ	B	B	B
𐤂	⏋	Γ	C G	C, G
⊲	Δ	Δ	D	D
𐤄	⋺	E	E	E
Y	Y	F	F V	F, V, U
⊒	I	I	...	Z
H	B	B	H	E, H
⊕	O	⊗	...	TH, PH
⇃	⸓	⸓	I	I
⅄	⼂	K	...	K, KH
⌒	∨⌐⌐	L ∧	L	L
⌐	M	M	M	M
⌐	M	N	N	N
𐅢	⊞	⊞	X	X
o	o	o	O	O
𐅡	⌐	⌐	P	P
⌐	M	M	...	S
φ	φ	φ	Q	Q
⌐	⌐	P	R	R
W	⌇	⌇	S	S
X	T	T	T	T

TABLE SHOWING HOW THE PHOENICIAN LETTERS PASSED THROUGH GREEK AND LATIN FORMS TO REACH THEIR PRESENT ENGLISH FORMS

They noticed that there were no Phoenician letters standing for vowels. They also noticed in the Phoenician alphabet a few letters representing consonants that did not exist in Greek speech. These letters they began to use for the Greek vowels. They thus took the final step in the process of devising a complete system of alphabetic writing.

Along with the alphabet, pen, ink, and paper came for the first time into Europe. The Greeks received all their paper from Egypt through the Phoenicians. Hence our word " paper ", derived from " papyrus ". The Greeks also called papyrus " byblos ", after the Phoenician city of Byblos, from which they received it. Thus arose the Greek word " biblia " for books, and from this word has come our word " Bible ".

71. Homer and the Gods

The Greeks loved to sing of brave men on the field of battle and to tell the great deeds of mighty heroes. In the pastures of Thessaly, where the singer looked up at the cloud-veiled summit of Mount Olympus, the home of the gods, there early grew up a group of such songs telling many a story of the feats of gods and heroes, the earliest literature of the Greeks. Into these songs were also brought memories of remote wars which had actually occurred, especially the war in which the Greeks had captured and actually destroyed the splendid city of Troy in Asia Minor. Probably by 1000 B.C. some of these songs had crossed to the coasts and islands of Ionia on the Asiatic side of the Aegean Sea. There arose a class of bards who graced the feasts of king and noble with songs of battle and adventure recited to the music of the harp.

After the separate songs had greatly increased in

number, they were finally collected together. They were not the work of one man, but a growth of several centuries of singers, some of whom were still living even after 700 B.C. It was then that they were first written down. Among these ancient singers there was one of great fame whose name was Homer. Once he was thought to have written all these songs and verses, but later it was thought that he wrote only the *Iliad*, the story of the Greek war against Troy, and perhaps the *Odyssey*, or the tale of the wanderings of Odysseus on his return from Troy. At that time the Greeks had no sacred book, and the songs of Homer became almost the Bible of Greece.

AN IDEAL PORTRAIT OF HOMER

In the Homeric songs and in the early tales about the gods, which we call myths, the Greeks heard how the gods dwelt among the clouds on the summit of Mount Olympus. There in his cloud palace, Zeus, the sky-god, with the lightning in his hand, ruled the gods like an earthly king. Each of the gods controlled a part of nature or the affairs of men. Apollo, the sun-god, whose beams were golden arrows, was the deadly archer of the gods. Apollo also shielded the flocks of the shepherds and the fields of the ploughmen, and he was a great musician. Above all, he knew the future ordained by Zeus and could, when properly consulted, tell what the future had in store. Apollo became the most beloved god of the Greek world.

Athena, the greatest goddess of the Greeks, seems in the beginning to have ruled the air, and she was mistress of the storms. Such power made her a warrior goddess, and the Greeks loved to think of her with shining weapons protecting the Greek cities. But she held out her protecting hand over them also in times of peace, as the potters shaped their jars, the smiths wrought their metal, or the women wove their wool.

APOLLO

Athena, too, had brought them the olive tree as they believed, and thus she became the goddess of the peaceful life of industry and art. As the foster-

GROUP OF GODS AND GODDESSES
(From the frieze of the Parthenon)

mother of all that was best in Greek life, she was the loveliest of the protecting powers which the Greeks felt everywhere watching over the life and work of men.

These three, then, Zeus, Apollo, and Athena, were the leading gods in the Greek world. The Greeks had many other gods and goddesses, a list of some of whom we give here.

> Zeus : the father of gods and men.
> Poseidon : ruler of the sea.
> Apollo : god of light, music, prophecy.
> Ares : god of war.
> Hephaestus : god of fire.
> Hermes : god of the wind.
> Hera : queen of Zeus.
> Athena : goddess of wisdom.
> Artemis : goddess of the chase.
> Aphrodite : goddess of love and beauty.
> Hestia : goddess of the hearth.
> Demeter : goddess of harvests.

72. CITIES AND UNIONS

We have seen Greek civilization beginning under influences from the East. In *government* the Greek world developed in a different way from that of the Orient. There each group of states finally became a large and powerful nation like Egypt on the Nile or Babylonia on the Two Rivers. In Greece, however, it was not easy for the city-states to unite into one nation. The chief reason was that the country was cut up by mountain ranges and deep bays so that the different cities were quite separated. Moreover, the Greeks of the mainland were likewise separated from the Greeks in the islands and in Asia Minor.

But there were four regions on the mainland of Greece which permitted the union of city-states into a

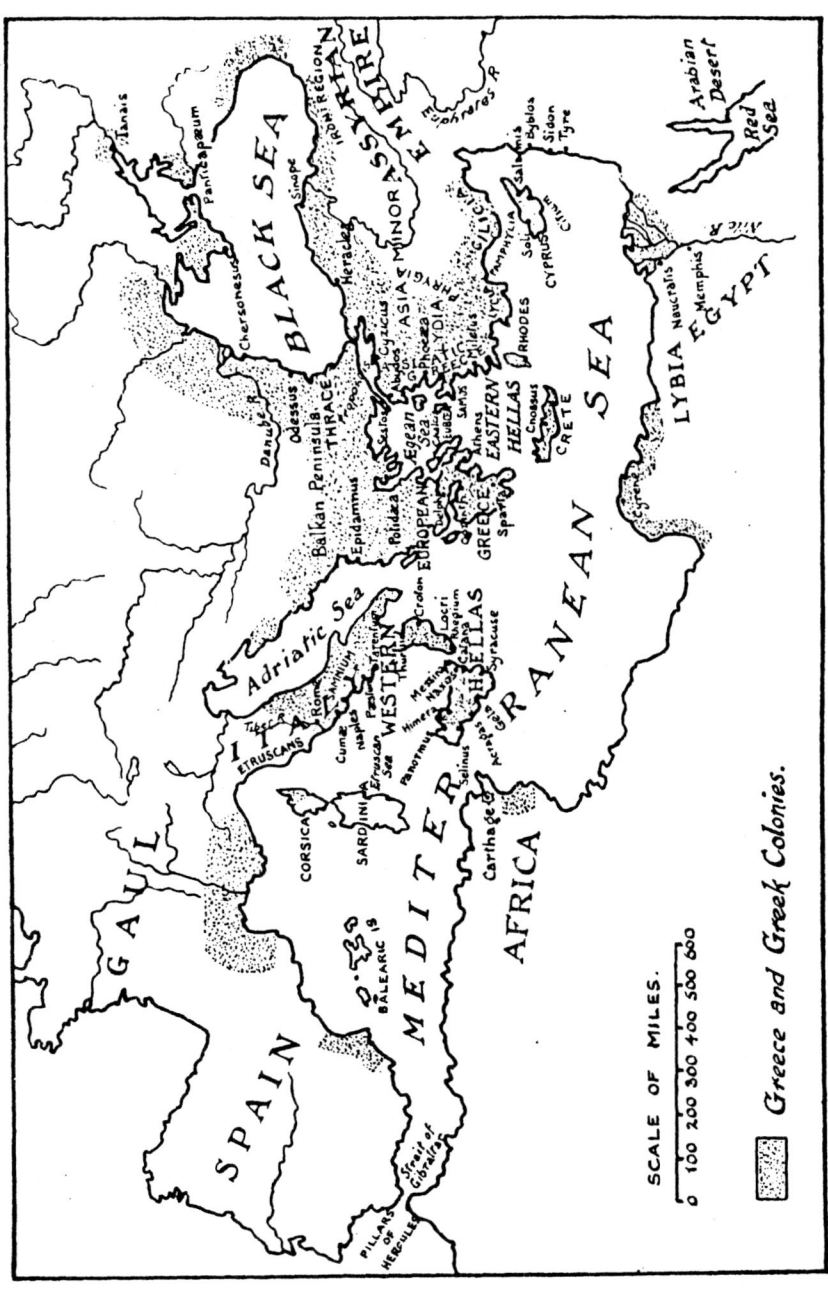

GREEK COLONIES AND SPHERE OF INFLUENCE DOWN TO THE SIXTH CENTURY B.C.

larger nation. These were the districts of Argos, Sparta, Athens, and Thebes. The oldest of these larger nations was Argos. The town of Argos had conquered the ancient Aegean strongholds and had created the nation of Argos. In the same way the kings of Sparta conquered the two peninsulas on the south of them and also the land of the Messenians. The two kingdoms of Argos and Sparta thus held a large part of the Peloponnesian peninsula.

In the peninsula of Attica, likewise, the little city-kingdoms were slowly conquered by Athens, which at last gained control of the entire peninsula. On the northern borders of Attica the region of Boeotia fell under the leadership of Thebes. Elsewhere no large and permanent unions were formed. Sparta and Athens led the two most powerful unions among the Greeks. Such a union or nation was called a city-state, in spite of its increased territory. The union occupying the peninsula of Attica was called Athens, and every peasant in Attica was an Athenian.

In governing such a little city-state, the Greeks entered upon a new stage in their progress about 750 B.C., when the common people began to struggle to improve their lot. It was a long and bitter struggle, and finally resulted in giving the people in some of the Greek states so large a share in governing that the form of government might be called " democracy ". This is a word of Greek origin meaning " the rule of the people ", and the Greeks were the first people of the ancient world to attempt it. But this did not come about in these city-states, especially Athens, until the sixth century B.C. In the period between the eighth century and the sixth century the struggle

The Greeks

towards democracy was going on, and the Greek states then passed through two stages of government before some of them gave great powers to their people.

These two periods were the Age of the Nobles, from about 700 to 600 B.C., and the Age of the Tyrants, from about 600 to 500 B.C. The nobles in many of the city-states began to rule instead of the kings towards 750 B.C. In both these Ages the Greek city-states made great progress in industry, commerce, colonization, art, literature, and science.

73. Ships and Colonies

In the Age of the Nobles the Greeks became the rivals of the Phoenicians in commerce and in founding colonies. As the Greek merchants gradually took up sea trade, the demand for ships led the Greek mechanics to undertake shipbuilding. They built their new craft on Phoenician models, the only ones with which they were acquainted.

The earliest ships in the Mediterranean, those of Egypt, were turned up at both ends, and the early Aegean ships were copies of this Egyptian model. The Phoenicians, however, introduced a change in the model by giving their ships at the bow a sharp projecting beak below water. Such a ship is shown on the next page in (B). The Greeks did not adopt the old Aegean form turned up at both ends, but took the Phoenician form with beaked prow, as shown in a vase painting from which the drawing of an eighth-century Greek ship (A) has been copied.

The Greeks became able sailors and adventurous merchants, and they also developed into good colonists.

Greek merchants were not only found trading in the northern Aegean, but their vessels had entered the great sea which they called the Pontus, known to us as the Black Sea. By 600 B.C. they had girdled the Black Sea with their towns and villages, reaching the broad grain-fields along the lower Danube and the iron mines on the south-eastern coast of the Black Sea.

But it was the unknown West which became the " America " of the early Greek colonists. Many a

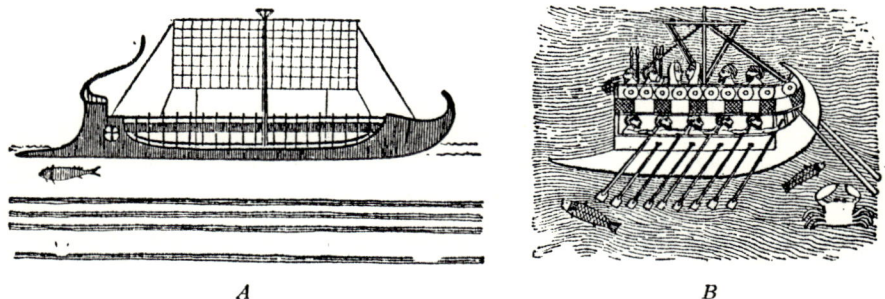

AN EARLY GREEK SHIP AND THE PHOENICIAN SHIP AFTER WHICH IT WAS MODELLED

Columbus pushed his ship into this strange region of mysterious dangers on the distant borders of the world, where the heroes were believed to live in the Islands of the Blest. Looking westward from the western coast of Greece the seamen could see the shores of the heel of Italy, only fifty miles distant. When they had once crossed to it, they coasted around Sicily and far into the West. Here was a new world. Although the Phoenicians were already there, its discovery was as important for the Greeks as that of America for later Europe.

By 750 B.C. the Greek colonies appeared in this new western world, and within a century they fringed southern Italy from the heel to a point well above the instep north of Naples, so that this region of southern Italy came to be known as "Great Greece". Here the

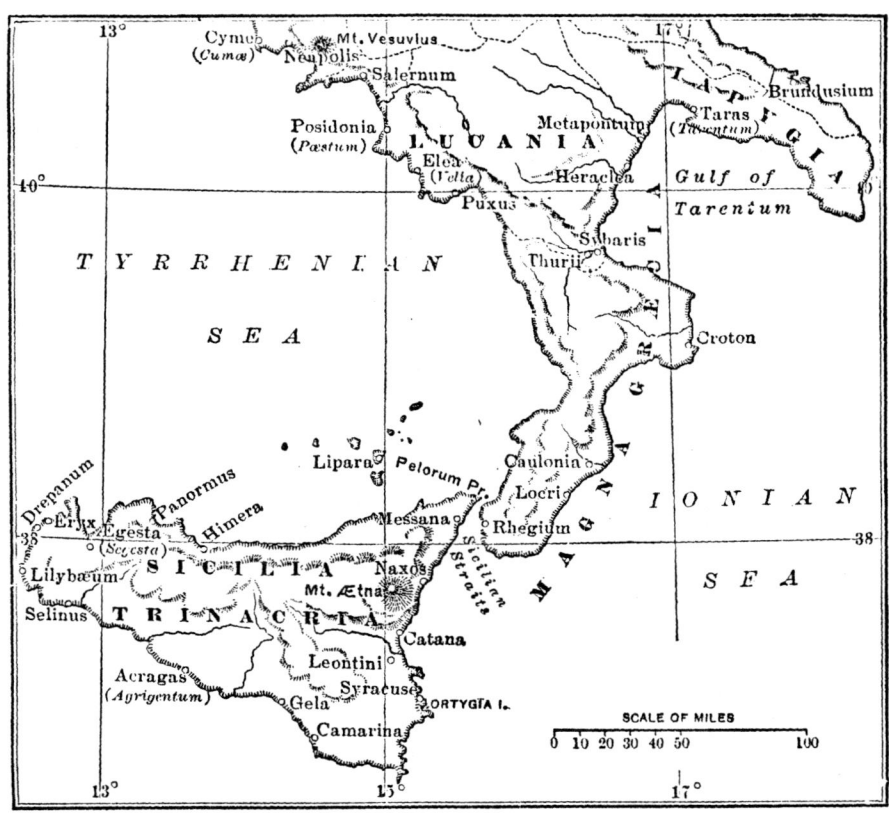

MAGNA GRAECIA AND SICILY

Greek colonists looked northward to the hills crowned by the rude settlements which were destined to become Rome. They little dreamed that this small town would yet rule the world, making even the proud cities of the homeland its vassals.

In spite of Eastern luxuries like gaudy clothing and rich tableware, Greek life in the Age of the Nobles was still rude and simple. The Greek cities of which we have been talking were groups of dingy sun-dried brick houses, with narrow winding streets which we should call alleys. On the height where the palace or the castle of the king once stood was an oblong building of brick, like the houses of the town below. In front it had a porch with a row of wooden posts, and it was covered by a " peaked " roof with a triangular gable at each end. This rude building was the earliest Greek temple. As for sculpture in this age, the figure of a god consisted merely of a wooden post with a roughly hewn head at the top. When draped with a garment it could be made to serve its purpose.

74. Hellenes

There were several strong influences which tended to keep the Greek states apart and prevented their union as a single nation. There were also influences which tended towards unity. Among these were the athletic games which arose from the early custom of honouring the burial of a hero with such contests. In spite of the great rivalry between the cities at these games, they gave a sense of unity by their celebration and by the fact that they were organized in common. They finally came to be practised at stated seasons in honour of the gods. As early as 776 B.C. such games were held as public festivals at Olympia. Repeated every four years, they finally aroused the interest of all Greece. The chief contests were the foot-race, boxing, wrestling, spear-throwing, and chariot races. Spectators from all parts crowded to the festival. A crown of olive was the only prize given to the victor, but his fellow-citizens on his return home received him as a conquering hero, sometimes throwing down a section of the city wall through which he entered in triumph. Statues of him, made by the most famous sculptors, were set up in Olympia and in his own city. Poets and orators produced some of their best work in singing his praises as one who had brought immortal fame upon his native town.

Religion also became a strong influence towards unity, because there were some gods at whose temples all the Greeks worshipped. The different city-states formed several religious councils made up of representatives from the various cities. Thus each city had a voice in the joint management of certain affairs. A famous council of this kind had control of the Olympic games.

Greek unity was strengthened also by a common language and by common traditions such as the Homeric songs, with which every Greek was familiar. Thus bound together by ties of custom, religion, language, and tradition, the Greeks gained a feeling of race unity which set them apart from other races. They called all men not of Greek blood *barbarians*, and they called themselves *Hellenes*, and found pleasure in the belief that they had all descended from a common ancestor called Hellen. You must carefully note that this name does not represent a Greek nation or single state, but only the group of Greek-speaking states, often at war with one another.

CHAPTER XII

THE AGE OF THE TYRANTS

75. THE TYRANTS

By the sixth century the Age of the Nobles had given way to the Age of the Tyrants, which means that the cities had become tired of the rule of the aristocracy whom the lower poor classes and the wealthy middle classes hated, and had given themselves up once more to be governed by one man, who in this case was not a king but a "tyrant". We must note carefully that "tyrant" in Greek does not mean one who ruled in a harsh way. It simply means a man who has managed to gather the chief power of a city-state in his own hands, partly by force in putting down his rivals, and partly by persuading the new commercial class of citizens and the poor oppressed peasants to rally round him. The word "tyranny" was merely a name for the high office held by such a ruler.

Many of these rulers were good men and looked after the rights of the people, curbed the nobles, gave great attention to public works like harbour improvements, state buildings and temples, and cultivated art, music, and literature. The Tyrants were so devoted to building that architecture made very important advances. The Greek cities, including the buildings of government, had been, as we have seen, simply groups of sun-dried brick buildings, but now the rough Greek temples of sun-dried brick were rebuilt by the Tyrants in limestone.

The Age of the Tyrants

At no time before or since were so many Greek temples erected as in the Greek world during the Age of the Tyrants.

Such temples as we see here were surrounded by lines of plain stone columns in a style which we call Doric. Although the Greeks borrowed the idea and the form of these columns from Egypt, they improved them until they became the most beautiful ever designed

DORIC TEMPLE AT PAESTUM

by early architects. We can see in the diagram on the next page the resemblance and the difference between the Greek and the older Egyptian columns. The earliest form of column used by the Greeks was a fluted shaft of stone (B) closely resembling the simplest form (A) which existed in Egypt about 2000 B.C.

The temples were now adorned, in the gable ends, with sculptured figures of the gods, grouped in scenes representing incidents in the old stories. At first the sculpture of the Greeks was very stiff. This was because they imitated Egyptian models, as can be seen from the picture given on p. 173.

The Egyptian portrait (*B*) is over two thousand years older than the Greek figure (*A*). The noble (*B*), one of those whose estate we visited on the Nile, stands in the usual pose of such figures in Egyptian

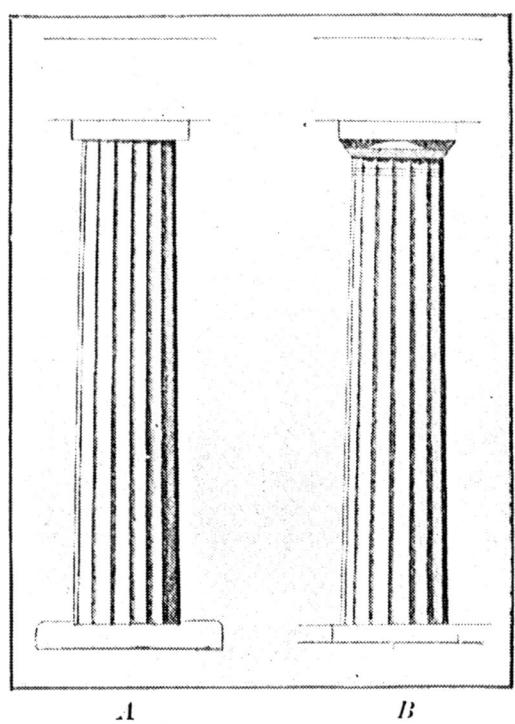

AN OLD EGYPTIAN COLUMN AND THE DORIC COLUMN DERIVED FROM IT

art, with the arms hanging down and the left foot thrust forward. The Greek figure (*A*) stands in the same pose with the foot thrust forward. Both look straight ahead, as was customary in early art. The Greek figure shows clearly the influence of Egyptian sculpture. It is still stiff and ungraceful.

But in course of time Greeks began to rid themselves

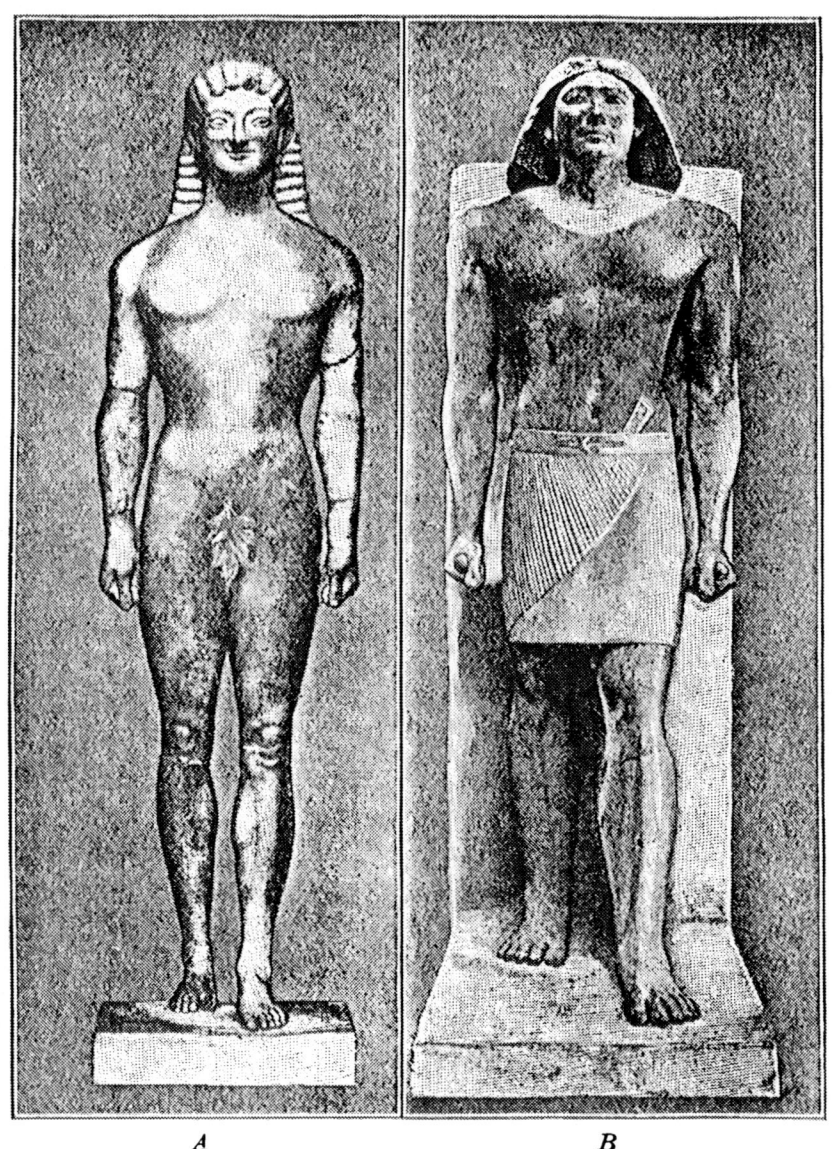

A   B

EARLY GREEK STATUE AND EGYPTIAN PORTRAIT STATUE BY WHICH IT WAS INFLUENCED

of the Egyptian influence in their sculpture, as we can see from the next picture, which is a statue of two

Athenian youths. The figures in the group are not so stiff as the ones we have seen above, and this shows us that progress was being made in the art of carving figures to represent a living, free human being.

MONUMENT OF THE TYRANT SLAYERS OF ATHENS, HARMODIUS, AND ARISTOGITON, FROM TWO POINTS OF VIEW

76. EARLY SCIENCE

The early Greeks believed that the gods ruled Nature and that there were no regular laws of Nature. In the Age of the Tyrants some men began to question the idea that Nature could be controlled by the gods. They believed that, if men only knew enough about Nature they could find out the rules by which Nature carried out her work. The chief of these new thinkers was Thales of Miletus, a Greek town of Ionia in Asia Minor. Thales had learned mathematics and astronomy from the Egyptians and the Phoenicians, and he had

The Age of the Tyrants

received from Babylonia a list of the movements of the sun and the stars. From such lists the Babylonians had already learned that eclipses of the sun took place at certain times. With these lists in his hands Thales was able to work out when the next eclipse would take place. He therefore told the people of Miletus that they might expect an eclipse of the sun before the end of a certain year. When the eclipse took place as he had foretold, the fame of Thales spread far and wide. Before this the Greeks thought that an eclipse was some sign from the gods. Now they were beginning to see that it happened naturally or according to a natural law.

Another citizen of Miletus, perhaps a pupil of Thales, explained the origin of animals by saying that the higher forms had developed from the lower forms, which is an idea believed by most people in modern days and which is called the Theory of Evolution. Yet another citizen of Miletus was Hecataeus, a geographer and historian. He travelled widely, including a journey up the Nile, and he wrote a geography of the world. We can see his idea of the world from his map on the next page.

Pythagoras was another Ionian thinker who moved to southern Italy. He and his pupils made some wonderful discoveries in science. One of the most important problems in Euclid's Geometry is known to every schoolboy as Pythagoras' Theorem (Book I, Proposition 47). These men also found out that the length of a musical string is in exact relation to its tone. They also were the first to make the discovery that the earth is a sphere having its own motion.

These are only a few of the great things discovered

at this time by the Greeks about Nature. In modern times we are constantly discovering many more of the laws of Nature by means of science. But we must bear in mind that such men as Thales and his followers first started the world on the wonderful road of science. Their work will ever remain one of the greatest of human achievements.

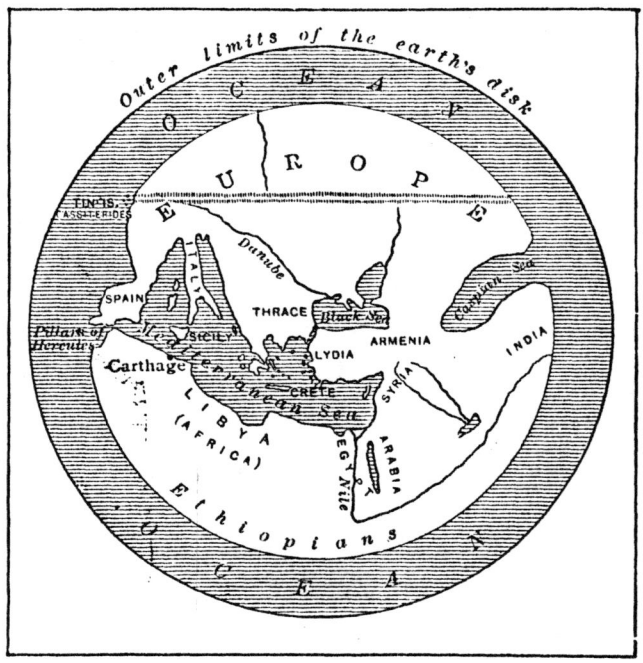

MAP OF THE WORLD BY HECATAEUS (517 B.C.)

77. SPARTA

This Age of the Tyrants which we are considering briefly was one of the great epochs of the world's history. Then it was that the Greeks overtook and passed the Orient in civilization. This age of rapid progress in business, in government, in art, and in science ended about 500 B.C., to give way to the still more glorious age of the fifth century.

We must not think that every city-state in Greece was governed in this time by a tyrant. Sparta, for example, did not depart from the old custom of kingship. The only change in Sparta had been to have two kings instead of one. Sparta was quite different from the other cities of Greece, and especially different from Athens, its chief rival. Sparta was a military state. Athens was a great centre of industry and commerce. Sparta had no literature, no art, no science; Sparta was old-fashioned and conservative and proud. Athens was progressive, eager for new things, new knowledge, and new movements. Above all, Sparta was aristocratic and believed in the rule of the upper classes, while Athens was becoming more and more democratic, giving the people an ever greater share in the government of the city-state.

In the sixth century (600–500 B.C.) both Sparta and Athens were increasing in power. Long before 500 B.C. the Spartans had forced their neighbouring states into a union called the "Spartan League", which included nearly the whole of the Peloponnese. As the leader of this league, Sparta was the most powerful state in Greece. She gained this power by means of a very strict military system. The Spartan citizens were all soldiers and devoted themselves entirely to military training. The state provided public meals where each soldier-citizen ate with a group of about fifteen of his friends, all men, at the same table every day. The lands of the citizen were cultivated for him by slaves, and his only occupation was military drill and exercises.

Sparta remained a group of straggling villages not deserving the name of city, and entirely without fine public buildings or great monuments of any kind. Like a large military club or camp, it lived off its own slave-worked lands and from the taxes it squeezed out of its subject towns without allowing them any vote in their government.

The character of the Spartans and the Spartan state is clearly seen in the strict training of the children, who were looked upon as belonging to the state and not to their fathers and mothers. Every boy baby was brought before the Council and examined. If he did not look strong enough to become a good soldier the Council condemned him to die by being left in a cold mountain valley. At the age of seven the boys were handed over to public teachers, who would train and educate them to become good and strong soldiers. The training was that of the barrack square. The Spartans had little use for the gentler side of education. They did not encourage eloquent speakers and poets. Their aim was to talk as little as possible. Boys were taught always to reply to anything in the fewest words possible. At the public tables they were compelled to sit " silent as statues ". This education did not develop the mind, for all the attention was given to the training of the body, and the Spartan boys became very expert in running, leaping, wrestling, and hurling the spear. The greatest ideal of the Spartans was to train their youth to bear pain without murmuring or even flinching. Many methods were adopted to bring this about. The boys were trained to withstand the cold of winter by wearing only their light summer dress. They were often scourged heavily to accustom them to bear pain bravely. Sometimes the whipping caused death. A story will help you to realize the type of courage this system of training produced. Once a Spartan youth stole a young fox, and he was caught. The rules of Sparta made the punishment heavy—not for stealing, but for being caught. The boy hid the fox beneath his tunic. The fox began to bite the boy's stomach and to tear out his vitals. But the boy, so well disciplined in suffering pain, showed no sign and allowed no muscle of his face to betray him.

78. ATHENS

Athens, on the other hand, was making progress along other lines. She was a busy centre of industry and commerce. She cultivated art, architecture, and literature. She encouraged her people to take a more direct share in their own government.

The beautiful Athenian vase shown on the next page gives an idea of the artistic and business enterprise of Athens in the sixth century. It was found in an Etruscan tomb in Italy. It is signed by the potter Ergotimos, who gave it its beautiful shape, and also by the painter Clitias, who painted the beautiful scenes on it. The potters of Athens had their workshops in a large quarter of the town. These Athenian factories must have been of considerable size, for of the painted Greek vases discovered by excavation and which are signed by the artist, about half are found to have come from only six factories in Athens. It is interesting at the present day to see the modern excavator opening tombs in Asia Minor and taking out vases bearing the signature of the same Athenian vase-painter whose name you may also read on vases dug out of the Nile Delta in northern Africa, or taken from tombs in the cemeteries of the Etruscan cities of Italy.

Then again in the sixth century Athens made great progress in government. She did not remain old-fashioned and conservative like Sparta, and, above all, Athens was not afraid of giving the people a share in

AN ATHENIAN PAINTED VASE OF THE EARLY SIXTH CENTURY B.C.

government. In 594 B.C. there was a great leader in Athens called Solon. He made a law that anyone who had lost a law-suit could appeal to a jury of citizens over thirty years of age selected by lot. This change and some others greatly improved a citizen's chances of securing justice. Solon also divided the Athenian citizens into four classes according to their income. The wealthy nobles were the only ones who could hold the highest offices, and the peasants were permitted to hold only the lower ones. The humblest

The Age of the Tyrants

free citizen could, however, be certain of the right to vote in the Assembly of the people.

Thus Athens, unlike Sparta, was becoming more democratic. She made further progress in this direction as time went on. In the period between 540 and 528 B.C. Pisistratus ruled in Athens as a tyrant. He governed with great wisdom and success. He carried out many public improvements. Athenian manufactures flourished as never before, and when Pisistratus died in 528 B.C., he had laid a foundation to which much of the later greatness of Athens was due.

Pisistratus was followed by his two sons as tyrants. But the Athenian people did not like being ruled by tyrants, and one of the sons of Pisistratus was killed, while the other was compelled to flee. So it was that shortly before 500 B.C. Athens was freed from her tyrants.

The Athenian people were now able to gain further power by the efforts of Clisthenes, a nobleman friendly to the lower classes. In order to avoid the rise of a new tyrant, Clisthenes established a law that once a year the people might by vote declare any prominent citizen dangerous to the State and banish him for ten years. To cast his vote against a man, a citizen had only to pick up one of the pieces of broken pottery lying about the market-place, write upon it the name of the citizen to be banished, and place it in the voting urn. Such a bit of pottery was called an "ostracon", and to "ostracize" a man (literally, "to potsherd" him) meant to banish him.

By these and other means Athens had (about 500 B.C.) gained a form of government which gave the people a high degree of power. The State was in large measure a democracy. This picture shows a potsherd bearing the name of Themistocles. It was written there by some citizen of Athens who desired and secured his ostracism in 472 B.C.

An Ostracon

79. The Persian Wars

At length, with the rise of the fifth century (500–400 B.C.), began the long foreseen struggle between the Persian Empire and the Greek city-states. In this struggle Athens played the chief part in the defence of Greece and, because she was victorious, became for a time the leading and most famous city in the Greek world. Persia had conquered the Greek cities of Asia Minor before 500 B.C., and Athens attempted to help some of these cities to revolt against the Persian king. In this effort the Athenians burned the city of Sardis. On learning of this Darius, the great Persian ruler, asked who the Athenians were. He then called for his bow and, placing an arrow on the string, shot it upwards into the air, saying, " Grant, O Zeus, that I may have vengeance on the Athenians ". Then he ordered one of his servants every day when his dinner was spread to repeat to him three times these words :

" Remember the Athenians ".

The Age of the Tyrants

In 490 B.C. Darius sent a great army of vengeance into Greece. It landed at Marathon barely a day's journey from Athens. The danger was very great. The Athenians faced it with courage, and marched out to offer battle on the field of Marathon. Their bravery and their brilliant tactics saved Greece. The Persian army was driven with great slaughter to the ships in which it had come. Marathon is one of the world's great and decisive battles. If the Persians had won they would have crushed the freedom of Greece with the tyranny of the East, and the world would have lost some of its finest ideas and some of its wonderful treasures in art.

Marathon was not the last word in the struggle between Greece and Persia, for the Persians were determined to wipe out the disgrace of this overwhelming defeat. Darius died, but his son Xerxes planned an enormous attack on Greece. For eight years he made his preparations. It took three years to dig a canal across the promontory of Mount Athos, in order to provide a safe passage for the ships carrying his troops when the expedition was ready. Across the Hellespont itself a gigantic double bridge of boats about a mile and a half long was constructed. Then in 480 B.C. the attack began.

The Persians marched through Thrace and Macedonia into Thessaly. The Greeks had decided to offer the first resistance to the Persians at Thermopylae. This was a very narrow pass leading from Thessaly into central Greece. On one side lay the sea and on the other the rugged mountains. The Greeks were more united and better prepared than before Marathon. The Spartans held the pass, from which they could not be driven except by an attack in front, as the fleet of Athens prevented a force from being landed in their rear. The Persians attacked the pass, but so narrow was it, and so bravely did the Spartans defend it, that their efforts were in vain. Then a Greek traitor showed the Persians a path leading over the mountains

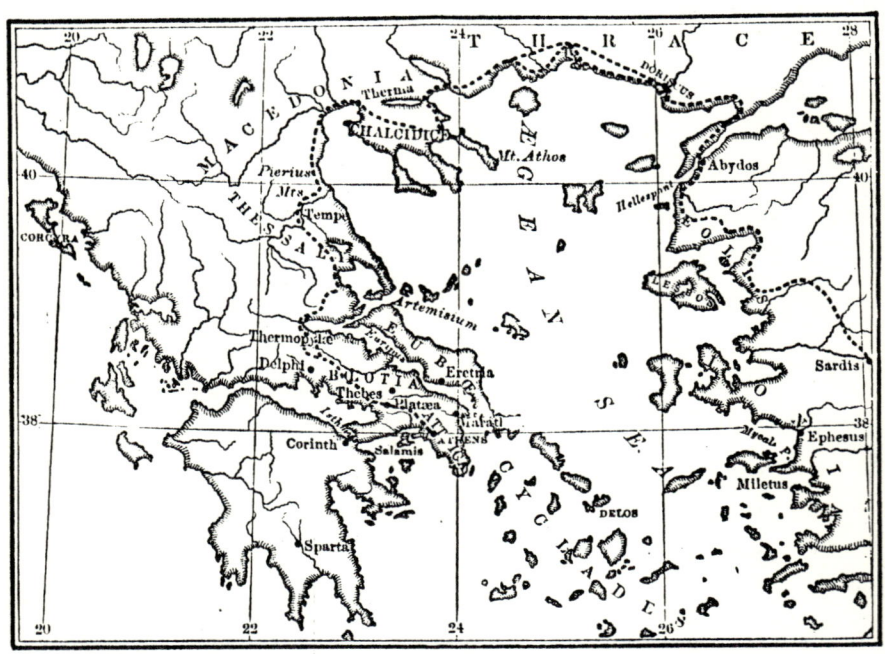

MAP ILLUSTRATING THE INVASION OF GREECE BY XERXES

to the rear of the Greeks. This settled the issue. But the Spartans, rather than give in, died to the last man, and their story has been related ever since as one of the world's greatest heroisms.

The Spartans had done their best at Thermopylae, but they had been unable to stop the Persians, and Greece was in danger. Athens once more saved the situation, and Athens was ready because, under the leadership of her great statesman Themistocles, she had been preparing a navy ever since the victory of Marathon. The Athenians knew that the Persians would one day come again to avenge that defeat.

After the disaster at Thermopylae Athens was an easy prey to the Persians. Immediate action was necessary. The Athenians decided to trust to their fleet and leave Athens to its fate. The women and children were removed out of the country to different places of safety. The soldiers of Athens were all crowded into the fleet. The Persians advanced over the empty plains of Attica, and shortly the city of Athens was in flames. But the Athenian fleet was waiting near the island of Salamis, which is separated from Attica by a narrow strait. The Persian ships attacked the Greek ships and suffered a great defeat. Their fleet was broken, two hundred of their ships were destroyed, and Xerxes the Persian tyrant was compelled to withdraw to Asia. But Xerxes left a Persian army behind him in Greece under an able general, Mardonius. Greece was therefore not yet safe, despite the victory at Salamis. So in the following year, 479 B.C., a combined force of Spartans and Athenians attacked the Persians at Plataea, and finally defeated them. No Persian army ever set foot in European Greece again.

80. THE NEW ATHENS

When the Athenians returned and looked out over the ashes of what was once Athens, amid which rose the smoke-blackened heights of the Acropolis, they began to realize the greatness of their victory and their deliverance. With the none too willing help of Sparta they had met and crushed the ancient power of

Asia. They felt themselves masters of the world. The past seemed narrow and limited. A new and greater Athens dawned upon their vision.

This was all very different from the feeling of the stolid Spartans, whose whole state, it will be remembered, was little more than a large military club or camp. Sparta still represented the past and the privileges of the few, and looked with distrust and jealousy upon the larger world which was opening to Greek life.

Athens, on the other hand, represented the future and the rights of the people. Thus Greece fell into two camps, as it were: Sparta, the home of tradition; Athens, the champion of progress. Accordingly, the brief union of Athens and Sparta against the Persians was followed by a deadly rivalry between these, the two leading states of Greece.

Immediately after the defeat of the Persians Athens was rebuilt. Under the leadership of Themistocles new walls were erected around a new and larger city. The Piraeus, the port of Athens, was strongly fortified, and from this base the Athenian fleet became masters of the Aegean. Then the Athenians formed a league with the Greek cities of Asia Minor and the Aegean Islands. The cities were to give money or ships, and Athens was to command the united fleet. The treasury of this league, of which Athens was in charge, was on the island of Delos, hence the union was called the Delian League. In creating this league Athens was really creating an Empire for herself, and this prospect caused great jealousy and distrust in Sparta.

In 460 B.C. there came forward in Athens a brilliant young citizen named Pericles. He desired to build up the splendid Athenian Empire of which Themistocles had dreamed. He put himself at the head of the party of progress in Athens which desired to increase the power of the people. He was elected leader of Athens year after year (460–429 B.C.), and he proved himself to be one of the most successful rulers in the world's history. Not long after Pericles gained the leadership of the people the jealousy between Sparta and Athens developed into war. This is often called the First Peloponnesian War. It lasted nearly fifteen years (459–446 B.C.), with varying fortunes on both sides. Each city was greatly weakened by the war. Nevertheless, much progress was made in Athens, and in the next chapter we shall glance briefly at the new and glorious Athens now developing under the leadership of Pericles.

CHAPTER XIII

FIFTH-CENTURY ATHENS

81. ATHENIAN HOUSES

THE hasty rebuilding of Athens after the Persians had burned it did not produce any noticeable changes in the houses, nor were there any of great size or splendour. Since the appearance of the first European houses many thousand years had passed, but there were still no beautiful houses anywhere in Europe such as we found on the Nile. The one-story front of even a wealthy man's house in Athens was simply a blank wall, usually of sun-dried brick, rarely of broken stone masonry. Often without any windows, it showed no other opening than the door, but a house of two stories might have a small window or two in the upper story. The door led into a court open to the sky and surrounded by a porch with columns. Here in the mild climate of Greece the family could spend much of their time as in a sitting-room. In the middle of the court stood an altar of the household god Zeus, the protector of the family; while around the court opened a number of doors leading to a living-room, sleeping-rooms, dining-room, store-rooms, and also a tiny kitchen.

The Greek house lacked all conveniences. There was no chimney, and the smoke from the kitchen fire, though intended to drift up through a hole in the roof, choked the room or floated out through the door. In winter gusty drafts filled the house, for many doorways were without doors, and glass in the form of flat panes for the windows was still unknown. In the mild Greek climate, however, a pan of burning charcoal, called a brazier, furnished enough heat to warm the chilly air of a room. Lacking windows, the ground-floor rooms depended entirely on the doors opening into the court for light. At night the dim light of an olive-oil lamp was all that was available. There was no plumbing or piping of any kind in the house, no drainage, and consequently no sanitary arrangements. The water supply was brought in jars by slaves from the nearest well or flowing spring.

The simplicity of the Athenian houses themselves was in great contrast with the beautiful furniture which the Greek craftsmen were now producing. There were many metal utensils; among them ladies' hand mirrors of polished bronze were common; the

Fifth-Century Athens

most numerous of all were lovely painted jars, vases, and dishes, along with the more ordinary pottery forming the household "crockery".

This picture gives us a glimpse into the house of a Greek bride the day after her wedding. At the right, leaning against a couch, is the bride. Before her are two young friends, one sitting, the other standing, both playing with a tame bird. Another friend

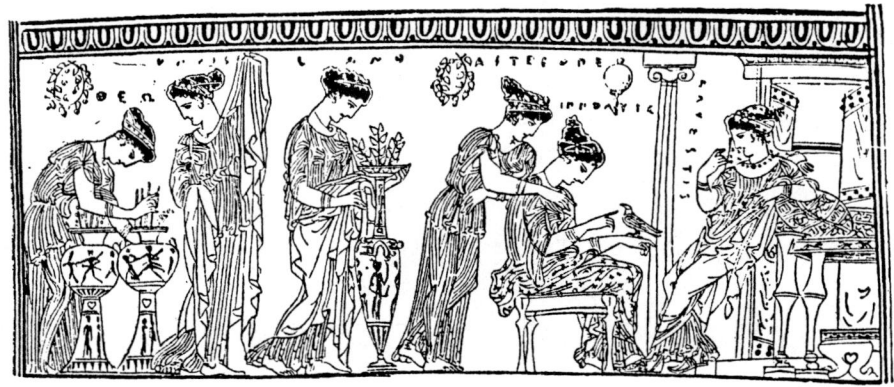

SCENE IN THE HOUSE OF A GREEK BRIDE

approaches carrying a tall and beautiful painted vase as a wedding gift. At the left a visitor arranges flowers in two painted vases, while another lady, adjusting her garment, is looking on. The walls are hung with festive wreaths. The furniture of such a house was usually of wood, but if the owner's wealth permitted, it was adorned with ivory, silver, and gold. It consisted chiefly of beds, like the couch in the picture, chairs, footstools (as at the foot of the couch), small tables, and clothing chests which took the place of cupboards.

82. Streets, Costumes, and Schools

The streets of Athens were merely lanes or alleys, narrow and crooked, winding between the bare mud-brick walls of the low houses standing wall to wall. There was no pavement, and a stroll through the town after rain meant wading through the mud. All household rubbish was thrown into the street, and there was no system of sewage. The few wells and fountains fed by city water-pipes did not furnish enough water to flush the streets, and there was no system of street cleaning. During the hot summers of the South, therefore, Athens was not a healthy place of residence.

All Athens lived out of doors. Athenian life at this time was beautifully simple. Almost all citizens appeared in the simple white garments which we of modern times have come to associate with the classical Greeks. Gorgeous costumes which had been usual in the old days disappeared in Greece, as they did among us in the days of our great-great-grandfathers. Nevertheless, the man of elegant habits took great pride in draping his costume, and was proud of the graceful and sweeping lines in which he could arrange its folds. The picture opposite of a statue of the poet Sophocles shows us the wonderful beauty of a well-draped Greek costume.

There were no schools for girls, but when a boy was old enough he was sent to school in charge of an old slave called a " pedagogue " (*paidagogos*), which really means " leader of a child ". He carried the boy's books and outfit. There were no schools maintained by the State and no schoolhouses. School was conducted in his own house by some poor citizen who had perhaps lost his means, or by some other poor

Fifth-Century Athens

person, perhaps an old soldier or even a foreigner. He received his pay from the parents; but there was a board of state officials appointed to look after the schools and to see that nothing improper was taught.

STATUE OF THE TRAGIC POET SOPHOCLES

Without special training for his work, the teacher merely taught the old-time subjects he had learned in his youth. Music was a very important subject in Greek education, not merely for entertainment, but also and chiefly as an influence towards good conduct. Besides learning to read and write, the pupil learned by heart many passages from the old poets, and here and there a boy with a good memory could repeat the entire *Iliad* and *Odyssey*. On the other hand, the boys had no instruction in mathematics, geography, or science.

The scenes on p. 192 are painted round the centre of a shallow bowl, which accounts for their peculiar shape. In (*A*) we see at the left a music teacher seated at his lyre, giving a lesson to the lad seated before him. In the middle sits a teacher of reading and literature, holding an open roll from which the boy standing before him is learning a poem. Behind the boy sits a slave (pedagogue), who brought him to school and carried his books. In (*B*) we have at the left a singing lesson, aided by the flute to fix the tones. In the middle the master sits correcting an exercise handed him by the boy standing before him, while behind the

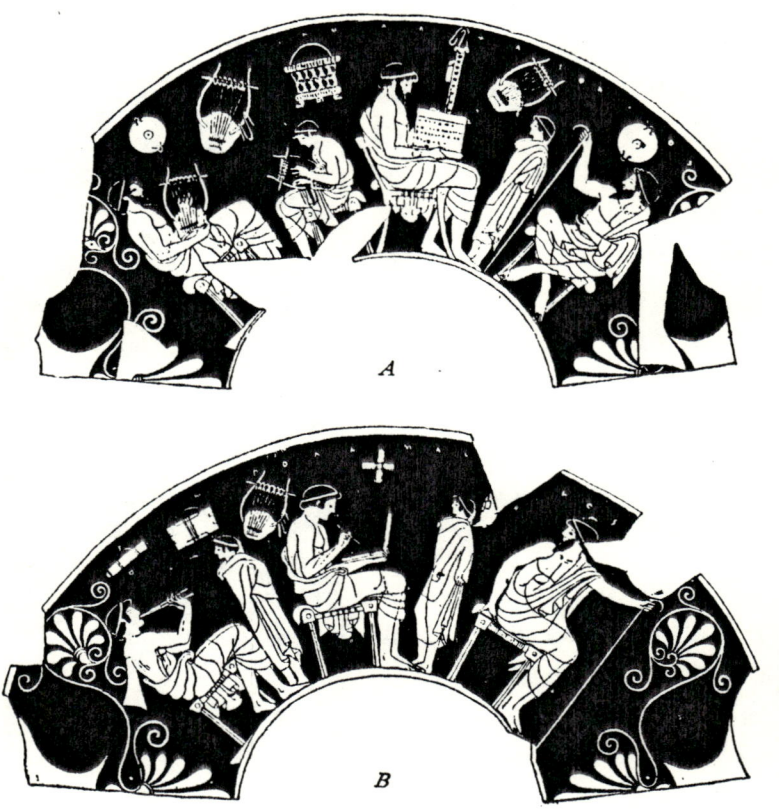

AN ATHENIAN SCHOOL IN THE AGE OF PERICLES

boy sits the slave (pedagogue) as before.

After a time life among the Athenians was quickened by the appearance of more modern private teachers called Sophists, a class of new and clever lecturers who wandered from city to city. Many a bright youth who had finished his music, reading, and writing at the old-fashioned private school annoyed his father by insisting that such schooling was not enough and by demanding money to pay for a course of lectures delivered by one of these new teachers. For the first time higher education was thus open to young men who had hitherto thought of little more than a victory in the Olympic games or a fine appearance when parading with the crack cavalry of Athens.

The appearance of these new teachers, therefore, marked a new age in the history of the Greeks, and especially in that of Athens. In the first place, the Sophists recognized the importance of good public speaking in addressing the large citizen juries or in speaking before the Assembly of the people. The Sophists, therefore, taught oratory with great success, and many a father who had no gift for speaking had the pleasure of seeing his son a practised public speaker. It was through the teaching of the Sophists, also, that the first successful writing of Greek prose began. At the same time they really founded the study of language, which was yet to become grammar. They also taught mathematics and astronomy, and the young men of Athens for the first time began to learn a little science. Thus the truths which the Greek philosophers began to observe in the days of Thales were, after a century and a half, beginning to spread among the people.

83. An Open-air House of Commons

Athens was by this time a democracy, that is, a state in which the people took a great interest and a great part in government. This is a picture of the meeting-place of the Assembly of the people. The speaker's platform with its three steps is immediately in the foreground. The listening Athenian citizens of the Assembly sat on the ground now sloping away to the left, but at that time probably level. The ground

THE PNYX, THE ATHENIAN PLACE OF ASSEMBLY

they occupied was enclosed by a semicircular wall, beginning at the farther end of the straight wall seen here on the right, extending then to the left, and returning to the straight wall again behind our present point of view. This was an open-air House of Commons where, however, the citizen did not send a representative, but came and voted himself as he was influenced from this platform by great Athenian leaders, like Themistocles, Pericles, or Demosthenes. Note the Acropolis and the Parthenon, to which we look eastward from the Pnyx.

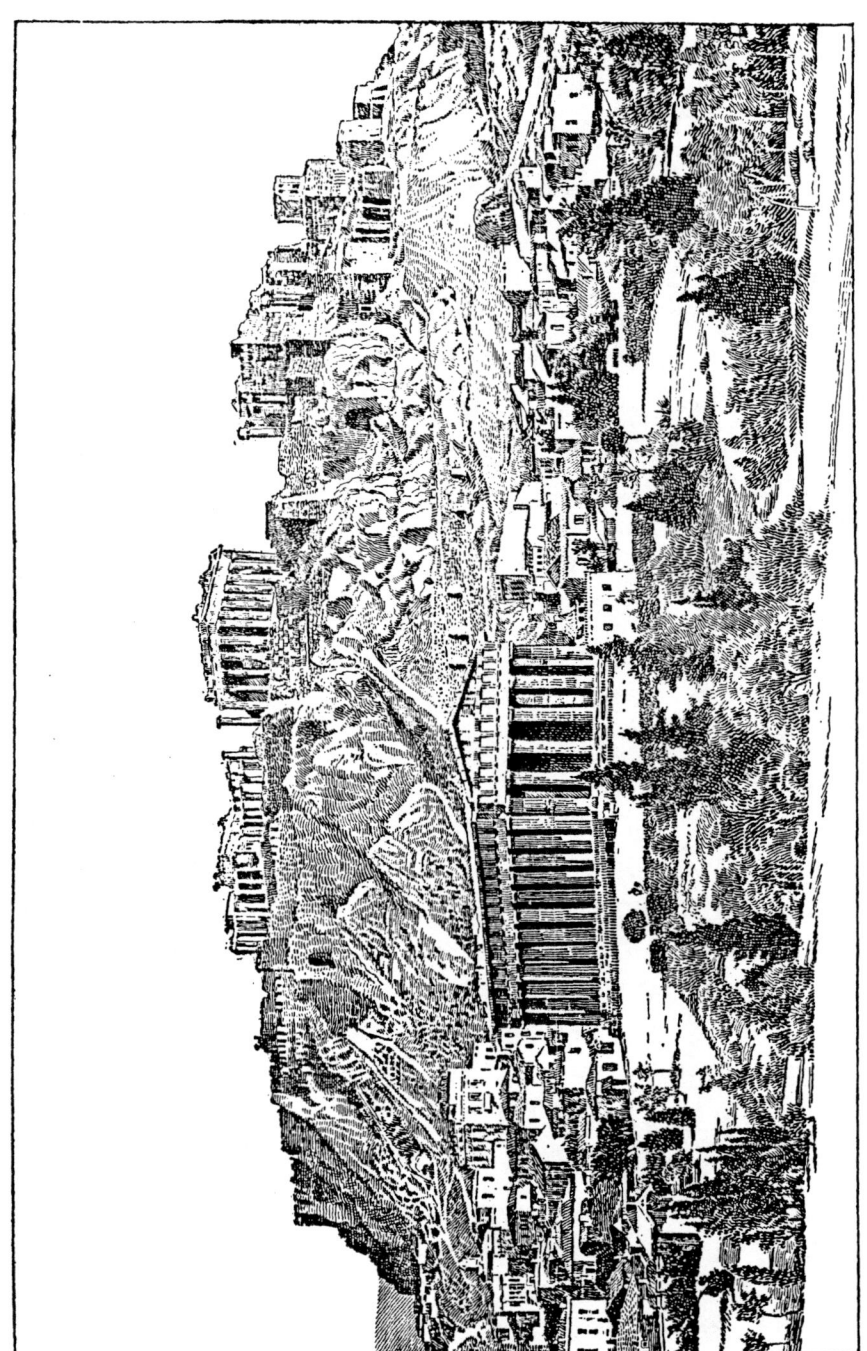

The So-called Temple of Theseus, the Areopagus, and the Acropolis of Athens

84. THE ACROPOLIS

The Acropolis, the rock citadel of Athens, is the most famous part of the city. There on its summit had always been the dwelling-place of Athena, whose arm was ever stretched out in protection of her beloved Athens. But for long years after the defeat of the Persians, the Acropolis rose smoke-blackened over the rebuilt houses of the city, and no temple of Athena appeared to replace the old building of Pisistratus, which the Persians had burned.

In time, however, the citizens of Athens, under the direction of Pericles, and with the aid of the world's greatest architects and sculptors, set up their victory buildings on the Acropolis. Let us examine the reconstructed picture of the Acropolis shown here. The lower entrance (A) is of Roman date. Beyond it we have on the right the graceful little temple of Victory (B), while before us rises the colonnaded entrance building (C) designed by Mnesicles. As we pass through it we stand beside the colossal bronze statue of Athena (D) by Phidias, beyond which at the left is the ancient sanctuary of the Erechtheum (F). To the right, along the south edge of the hill, is the wonderful temple of the Parthenon (E). Its farthest corner looks down upon the theatre (H). The other theatre-like building (I) in the foreground is a concert hall, built by Herodus Atticus, a wealthy citizen, in Roman times (second century A.D.). (G) is the foundation of an ancient temple (now destroyed) older than the present Parthenon.

Fifth-Century Athens

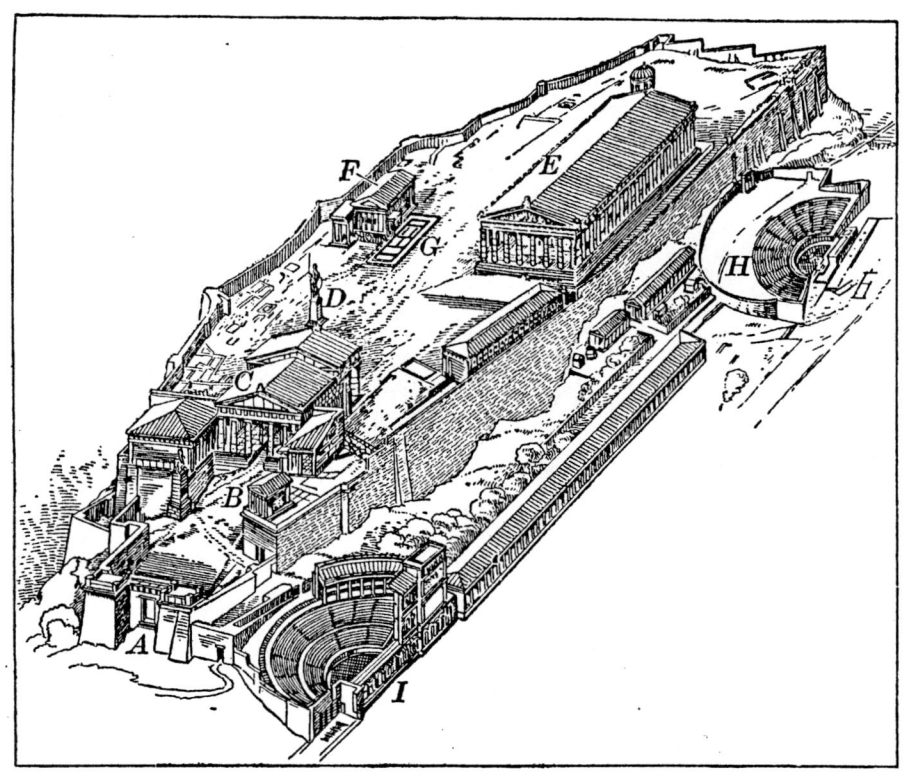

RESTORATION OF THE ATHENIAN ACROPOLIS

The most famous of all Greek buildings is the Parthenon on the Acropolis. The first picture overleaf is from a photograph of the ruins as they are to be seen to-day. The Parthenon was destroyed in 1687 during a war between the Turks and the Venetians. The Turks used the beautiful temple as a powder magazine. A bomb set fire to the magazine and more than half of the building was blown up.

The next picture is a restoration of the Parthenon as it was in the fifth century B.C., and it shows the wonderful beauty of the columns as they were when they left the hands of the builders.

THE PARTHENON
(From a photograph)

RESTORATION OF THE PARTHENON, AS IT WAS IN THE FIFTH
CENTURY B.C. (After Thiersch and Michaelis)

85. The Greek Orders

Let us here consider some of the details of Greek architecture. By the fifth century B.C. the Greeks had developed a style of temple building that has had an influence on buildings all over the world ever since. We have already referred to the development of the Greek column out of the Egyptian. The Greeks made it more beautiful in shape. In our view of the Acropolis we noticed the general style of a Greek temple. A closer examination of these temples shows us that there were three types, and these are called the Doric, Ionic, and Corinthian orders. From a distance the three orders appear very similar, but a closer study shows us some very important differences.

Look at the two little temples in the diagram on p. 200 : The little Doric building (*B*) is the treasury of the Athenians at Delphi, containing their offerings of gratitude to Apollo. On the low base at the left side of the building were placed the trophies from the battle of Marathon. Over them on the walls are carved hymns to Apollo with musical notes attached, the oldest musical notation surviving. The beautiful Ionic building (*D*) is a restoration of the Temple of Victory on the Athenian Acropolis. Compare the slender Ionic columns with the thicker shafts of the Doric style, and it will be seen that the Ionic order is a more delicate and graceful style. (*A*) and (*C*) show details of both styles. The following distinctions should be carefully noted :

(1) The Doric column is sturdy, strong, and yet refined in outline.
The Ionic column is slender and more graceful.

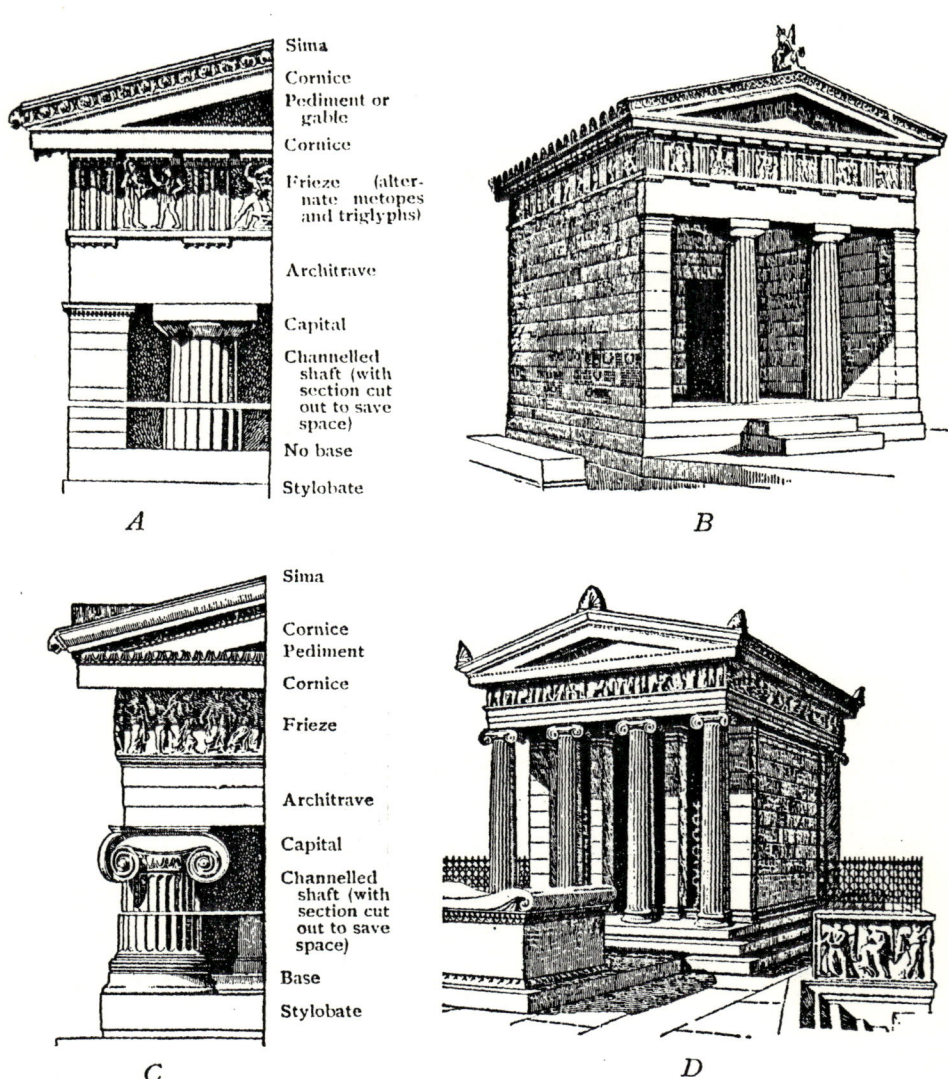

COMPARATIVE DIAGRAM OF THE TWO LEADING GREEK STYLES OF ARCHITECTURE, THE DORIC (*A* AND *B*) AND THE IONIC (*C* AND *D*)

(2) The Doric column has no ornamental base. This gives the style strength and directness. The Ionic column has a definite base, which is part of the ornamental scheme.

Fifth-Century Athens

(3) The capital of the Doric style is simple and square.

The Ionic capital is composed of spiral scrolls called volutes, which are the chief distinguishing marks of the style.

(4) The Ionic frieze is continuous.

The Doric frieze is divided and consists of alternate *metopes* and *triglyphs*. The object of the triglyphs is to carry upwards the line of the flutings in the column to prevent the temple from appearing too squat.

(5) The Doric *architrave* is a single block. The Ionic architrave is in three layers, which again adds to the delicacy of the latter style.

Finally, note that each style has its own appeal to our sense of beauty. Each is a definite contribution to the architecture of the world.

A new style developed in Greece about the fourth century B.C., though it was not much used before the time of Alexander the Great. This new style was called the Corinthian order. Egyptian architects had long before crowned their columns with a capital representing flowers or palm-tree tops, as we see in this sketch (left).

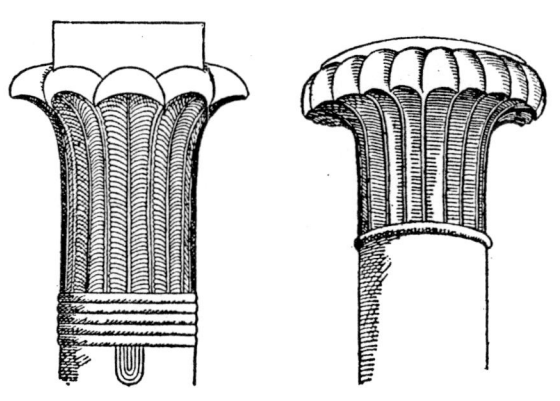

EGYPTIAN PALM-TREE CAPITAL (*left*): GREEK ADAPTATION (*right*) AT PERGAMUM

The Greeks now profited by this hint. Perceiving the great beauty of their own acanthus plant, they designed a capital adorned with a double row of acanthus leaves, as shown in the next sketch. The effect of this capital was peculiarly rich. Compare it with the Doric and Ionic capitals, and you will understand why we speak of " the *severe* Doric, the *graceful* Ionic, and the *ornate* Corinthian " styles.

A Corinthian Capital

We have already seen the Acropolis adorned with its beautiful temples. Let us now look at Olympia, another scene famous in Greek life, in order to judge the effect produced by the artistic use of these Greek ideas of architecture.

The total effect of these fine buildings with their shapely columns, all fitting in with the natural scenic background, is one of great beauty. We must remember that beauty appealed to the Greeks so much that they believed that beauty and goodness were one and the same thing. Note in the picture the great Doric temple in the centre foreground, the splendid theatre in the background, and on the extreme right the famous stadium where the Olympic contests took place.

General View of Olympia (A restoration by Thiersch)

86. Sculpture

As the Greeks developed architecture, so did they proceed with the art of sculpture. We have already seen an early example of Greek sculpture and have noticed that the influence of Egyptian statues is evident in the early work. Here on the left is another example. It is drawn from a relief statue on a tombstone. The limbs are stiff. The work is not free. In order to understand how different the Greek work became when it had shaken off the Eastern influence,

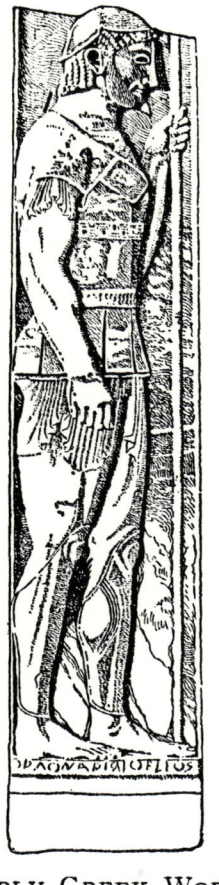

Early Greek Work

The Wrestlers

look at the illustration on the right. There is no stiffness in this group of wrestlers. We see here the natural grace and bending charm of the human body. That was the great achievement of the Greeks; they outlined man as he was. There are many famous names

Fifth-Century Athens

of sculptors in Greek history. We must be content with mentioning Myron, Phidias, and Praxiteles. Myron produced his best work about 460 B.C. His most famous statue is the Disc Thrower. It has been called one of the most wonderful of human works. It shows a freedom of treatment, a knowledge of form, and a love of humanity that is above all criticism. But Phidias is the greatest of the sculptors of Athens. In a long band of carved marble extending entirely round the four sides of the Parthenon, at the top inside the colonnades, Phidias and his pupils have shown the people of Athens moving in the stately procession of the Pan-Athenaic festival. These are not individual portraits of actual Athenian folk, but only types which lived in the mind of the sculptor,

THE DISCUS THROWER

and not in the streets of Athens. Such sculpture had never been seen before. Inside the Parthenon stood the colossal figure of Athena, wrought by the cunning hand of Phidias in gold and ivory. Even from the city below the citizens could see, touched with bright colours, the figures of the gods with which Phidias had filled the triangular gable ends of the building. Out in the open area behind the entrance rose another great work of

Phidias, a colossal bronze statue of Athena, seventy feet high. With shield and spear the goddess stood, and the glittering point of her spear could be seen shining like a beacon far across the land, and even by the sailors far out at sea as they sailed homeward.

ATHENIAN YOUTH IN PROCESSION
(From the frieze of the Parthenon)

87. DRAMA

Let us accompany an Athenian citizen to the theatre of Athens that lies at the foot of the Acropolis. The people are already entering, for the spring feast of Dionysus has arrived. It is natural that the people should feel that the theatre and all that is done there should belong to them, especially as they look down upon the orchestra circle and recognize their friends and neighbours and their own sons in the chorus for

Fifth-Century Athens

the day's performance. The play would seem very strange to us, for there is little or no scenery; and the actors, who are always men, wear strange masks. The story of the play is largely told in song by the chorus, but this is varied by the dialogue of the actors, and the whole is not unlike an opera.

The three greatest Greek dramatists were Aeschylus, Sophocles, and Euripides. Their plays are immortal.

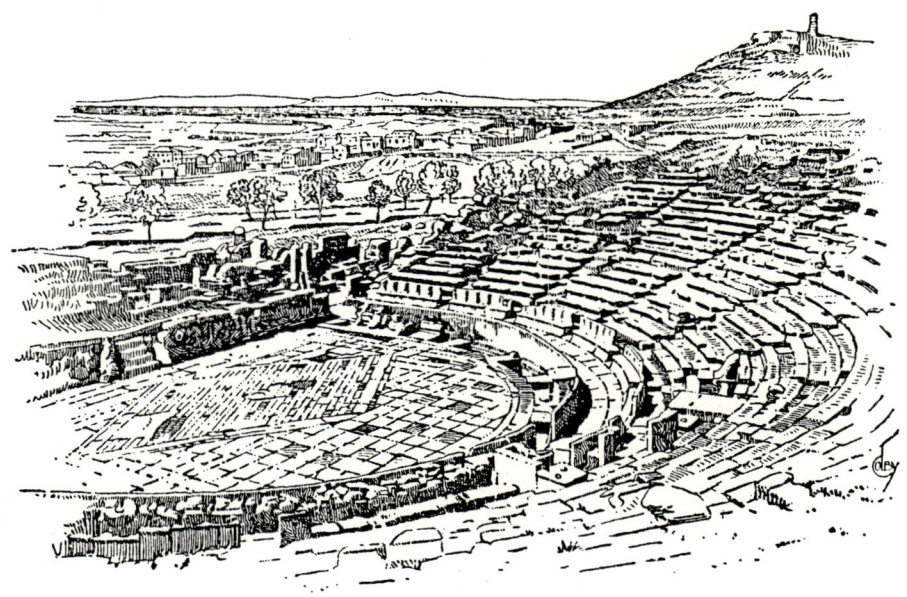

THE THEATRE OF ATHENS

This is a picture of the theatre of Athens. It was the centre of the growth and development of Greek drama which began as a part of the celebration of the spring feast of Dionysus, god of the vine and of the fruitfulness of the earth. The temple of the god stood just on the left of our picture. Long before anyone knew of such a thing as a theatre, the people gathered at this place to watch the celebration of the god's spring feast, where they formed a circle about the chorus, which narrated in song the stories of the gods. This circle (called the orchestra) was finally marked out permanently, seats of wood for the spectators were erected in a semicircle on one side, but the singing and action all took place in the circle on a level with the ground. On the side opposite the public was a booth, or tent (Greek *skene*, " scene "), for the actors, and out of this finally developed the stage. In the picture we see the circle of the orchestra with the stage cutting off the back of the circle. The seats are of stone and accommodated possibly seventeen thousand people. The fine marble seats in the front row were reserved for the leading men of Athens. The old wooden seats were still in use in the days when Aeschylus, Sophocles, and Euripides presented their dramas in competition for prizes awarded for the best plays.

88. Civil War

We must now proceed with the further story of Greece. The fifth century ended with war as it had begun with war. The defeat of the Persians had produced a new and brilliant Athens, but it did not result in a united Greece. Sparta became more and more jealous of the new Athens and of the power she had over countless neighbouring cities, and eventually this jealousy ripened into war. We have already referred to the First Peloponnesian War. A Second Peloponnesian War broke out in 431 B.C. After ten years of devastation a peace was declared in 421 B.C. Each side agreed to give back the conquests it had made. It is sad to relate that a Third Peloponnesian War broke out between the rivals almost immediately. This proved to be final, and Athens was completely defeated (404 B.C.). " Never," says Thucydides, " never were so many cities captured and depopulated. Never were exile and slaughter more frequent, whether in war or brought about by cruel strife." Sparta imposed hard terms on her rival. The Long Walls which had been built from Athens to the Piraeus as well as the fortifications of the Piraeus were torn down. The Athenian fleet had already been almost totally destroyed and the remnant of it was handed over to Sparta. All her foreign possessions were given up, and Athens was forced to enter the Spartan League.

Thus the fifth century, which had so gloriously begun for Athens with the repulse of Persia, the century which, under the leadership of such men as Themistocles and Pericles, had seen her rise to supremacy in all that was best and noblest in Greek life, closed with the destruction of the Athenian Empire.

Sparta managed to maintain her leadership of Greece for over thirty years. But she had to face frequent revolts on the part of cities which hated her rule. The city of Thebes finally united with Athens to crush Sparta (371 B.C.). It then remained to see whether Thebes, the new victor, could do what Athens and Sparta had failed in doing and could create a Greek *nation*. But it was not to be. The power of Thebes collapsed in 362 B.C.

Thus the only powerful Greek states which might have united the Hellenic world into a nation had crushed each other, and before long Greece fell into the power of a conqueror from the outside. Yet, in spite of these disasters during the two generations after Pericles, the Greeks and especially the Athenians made such marvellous progress in art, architecture, literature, philosophy, and science that this period is regarded as one of the greatest in the history of man. We shall now examine some of this later progress.

89. Praxiteles

The greatest of the Greek sculptors in the fourth century B.C. was Praxiteles. He produced his chief works about 360–340 B.C. His native city being without money for great monumental works, Praxiteles wrought individual figures of life size, and most of these for foreign states. Unlike the majestic and exalted figures of Phidias, the gods of Praxiteles seem near to us. They at once appeal to us as being human like ourselves, interested in a life like ours, and doing things which we would like to do ourselves. As they stand at ease in attitudes of repose, the grace and balance of the flowing lines give them a splendour of beauty unattained by any earlier sculpture of the Greeks.

Notice the wonderful ease and grace with which the figures of Apollo and the Satyr are posed. In a country where lizards were darting along every sunny wall, a lad with a stone poised to throw was a frequent sight. This common human action is the one which Praxiteles chose for his Apollo, and another equally common, the pouring of wine, he has depicted in the figure of the Satyr. These very human gods were quite different from those of Phidias.

Fifth-Century Athens

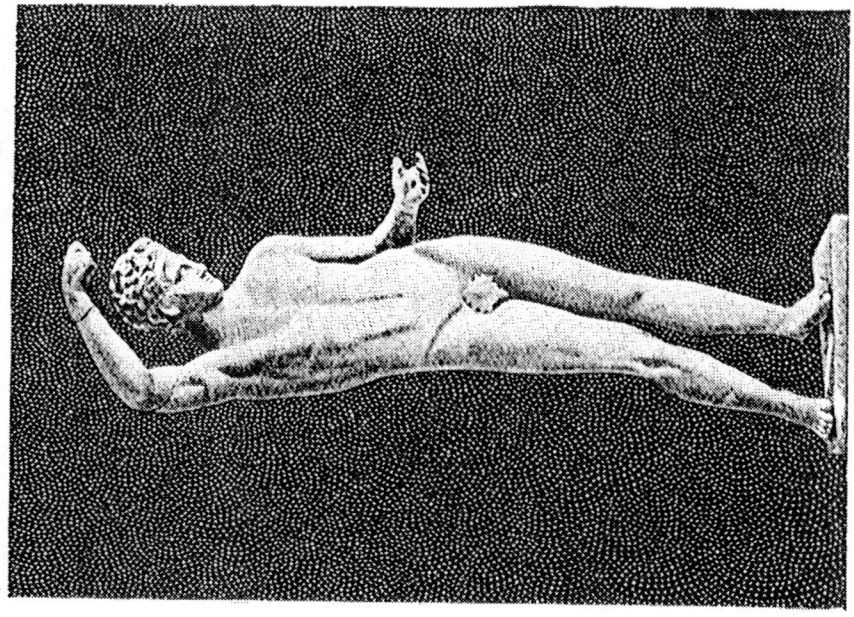

Satyr

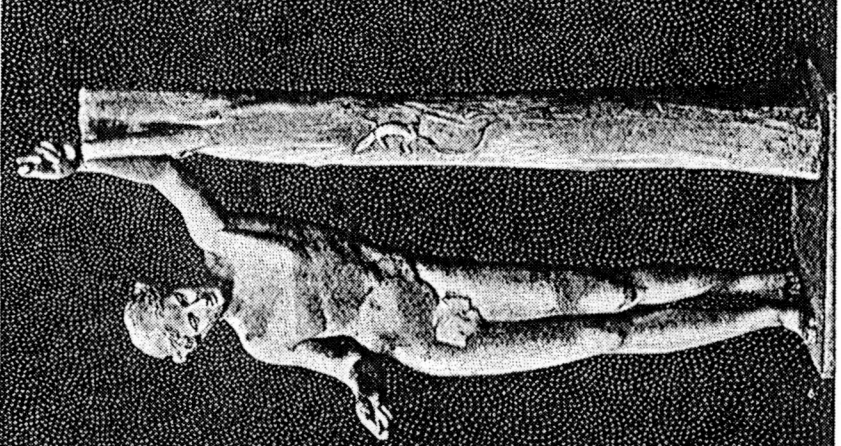

Apollo

A Brief History of Ancient Times

PRAXITELES' FIGURE OF HERMES PLAYING WITH THE CHILD DIONYSUS

This wonderful statue of Hermes by Praxiteles shown in the above picture was discovered in the ruins of the temple of Hera at Olympia, and is one of the few original works of the great Greek sculptors found in

Greece. Nearly all such Greek originals have perished, and we know them only in Roman copies. In his uplifted hand (now broken off) the god probably held a bunch of grapes, with which he is amusing the child.

90. THE GREATEST GREEK

The meaning of the Greek word " philosopher " is " a lover of wisdom ". Philosophy is a science which searches for the reason and causes of things. The Greeks began this science, and the study of philosophy has occupied the minds of great men from that day to this. There were three very important Greek philosophers: Socrates, Plato, and Aristotle.

PORTRAIT OF SOCRATES

Socrates was the son of a stone-cutter, or small sculptor. The ill-clothed figure and ugly face of Socrates had become familiar in the streets to all the folk of Athens since the outbreak of the second war with Sparta. He was accustomed to stand about the market-place all day engaging in conversation with anyone he met, and asking a great many questions. Socrates' arguments left the citizens of Athens in a very confused state of mind, for they seemed to call in question everything which had once been regarded as settled.

Yet this familiar and homely figure of the stone-cutter's son represented the best and highest in Greek genius. Without desire for office or a political career, Socrates' supreme interest nevertheless was the State. He believed that the State, made up as it was of citizens, could be saved and purified only by the improvement of the individual citizen through the education of his mind to recognize virtue and right.

The simple personality of this greatest of Greek teachers often opened to him the houses of the rich and noble. His fame spread far and wide, and a group of pupils gathered about him, among whom the most famous was Plato. But his aims and noble efforts on behalf of the Athenian state were misunderstood. His keen questions seemed to throw doubt upon all the old beliefs. So the Athenians summoned Socrates for trial for corrupting the youth with all sorts of doubts and teachings against the gods. Socrates might easily have left Athens when the complaint was lodged against him. Instead, he appeared for trial, made a powerful and dignified defence, and when the court voted the death penalty, passed his last days in quiet conversation with his friends and pupils, in whose presence he quietly drank the "fatal hemlock".

Plato (427–347 B.C.), the most brilliant of the pupils of Socrates, wrote out much of his master's teachings in the form of imaginary conversations between Socrates and those who flocked around him to discuss the deep problems of man's nature and duty. These *Dialogues* are at once so charming and so full of deep thought that they are still counted among the most wonderful books of all the ages. They give us a good idea of the informal way in which the leading Athenians were accustomed to meet in the market-place or in the house of some thoughtful citizen and confer together on the good, the true, and the beautiful. It is through the writings of Plato that we learn most of what we know of Socrates, for he himself wrote nothing.

Aristotle (384–322 B.C.) was a student of Plato's and he became as famous as his master. With the help of his own students Aristotle wrote books on almost every important subject—politics, ethics, economics, psychology, zoology, astronomy, poetry, and the drama. It seems to have been his ambition to tell everything that had ever been discovered and to present this information in such a way that others could easily learn it. His knowledge was so great that in the Middle Ages his books were almost the only ones studied in the universities of Europe, and he is still looked upon as perhaps the greatest scholar that the world has ever produced.

91. Summary

The constant conflicts among the Greek cities, which proved so fatal to their political unity, had nevertheless spurred on each one of them to surpass its rivals in art and literature and all that is finest in civilization. Great as was the age of Pericles, the age that followed was still greater. The tiny Athenian state, having at most twenty-five or thirty thousand citizens, had furnished in this period a group of great artists and thinkers such as never in the whole history of the world arose elsewhere in so small a community.

Their names and their achievements are accounted to-day as among the most famous in human history.

We shall now see how the Greek cities, because of their lack of unity, fell into the hands of the king of Macedonia, and we shall read how Alexander the Great spread Greek civilization throughout the East.

CHAPTER XIV

THE HELLENISTIC AGE

92. ALEXANDER THE GREAT

IN the fourth century B.C. a new power was developing to the north of the Greek cities, which was destined to play a leading part in Greek affairs. This was Macedonia. Its first king of importance was Philip, the father of Alexander the Great. Philip himself had enjoyed a Greek education, and when he gained the power over Macedonia in 360 B.C. he understood perfectly the situation of the disunited Greek world. He planned to make himself its master, and he began his task with the ability both of a skilled statesman and an able soldier.

After the death of Philip in 336 B.C. the power in Macedonia passed into the hands of his son Alexander, a youth of only twenty years of age. Seven years before, when Alexander was thirteen years old, his father had summoned to the Macedonian court the great philosopher Aristotle, a former pupil of Plato, to be the teacher of the young prince. Under his instruction the lad learned to know and love the masterpieces of Greek literature, especially the Homeric

The Hellenistic Age

songs. The deeds of the ancient heroes touched and aroused his young imagination, and as he grew older his love for Greek culture increased to such an extent that it inspired all his work. Alexander became, before he was thirty years of age, one of the greatest conquerors the world has ever known, but that fact must not make us forget that he was a statesman who knew the value of Greek civilization and whose main object was to make his conquests the means by which the culture of Greece could be spread throughout the eastern world. The work of Alexander was to create for Greek civilization a great world in Asia in which it could develop.

But Asia had to be conquered first, and this amazing boy set out to do this. It was first necessary for him to be master of Greece itself. The Greek states fancied they could easily overthrow so young a ruler as Alexander. They were soon to learn how wise a head was on his young shoulders. When Thebes revolted against Macedonia, Alexander captured and destroyed the city, sparing only the house of a great Greek poet called Pindar. All Greece was thus taught to fear and respect his power, learning at the same time how he valued and respected Greek genius. After this the Greek states, with the exception of Sparta, formed a league and elected Alexander as its leader and general. As a result they all sent troops to increase his army. Alexander then decided to lead the united Greeks against the Persian lord of Asia, looking upon himself as the champion of Hellas against Asia. He first decided to master Asia Minor, where there were many Greek cities which had been long subject to the Persians. His first great victory over the Persians was at the battle of Granicus (334 B.C.), and it resulted in the conquest of Asia Minor, which was thus freed for ever from the Persian yoke. Then Alexander reached the north-east corner of the Mediterranean. Before him lay a vast Asiatic world of forty million souls, where the family of the Great King of Persia had been supreme for two hundred years. In this great arena Alexander was to be the champion for the next ten years (333–323 B.C.).

At this important point, by the Gulf of Issus, Alexander met the main army of Persia under the personal command of the Great King, Darius III, the last of the Persian line. The Persians were swept away from the field, and the retreat of Darius never stopped until it had crossed the Euphrates. Many a general would have been satisfied with this sweeping victory of the battle of Issus, especially when Darius the Great King sent a letter desiring terms of peace and offering to accept the Euphrates as a boundary between them, all Asia west of that river to be handed over to the Macedonians. Alexander's friends advised him to accept the terms. It was a dramatic and important moment, and we can imagine the figure of the young soldier standing with his letter in his hand. Here was a great offer. Here were old counsellors advising him most strongly to accept. But before the eyes of the young king there arose a vision of a still vaster empire controlled by Greek civilization, a vision to which the duller eyes about him were entirely closed. Alexander waved aside his advisers and determined to conquer the *whole* Persian Empire.

The picture on p. 219 shows Alexander attacking the Persian king at the battle of Issus. It is one of the

The Hellenistic Age

Alexander the Great charging the Bodyguard and Officers of the Persian King at the Battle of Issus

greatest scenes of heroism in battle ever painted. This splendid scene is made with pieces of coloured glass (mosaic) forming a floor pavement discovered in 1831 at the Roman town of Pompeii. It was originally laid at Alexandria and was afterwards moved to Italy by the Romans. It is really a copy of an older work, a painting done at Alexandria.

The artist who designed this great work has selected the supreme moment when the Persians (at the right) are endeavouring to rescue their king from the onset of the Macedonians (at the left). Alexander, the bareheaded figure on horseback at the left, charges furiously against the Persian king (Darius III), who stands in his chariot (at the right). The Macedonian attack is so impetuous that the Persian king's life is endangered. A Persian noble dismounts and offers his riderless horse, that the king may quickly mount and escape. Devoted Persian nobles heroically ride in between their king and the Macedonian onset, to give Darius an opportunity to mount. But Alexander's spear has passed entirely through the body of one of these Persian nobles, who has thus given his life for his king. Darius throws out his hand in grief and horror at the awful death of his noble friend. The driver of the royal chariot (behind the king) lashes his three horses, endeavouring to carry Darius from the field in flight.

93. Lord of the Ancient East

Having made his great decision to capture the whole empire of Persia, it was necessary for Alexander to make sure that he would not be surprised in the rear. His first task was to march southward along the eastern end of the Mediterranean. All the important Phoenician seaports on the way were captured. Then Alexander marched into Egypt, which was very feeble because it had been so long a Persian province. It fell an easy prey before the conqueror, who was now ready for his larger plans. He proceeded at once from Egypt through Palestine to Asia, where in turn he crossed the Tigris near the ruins of Nineveh. Here the Great King of Persia had gathered his forces for a last stand. A battle was fought at Arbela (331 B.C.). Although greatly outnumbered, the Macedonians crushed the Asiatic army and forced the Persians into disgraceful flight. In a few days Alexander was living in the winter palace of the King of Persia in Babylon.

Thus, at last, both the valley of the Nile and the valley of the Euphrates, the homes of the earliest two civilizations, were now in the hands of a European power and under the control of a newer and a higher civilization. Less than five years had passed since the young Macedonian had entered Asia. Another five years of triumph were to follow. In the course of these five years, while the Greek world looked on in amazement, the young Alexander seemed to disappear in the mists on the far-off eastern fringes of the known world. He marched his army in one vast loop after another through the heart of Irania, northward across the Oxus, southward again across the Indus and the very frontiers of India into the valley of the Ganges, where at last the complaints of his weary troops forced him to turn back. He descended the Indus and even sailed the waters of the Indian Ocean. More than seven years after he had left the great city of Babylon, Alexander entered it again.

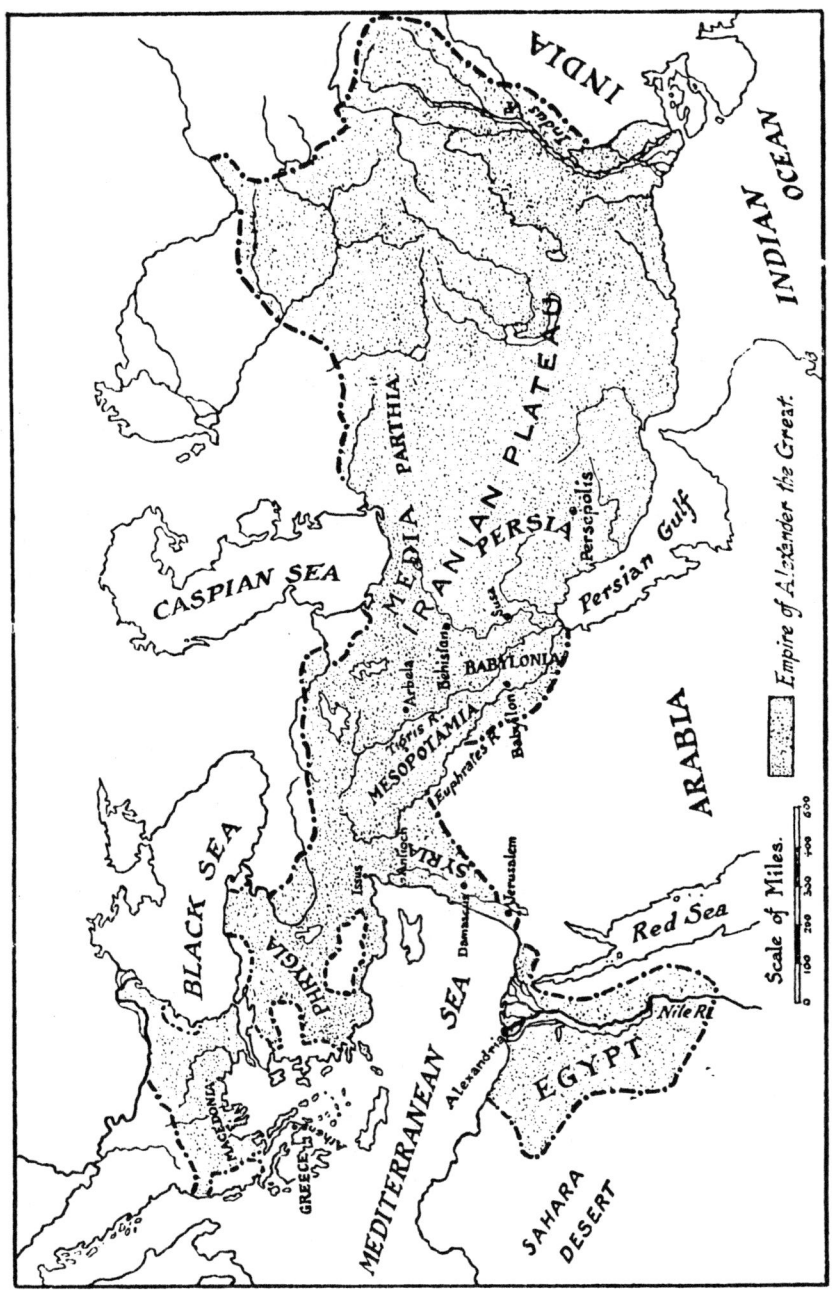

EMPIRE OF ALEXANDER THE GREAT

The Hellenistic Age

He had been less than twelve years in Asia and he had carried Greek civilization into the very heart of the Continent. At important points along his line of march he had founded Greek cities bearing his name and had set up kingdoms which were to be centres of Greek influence on the frontiers of India. Never before had East and West so mingled as in this amazing work of Alexander.

But the end came with striking suddenness. In 323 B.C. he fell sick and died after a few days. He was then thirty-three years of age. He has been well termed "the Great". Few men of genius, and certainly none in so short a time, have left so great a mark on the course of human affairs. He created a new age, in which Greek civilization led the way throughout a world extending from Sicily and South Italy eastward to the Persian Gulf. For this reason we call this period beginning with Alexander the "Hellenistic Age". In this age Greek became the common language of the Eastern Mediterranean and the Near East. This fact is well illustrated by the Rosetta Stone.

94. The Rosetta Stone

We can see how the Greek language was used in Egypt by studying the Rosetta Stone which was found there, and which is one of the most important relics of old times in our possession. This famous inscription is in two languages. It was written in Greek because the language of the government was Greek, and because there were so many Greek-speaking people in Egypt. At the same time, as the stone was to be a public record, it was necessary that it should be read by Egyptians who knew no Greek. The document was therefore first written out with pen and ink, just as we would

THE ROSETTA STONE, BEARING THE SAME INSCRIPTION IN GREEK (*C*) AND EGYPTIAN (*A* AND *B*)

do it, in ordinary Egyptian handwriting, now called *demotic*. This demotic copy was then cut on the stone where it occupies the middle. The priests also wrote out the document in the ancient sacred hieroglyphics, and they put this hieroglyphic form in the place of honour at the top of the stone, where the two corners have since been broken off and lost. Both of these two forms then are Egyptian—the upper corresponding to our print, the lower corresponding to our handwriting. The Greek translation of the Egyptian we see at the bottom.

The stone was intended as a public record of certain honours which the Egyptian priests were extending to the Greek king, one of the Ptolemies, in 195 B.C. After it fell down and was broken, the stone had been buried in rubbish for many centuries, when the soldiers of Napoleon accidentally found it while digging trenches near the Rosetta mouth of the Nile in 1779. Hence it is called the Rosetta Stone. It was afterwards captured by the British, and is now in the British Museum. By comparing the Greek version of the record with the Egyptian forms, scholars were able to understand the ancient Egyptian hieroglyphic writing.

95. The New Greek Cities

Alexander and his successors built a great many Greek cities in Asia Minor, Syria, Mesopotamia, and Egypt, especially upon the banks of the rivers of these different regions, along the main routes of travel, and at the important points of trade and commerce. They were furnished and adorned with Greek temples, theatres, gymnasia, and covered colonnades. The cities of Greece were thus reproduced throughout western Asia. In these cities the buildings and the Doric, Ionic, and Corinthian columns were as beautiful as those of the homeland. The following diagram gives us a striking restoration of one of these new Greek cities of Asia Minor.

This little city when excavated proved to be almost a second Pompeii, only older. Above (*A*), on the top of the cliff, was the citadel with a path leading up to it (*B*). (*C*) shows the masonry flume which brought the mountain water down into the town. Entering the town one passed through the gate at (*K*), and up a straight street to the little provision-market square (*L*). Just above the market was the temple of Athena (*I*), built by Alexander himself. Then one entered the spacious business market (agora) (*M*), surrounded by fine colonnades, with shops behind them, except on one side (under *N*), where there was a stately hall for business and festive occasions, like the basilica halls which were coming in at this time among the Greeks. Beyond at (*N*) were the offices of the city government, the hall in which the Council and Assembly met, and the theatre (*E*). At (*G*) was the temple of Isis, and in the foreground were the gymnasium (*P*) and the stadium (*Q*). The wash-room here still contains the marble basins and the lion-headed spouts from which the water flowed. An attached open hall was used for school instruction and lectures. Above the seats of the stadium (*Q*) was a beautiful colonnade six hundred feet long, for pleasure strolling between the athletic events, to enjoy the grand view of the sea upon which the audience looked down. Around the whole city was a strong wall of masonry, with a gate at the east (*H*) and west (*K*), while along the streets outside these gates were the tombs of the ancestors as at Athens. Such was the city of Priene in Asia Minor.

The Hellenistic Age

Restoration of the Hellenistic City of Priene in Asia Minor.
(After a Drawing by A. Zippelius)

A Brief History of Ancient Times

The public buildings of Pergamum, as seen in the next diagram, show us still more vividly the power of Greek ideas outside Greece itself. Pergamum, on the west coast of Asia Minor, became a flourishing city-kingdom in the third century B.C. under the successors of Alexander the Great. The dwellings of the citizens were all lower down, in front of the group of buildings

RESTORATION OF THE PUBLIC BUILDINGS OF PERGAMUM, A HELLENISTIC CITY OF ASIA MINOR. (After Thiersch)

shown here. These public buildings stand on three terraces—lower, middle, and upper. The large *lower* terrace (*A*) was the main market-place, adorned with a vast square marble altar of Zeus, having colonnades on three sides, beneath which was a long sculptured band (frieze) of warring gods and giants. On the *middle* terrace (*B*), behind the colonnades, was the famous library of Pergamum, where the stone bases of library shelves still survive.

The Hellenistic Age

96. Laocoön

Sculpture flourished especially in Pergamum in the Hellenistic Age under the Athenian influence. We will

A Gallic Chieftain in Defeat slaying his Wife and Himself

THE DEATH OF LAOCOÖN AND HIS TWO SONS

look at two examples of this later art. Note the vigour, energy, and movement that has now come into the figures. The Gallic chieftain with one hand supports his dying wife, and, casting a terrible glance at the pursuing enemy, plunges his sword into his own breast. The tremendous power of the barbarian's muscular figure is in startling contrast with the helpless limbs of the woman. The beholder feels both terror at the wild strength of the northern barbarian, and at the same time sympathy with his courage, which prefers death, for himself and his loved one, to shameful captivity.

This famous group, "The Death of Laocoön", was wrought some time in the first century B.C. by Agesander of Rhodes and two other sculptors, perhaps his sons. It shows the priest Laocoön in a last agonizing struggle with the deadly serpents which enfold him and his two sons. It is one of the most marvellous representations of human suffering ever created by art, but it does not move us with such sympathy as the death of the Gallic chieftain. These works are among the supreme creations of ancient art.

97. Alexandria

In number of citizens, wealth, commerce, power, and in all the arts of civilization, Alexandria was in the Hellenistic Age the greatest city of the whole ancient world. Along the harbours stretched extensive docks, where ships which had braved the Atlantic storms along the coast of Spain and Africa moored beside Oriental craft which had sailed the Indian Ocean and collected goods from the vast Oriental world beyond. Side by side on these docks lay bars of tin from the British Isles with bolts of silk from China and rolls of cotton goods from India. The growing commerce of the city even required the establishment of government banks.

From far across the sea the mariners approaching at night could catch the gleaming of a lofty beacon shining from a great lighthouse tower which marked the entrance of the harbour of Alexandria. This wonderful tower, the tallest building ever erected by a Hellenistic engineer, was a descendant of the old Babylonian temple with which it was closely related. (See page 85.)

THE LIGHTHOUSE OF THE HARBOUR OF ALEXANDRIA IN THE HELLENISTIC AGE. (After Thiersch)

From the deck of a great merchant ship of over four thousand tons the incoming traveller might look citywards beyond the lighthouse and behold the great war fleet of the Ptolemies outlined against the magnificent royal gardens. Here rose the marble residence of the Ptolemies, the Greek kings of Egypt, occupying a point of land which extended out into the sea and formed the east side of the harbour. From the royal parks of the Persian kings and the villa gardens of the Egyptians the Hellenistic rulers and their architects had learned to appreciate the beauty of parks and gardens artistically laid out and adorned with tropical trees, lakes, fountains, and sculptured monuments. Thus the art of landscape gardening—an art long familiar to the architects of the Orient—was also being cultivated by Europeans.

At the other end of the park from the palace were grouped the marble buildings of the Royal Museum, with its great library, lecture halls, exhibition rooms, courts and porticoes, and living-rooms for the philosophers and men of science who resided in the institution. Farther in the city were the magnificent public buildings, such as gymnasiums, baths, stadiums, assembly hall, concert hall, market-places, and basilicas, all surrounded by the residential quarters of the citizens.

Science made great progress in the Hellenistic Age. There was a group of men in Alexandria who formed the greatest body of scientists in the ancient world. They lived together at the Museum, a sort of university where they were paid salaries and supported by the Ptolemies. Their books were regarded as authorities for nearly two thousand years, until the revival of science in modern times. The very first generation of scientists at the Alexandrian Museum boasted a great name in mathematics which is still famous among us— that of Euclid. His complete system of geometry was so well built up that Euclid's geometry is still used as a schoolbook—the oldest schoolbook in use to-day.

The most remarkable man of science of the time was probably Archimedes. He lived at Syracuse, and one of his famous feats was the arrangement of a series of pulleys and levers, which so multiplied power that the king was able by turning a light crank to move a large three-masted ship standing fully loaded in the dock, and to launch it into the water. After witnessing such feats as this the people easily believed his proud boast, " Give me a place to stand on and I will move the earth ". He devised such powerful and dangerous war machines that he greatly aided in defending his native city from capture by the Romans. But Archimedes was far more than an inventor of practical appliances. He was a scientist of the first rank. He was able to prove to the king that one of the monarch's gold crowns was not of pure metal, because he had discovered the principle of determining the proportion of loss of weight when an object is immersed in water. He was thus the discoverer of what we now call "specific gravity". Beside his skill in physics he was also the greatest of ancient mathematicians.

98. About 200 B.C.

As we have seen, a larger world had engulfed the old Greek city-states, and at the same time the influence of the Greeks had brought the world to a higher level of civilization than men had ever seen before. But this Hellenistic world of the eastern Mediterranean had by 200 B.C. reached a point when it was to feel the iron hand of a great new military power from the western Mediterranean. There in the West for some three centuries the city of Rome had been developing a power which was to unite both the East and West into a vast Empire, including the whole Mediterranean. We must therefore now turn to the story of Rome.

PART VI
ROME

CHAPTER XV

THE KINGDOM OF ROME

99. ITALY

THE most important land in the western Mediterranean world in early times was Italy. The Italian peninsula, thrusting far out into the sea, is nearly six hundred miles long. It is four times as large as Greece, and is not cut up by mountains into winding valleys and tiny plains. There are larger plains for the cultivation of grain than we find anywhere in Greece, and there is much more room for flocks and herds on the mountain slopes. The coast of Italy is not so cut up as that of Greece, and there are fewer good harbours. Hence agriculture and the rearing of cattle developed much earlier than trade.

The fertile plains and forest-clad slopes of Italy have always attracted the people of northern Europe to leave their own bleak and wintry lands and move to this warm and sunny peninsula in the southern sea. Probably not long after the Greeks had pushed into the Greek peninsula, the western tribes of Indo-European blood had entered Italy. The most important group that settled in the central and southern parts of the peninsula were the Italic tribes, the earliest Italians. Their name, first applied by the Greeks to the south, was finally given to the whole peninsula; hence the name "Italy". Probably within a few centuries these tribes had also overflowed into Sicily.

Besides the Italic invaders, there were in the western Mediterranean world three more rival peoples, all of whom had come from the eastern Mediterranean world. The first were the Etruscans, who probably had an earlier home in western Asia Minor and who were settled in Italy about 1000 B.C. They thrust back the Indo-European tribes, and finally gained control of the west coast of Italy from the Bay of Naples almost to Genoa, including much of the inland country as far back as the Apennines. It looked as though the Etruscans would become the final lords of Italy, and they continued as an important people of the West far down into Roman history.

The Carthaginians, descended from the Phoenicians of old, were the second of the three rivals of the Italic tribes. On the African coast opposite Sicily they had built a great city called Carthage, which was before long the leading harbour in the western Mediterranean. The Carthaginians soon held the northern coast of Africa westward to the Atlantic. Besides gaining southern Spain, they also settled on the islands of Corsica, Sardinia, and Sicily.

The Carthaginians were trying to make the western Mediterranean their own, when the Italic people saw their third rivals invading the West. They were the Greeks. We have already followed the expansion of the Greeks as they founded their city-states along the coast of southern Italy and in Sicily in the eighth century B.C. The strife among these city-states made it just as impossible for them to unite into a Greek nation of the West as it had been for the city-states in Greece itself to combine into a strong nation. The strongest of all the western Greek cities was Syracuse.

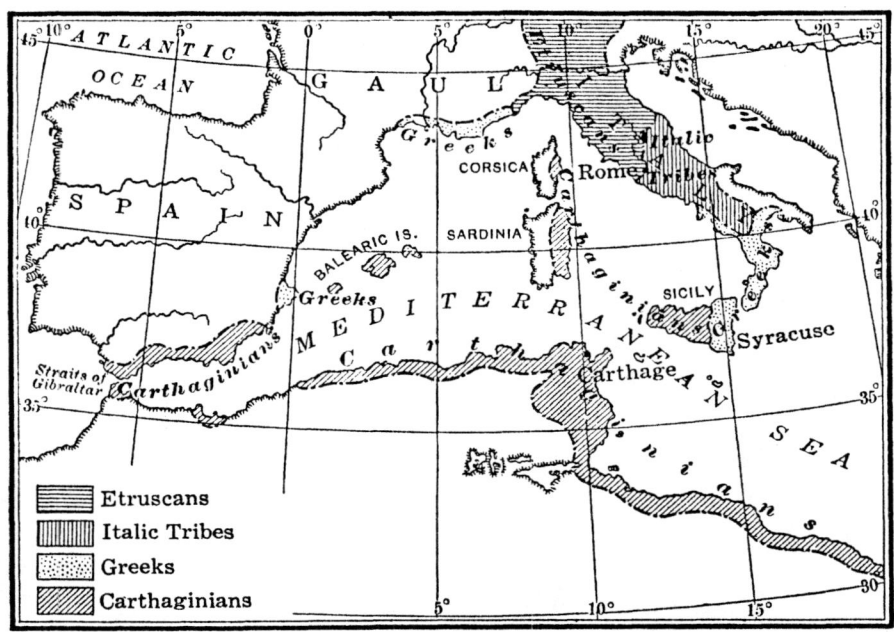

THE FOUR RIVAL PEOPLES OF THE WESTERN MEDITERRANEAN: ETRUSCANS, ITALIC TRIBES, GREEKS, AND CARTHAGINIANS

Let us now follow the career of the Italic tribes of central Italy under the leadership of Rome, and watch them slowly gaining power and civilization.

100. EARLY ROME

On the south or east bank of the river Tiber there was a group of Italic tribes known as the Latins. They occupied a plain less than thirty by forty miles. They called it Latium, from which comes their name—

Latins. They watched very anxiously the growth of the strong Etruscan towns on the other side of the Tiber, and they did what they could to keep the Etruscans from crossing to the Latin side.

When these Latin peasants needed weapons or tools, they were obliged to carry up a little grain or an ox to a trading post on the south side of the Tiber. Just

A Glimpse across the Plain of Latium and the Appian Way to the Distant Alban Mountains

above the coast marshes, which extended some ten or twelve miles inland from the mouth of the Tiber, there was an island and an easy ford across the river. Several neighbouring hills bore straggling villages, and a stronghold on a hill, called the Palatine, was their leader. Here, stopped by the shoals, moored now and then an Etruscan ship which had sailed up the Tiber, the only navigable river in Italy. On the low marshy ground, encircled by the hills, was an open-air market which they called the Forum. Here the Latin peasants could meet the Etruscan traders and exchange grain or oxen for metal tools or weapons. This group of villages on the Tiber was the beginning of Rome.

The Etruscan towns after 800 B.C. stretched far across northern Italy. Perhaps as early as 750 B.C. one of the Etruscan princes crossed the Tiber, drove out the last of the line of Latin chieftains, and took possession of the Palatine hill. From this place as his castle and palace he gained control of the villages on the hills above the Tiber, which then gradually joined together to become the city of Rome. These Etruscan kings soon extended their power over the Latin tribes on the plain of Latium, and the town of Alba Longa by the Alban Mount, which once led the Latins, disappeared. Thus Rome became a city-kingdom under the rule of an Etruscan king, like the other Etruscan cities which stretched from Capua far north to the harbour of Genoa. Although Rome was ruled by a line of Etruscan kings, it must be borne in mind that the population of Latium which the Etruscan kings governed continued to be Latin and to speak the Latin tongue. The Etruscans were constantly sailing their ships to trade in the harbours of Greece. There they learned to write their own language with Greek letters. Many tombs containing such inscriptions still survive in Italy. Although we know the letters and can pronounce Etruscan words, scholars are still unable to understand them.

This trading with Greece brought in beautiful painted Greek pottery, and the Etruscans quickly learned to make similar paintings. Many of these still cover the walls of Etruscan tombs and show us how the Etruscans looked, the clothing they wore, and the weapons they carried. Having learned to mine copper, they early produced fine work in bronze, and developed a flourishing commerce in this industry. They likewise borrowed a great deal from Grecian architecture,

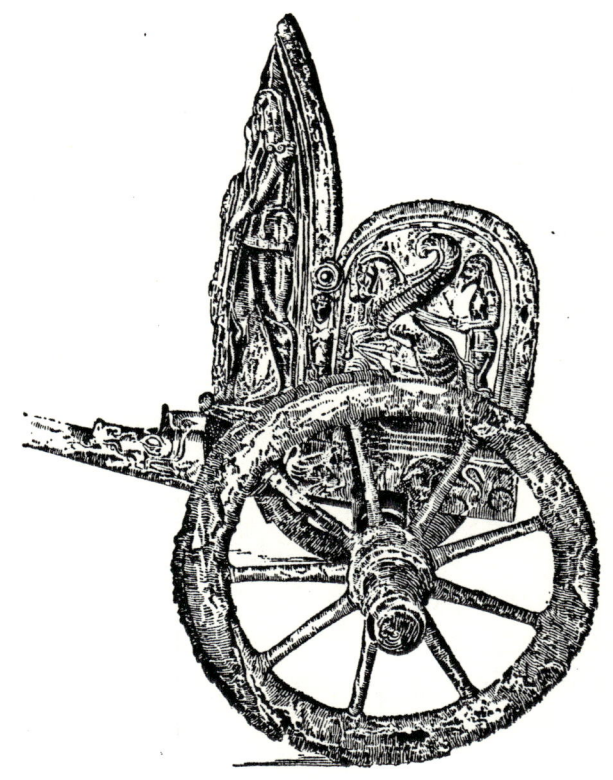

ETRUSCAN CHARIOT OF BRONZE

but unlike the Greeks they made plentiful use of the *round arch* which they had perhaps first seen in Asia Minor. We shall see an example of the use of this round arch in the construction of a drain in Rome in the next picture.

The Etruscan kings introduced great improvements into Rome. The Forum, the low market-place, was often flooded in the rainy season, and they built a stone

The Kingdom of Rome

drain arched at the top which carried off the water and made the city much more healthy. This ancient sewer drain still survives. On the hill called the Capitol, between the Forum and the Tiber, they built a temple to Jupiter, the state god, which lasted for centuries. About 500 B.C. the cruelty of the Etruscan rulers caused a revolt in Rome, and the kings of Rome were driven

A VIEW OF THE TIBER WITH THE AVENTINE HILL AND THE ETRUSCAN DRAIN

out. Thus it was that the career of Rome under kings came to an end; but the two and a half centuries of Etruscan rule left their mark on Rome, especially in architecture, religion, and early government.

101. MONEY

During this Etruscan period Greek influences were also felt in Rome. Down at the dock below the Tiber bridge, ships from the Greek cities of the South were becoming more and more common. Long before the

Etruscan kings were driven out, the Roman trader had learned to read the names of articles of trade in the bills handed him by the Greek merchants. Soon the Roman traders too were writing words and notes of their own with the same Greek letters, which thus became also the Roman alphabet, slightly changed to suit the Latin language. Thus the Eastern alphabet was carried one step further in the long westward journey, which finally made it the alphabet with which

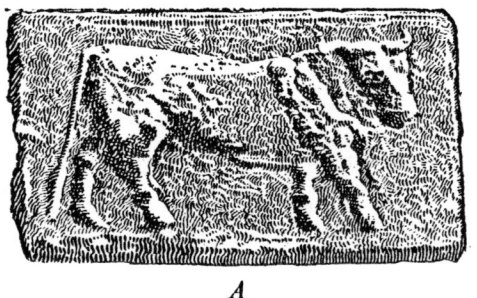

A　　　　　　　　　　　B

SPECIMENS OF EARLY ROMAN COPPER MONEY

this book is printed. The Phoenician alphabet and its descendants now stretched from India to the Atlantic.

There had been no *Roman* ships at the Tiber docks at first, but as time passed a Roman mechanic here and there learned to build a ship like those of the Greeks. As Roman business grew, it was found very inconvenient to pay bills with grain and oxen, while the Greek merchant at the docks paid his bills with copper and silver coins. For a long time instead of the oxen themselves rough bars of copper were used bearing the figure of an ox. It was not until more than a hundred and fifty years after the Etruscan kings had been driven out that the Romans issued actual copper coins. In this picture you see a specimen of a bar bearing the

The Kingdom of Rome

figure of an ox (*A*), and also an early copper coin (*B*). Later, as contact with the Greek cities increased, the Romans also began to issue silver coins. They also gradually adopted the Eastern measures of length and bulk with which the Greeks measured out to them the things they bought.

102. THE GODS

The Romans believed there was a god over each realm of nature and each field of human life. Jupiter was the great sky-god and king of all the gods; Mars, the patron of all warriors; Venus, the queen of love; Juno was protectress of women, of birth and marriage, while Vesta, too, watched over the household life, with its hearth fire surviving from the nomad age of the fathers on the Asiatic steppes two thousand years before; Ceres was the goddess who maintained the fruitfulness of the earth, and especially the grainfield (cf. English "cereal"); and Mercury was the messenger of the gods, who protected *mer*chandising, as his name shows.

As the Roman peasant came into contact with the Greeks, he heard also of the gods of Greece, and he was told that they were the counterparts of the originals of his own gods. The Roman learned that Venus was the Greek Aphrodite, Mercury was Hermes, Ceres was Demeter, and so on. The streets were full of Greek stories regarding the adventures of these gods when they were on earth.

Let us now see how the Roman state developed after the expulsion of the Etruscan kings.

CHAPTER XVI

THE REPUBLIC OF ROME

103. THE REPUBLIC

THERE are three main divisions in the great story of Rome :
1. Rome as a Kingdom (about 750 to about 500 B.C.)
2. Rome as a Republic (about 500 to 31 B.C.)
3. Rome as an Empire (31 B.C. to A.D. 476.)

We have dealt briefly with Rome as a Kingdom, during which time the seeds of civilization were planted among these people. In the next period, Rome as a Republic, we shall watch the amazing growth of Rome until it became the leading world power of its day.

When the Etruscan kings were driven out of Rome, about 500 B.C., the nobles, called *patricians*, were in control of the government. But none of their number was able to make himself king. Perhaps by arrangement with the people, the patricians agreed that two of their number should be *elected* as heads of the State. These two officers, called *consuls*, were both to have the same power. They were to serve for a year only and then give way to two others. To choose them, yearly elections were held in an assembly of weapon-bearing men, largely under the control of the patricians. Nevertheless, we must call this new state a republic, of which the consuls were the presidents, for the people had a voice in electing them. But as only patricians could serve as consuls, their government was very hard to bear. The people, called the " plebs " (compare

The Republic of Rome

with our word "plebeian"), especially among the Latin tribes, refused to submit to such harsh rule.

The patricians were unable to get on without the help of the peasants as soldiers in their frequent wars. They therefore agreed to give the people a larger share in the government by allowing them, in an assembly of their own, to elect a group of new officials, called *tribunes*. The tribunes had the right to cancel the action of any officer of the government—even that of the consuls themselves. When any citizen was treated unjustly by a consul he could appeal to the tribunes, and they could change the consul's decision and even save a citizen from sentence of death. The tribunes, therefore, gained great power because they could stop the carrying out of any law they thought unjust to the common people. Later, as government business increased, the number of tribunes was increased.

104. New Officers

In the beginning it would seem that almost all the business of government was in the hands of the consuls. They were the generals of the army in war, they had charge of the public money in the treasury, and they were the judges in all cases at law. It was difficult to combine all these duties. The consuls were often obliged to be absent from Rome for long periods while leading the army, and at such times they were of course unable to give any attention to law cases, so two citizens having a lawsuit might be obliged to wait until the war was over. Much other ordinary business, like that of the treasury, demanded more time than the consuls could possibly give it.

So it became necessary to create new officers for various kinds of business. To take care of government money, officers called *quaestors* were appointed. Two public officers called *censors* were required to keep lists of the people, to decide the amount of taxes each citizen owed, and to look after the daily conduct of the people and see that nothing improper was permitted. Our own use of the word " censor " comes from the name of these Roman officials. For the decision of cases in the law courts a judge called a *praetor* was appointed to assist the consul, and the number of such judges slowly increased. In times of great national danger it was usual to appoint some trusted leader as the supreme ruler of the State. He was called the " Dictator ", and he could hold power for but a brief period.

LICTORS WITH FASCES

The Romans had a deep respect for their officers. The consul appeared in public with twelve men called *lictors*, bearing the symbol of the State. Each man

The Republic of Rome

carried a bundle of rods, suggesting the consul's right to beat one who was guilty; in the middle of the bundle of rods was an axe, which was a sign of the consul's right to award the death penalty. The other officers of high rank were attended by a smaller group of lictors. The consuls and all the higher officials wore white robes edged with purple, a costume which only these men had a right to wear.

105. THE SENATE AND THE PEOPLE

There was in Rome an important council called the Senate (from Latin *senex*, meaning " old man "). At first only the patricians or nobles could be elected to the Senate as they had the sole right to be elected as consuls. A man of the people could be chosen tribune, but that was all. The tribunes could protect the people from some injustice and save their lives if they were wrongly condemned to death. But the tribunes could not secure for a citizen the right to be elected as consul or to become a senator. So the people of Rome pressed for more power and more rights from the patricians, and without fighting or bloodshed they secured these rights in the course of the first two centuries after the founding of the Republic. The people, for example, insisted upon a record being made in writing of the laws of Rome so that they might know by what rules they were being judged. Then the people demanded the right to share in the making of *new* laws, and to possess an assembly of the people which might pass new laws. In time these new laws increased the rights of the people to hold office. And in the end the Roman citizens elected their own neighbours as censors and quaestors, as judges, and at last even as consuls. And men of the people could be elected to sit in the great Senate itself.

At first the members of the Senate had been chosen from among the patricians by the consul. As the power of the people grew great changes took place in this system. A new law ordered the *censors* to make out the list of senators, and they were to give the preference to men who had been officers and magistrates. By this time many men of the people had been in turn chosen quaestors and censors and the like, so they were now given the chance of becoming senators. In this way the Senate was made stronger by bringing fresh blood from the ranks of the people. As a result, the Senate was made up of the three hundred men of Rome who had gained the most experience in government and in public affairs.

Although the consuls were at first more important than the Senate in the control of Roman affairs, as time went on the Senate gave orders to the consuls. The Senate became the real ruler of Rome. It was a large committee guiding the Roman State. It became the most famous and the greatest council of rulers which ever grew up in the ancient world or perhaps in any age.

106. THE PROGRESS OF ROME

At the time the Etruscan kings were expelled the territory of the Roman Republic was the mere city with the adjacent fields for a very few miles around. Then the Latin tribes on the south of Rome looked to the city for protection, and gradually Rome became the leader of Latium. The Roman Senate gave to the citizens of Latium privileges in Rome about equal to those of Roman citizens, and the Latins were therefore ready to fight for the defence of the city whose leadership they followed. But there were many enemies facing Rome outside Latium, and one by one they became the subjects of Rome. In 325 B.C. a fierce war broke out between Rome and the Samnites which lasted with interruptions until 295 B.C., when there was a great battle at Sentinum which decided the future of Italy for over 2000 years. The victory not only gave the Romans possession of central Italy, but it made them the leading power in the whole peninsula. To the north lay the Etruscans and the Gauls. In the south were the Greeks, with the Carthaginians in Sicily. Within

I. Italy at the Beginning of the Roman Republic (about 500 B.C.)

II. Roman Power during the Samnite Wars (down to 300 B.C.)

twenty years' time Rome made the Greek cities of southern Italy surrender one by one to her army, and they had no choice but to accept alliance with the Romans. Thus in two centuries and a quarter (500 – 275 B.C.) the tiny Republic on the Tiber had gained the mastery of the entire Italian peninsula south of the Po Valley.

III. Roman Power after the Samnite Wars (290 B.C.)

After these conquests, which proved Rome to be a master in the art of war, the Romans showed themselves also to be masters of peace. They had a way with them of keeping their conquests. Indeed, this is one of the secrets of the Roman genius: their method of keeping what they had won. In the first place, they did not try to annex or join up to Rome all the cities they had conquered, but made them

IV. Roman Power after the War with Pyrrhus (275 B.C.)

The Republic of Rome

"allies" instead. This would please the cities much more and would be more likely to keep them from revolt.

Secondly, these allies were given a kind of Roman citizenship; that is to say, Rome gave them many of the rights which she gave to her own citizens, such as protection in carrying on work and business, and equal rights with every Roman citizen in the law courts. This citizenship did not give the allies the right to vote in Rome. That did not matter much, for in order to vote it was necessary to go to Rome. The allied cities valued highly the rights and the protection given them. In return they allowed Rome to control their armies. All other local affairs, with the exception of the army, were managed and arranged by the towns themselves.

Thirdly, Rome showed her genius by sending out colonists and settling them in different parts of Italy. Roman peasants, obliged to bear Roman arms and having a voice in the government of Rome, were thus pushed out into Rome's new lands. These peasants were farmers, and they were given their farms to work in the distant places. This policy made the voice and the speech and the power of Rome felt throughout Italy, and above all it gave Rome an ever-increasing body of brave and hardy farmer-citizen-soldiers, tilling their own lands, and ready at all times to take up the sword on behalf of the State which shielded them. By these wise measures Rome gained and controlled all Italy.

107. THE GREEKS IN ITALY

Though Rome conquered the Greek cities of southern Italy, it must be carefully noted that the *civilization* of the Greek cities conquered Rome. The Roman soldiers beheld with wonder and admiration the beautiful Greek temples in such cities as Paestum and Tarentum. Here for the first time also they saw fine theatres, and they must have attended Greek plays, of which

GREEK TEMPLE AT PAESTUM IN SOUTHERN ITALY

they understood little or nothing. But the races and athletic games in the handsome stadium of such a Greek city must have been appreciated by the sturdy Roman soldiers.

The Romans at once felt the superiority of this new world of cultured life which they had entered in southern

The Republic of Rome

Italy. When a high-born Roman family like that of the Scipios wished to have carved a beautiful sarcophagus (stone coffin) for their father, they employed a Greek sculptor from the south. The sculpture shown in this picture is adorned with details of Greek archi-

GREEK STONE COFFIN IN ITALY

tecture, which clearly shows that it was done by a Greek artist. As Roman power expands, we shall see this conquest of the Romans by Greek civilization making greater and greater progress.

108. CARTHAGE

The most dangerous rival of Rome in the Mediterranean Sea was Carthage. The Carthaginians were descended from the Phoenicians. While Rome was only a small trading village on the Tiber, and before the Greeks ever entered these waters, the Phoenician merchants, the earliest explorers of the western Mediterranean, had found a good place for a city on the African coast opposite Sicily. Here, on the northern edge of the region now called Tunis, they had planted Carthage, the city which had become the commercial queen of the western Mediterranean and the most powerful rival of Rome.

The city of Carthage itself was large and splendid. It was in area three times as large as Rome. Behind wide docks and long piers, teeming with ships and merchandise, the city spread far inland, with spacious markets and busy manufacturing quarters humming with industry.

Carthage was pushing her empire of trade northwards into Sicily, Corsica, and Sardinia. Rome had made herself mistress of Italy. It was obvious that one day there would be a clash between these two great powers. This clash developed into three great wars between the rivals. The First Punic War (264–241 B.C.) ended in favour of Rome. The Romans had suffered much in the long war, and imposed very hard conditions on the enemy. The Carthaginians were required to give up Sicily and the neighbouring islands, and pay within ten years a huge war indemnity of thirty-two hundred talents. For the first time Rome now held territory outside the Italian peninsula, and this was but the beginning of a complete conquest of the Mediterranean countries. Shortly after the close of the first war Rome took possession of the large islands of Corsica and Sardinia. These, with Sicily, gave her three outposts against Carthage. At the same time Rome conquered the Gauls in the north of Italy and extended her boundaries to the Alps. Carthage tried to make up for this progress of Rome by turning her attention to the conquest of Spain, to which the Romans also laid claim. One of the Carthaginian generals in Spain, Hannibal, a young man of only twenty-four years of age, determined on the bold plan of attacking Rome from the north by leading a Carthaginian army from Spain through southern Gaul and across the Alps into Italy. Thus began the Second Punic War (218–202 B.C.).

The map below shows us the route and marches of this amazing young general from 218 to 203 B.C. For fifteen years he remained in Italy defying the might of the strongest military power of the time. Rome could call to her defence over seven hundred thousand

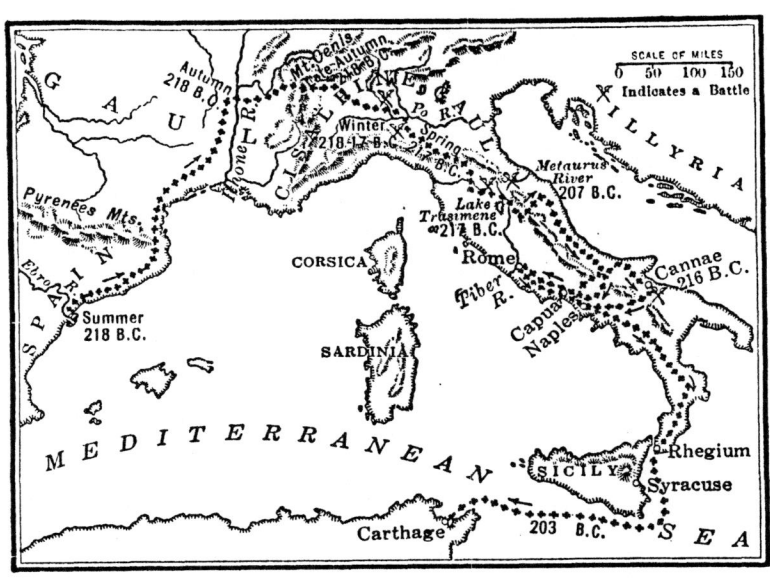

THE ROUTE AND MARCHES OF HANNIBAL FROM 218 TO 203 B.C.

men, citizens and allies. From this vast number Rome could recruit army after army. Hannibal had no such forces or possibilities of reinforcement. On leaving Spain he had about forty thousand men. The crossing of the Alps was very difficult. Overwhelmed by snowstorms, struggling over a steep and dangerous track, sometimes so narrow that the rocks had to be cut away to make room for the elephants that formed part of the army equipment, looking down over dizzy precipices, or up to snow-covered heights where hostile natives rolled great stones down upon them, the discouraged army of Hannibal toiled on day after day, exhausted, cold, and hungry. At every point along the straggling line, where help was most needed, the young Carthaginian general was always present, encouraging and guiding his men. When they issued from the Alpine passes they had suffered such losses that they were reduced to about thirty-four thousand men.

Hannibal knew a great deal about the best methods of warfare, and he had carefully studied the life and plans of Alexander the Great. The Roman consuls, commanding the Roman armies, had no special genius for war. They were simply magistrates, like our mayors. They were no match for the clever young Carthaginian. He began to gain victories over the Roman troops in northern Italy and was joined by many of the Gauls whom Rome had recently conquered. On the shores of Lake Trasimene he surprised a Roman army under the consul Flaminius, and the serious news reached Rome that her army was cut to pieces and its leader killed. Hannibal might now have advanced upon Rome itself, but he had no machinery for a siege. He desired another victory in the open in the hope that the allies of Rome would revolt and join him in attacking the city. He therefore carried on his operations in southern Italy. In 216 B.C. Rome sent an army of seventy thousand men to give him battle. Hannibal, with his thirty-two thousand men, met them at Cannae and won a brilliant victory. He surrounded the Roman army, and by the end of the day it was annihilated. Ex-consuls, senators, nobles, thousands of the best citizens of Rome had fallen in this terrible battle. Every family in Rome was in mourning. Of the gold rings worn by Roman knights as an indication of their rank, Hannibal is reported to have sent a bushel to Carthage. Even in modern times pieces of armour have been picked up on the battlefield.

Even after such a victory Hannibal was not strong enough to capture Rome, nor was Rome clever enough to defeat or capture Hannibal. He remained in Italy for fifteen years waiting his opportunity to strike the final blow. But the opportunity did not come, and by 203 B.C. the situation was becoming so serious near Carthage itself that Hannibal had to be called home to Africa. Rome had found a new general, Scipio. In him the Romans were to have at last a general who was a match for Hannibal. Scipio carried the war over into Africa. Hannibal led the forces against him. The two geniuses met at Zama. Hannibal was defeated, and the Second Punic War came to an end. The victory of Rome over Carthage made Rome the leading power in the whole ancient world. In the treaty which followed the battle of Zama the Romans forced Carthage to pay ten thousand talents in fifty years and to surrender all her warships but the triremes. Carthage lost her independence as a nation, and according to the treaty she could not make war anywhere without the consent of the Romans.

The Carthaginians were such a successful trading nation that they continued to prosper even while paying the heavy tribute with which Rome had burdened them. But Rome, the new mistress of the western Mediterranean, kept an anxious eye on her old rival. The Romans could not forget Hannibal and his wonderful victories and his long stay in Italy at the very doors of Rome. There was a famous old senator in Rome named Cato who was convinced that Carthage was still a danger to Rome. He finished all his speeches with these words, " Carthage must be destroyed ". Fifty years passed by. Cato's words were not forgotten. Carthage went to war with the Numidians in Africa without asking the consent of Rome. Rome charged

THE HARBOURS OF CARTHAGE AS THEY ARE TO-DAY

Carthage with breaking the treaty, and Rome decided to punish Carthage once and for all. In the three years' war (Third Punic War) which followed, the beautiful city of Carthage was captured and completely destroyed (146 B.C.). Its territory was taken by Rome and called the Province of Africa. A struggle of nearly one hundred and twenty years had resulted in the complete destruction of Rome's only remaining rival in the West. This long struggle between Rome and Carthage was a contest between the West and the East, between the Indo-Europeans and the Semites. Its result meant that the leadership of the West was to remain in the hands of the Indo-Europeans who had settled in the West. If Carthage had destroyed Rome, the Semitic Easterners would have ruled the Mediterranean, and the story of our civilization would have been a different one from that which you will follow in this book.

109. THE ARMY

How had Rome been able to gain so many victories? She did so by developing her citizen army until it became the best in the world. At first only those men who owned land served, and this rule limited the size of the army. Owing to the growth of Rome there were many men who owned no land and yet were wealthy because they owned money. The regulations were altered, and this new class of men having property in money was admitted into the army, which then grew considerably in size. Then the Senate decided to pay the citizens for their service in the ranks. This made a great difference, because it increased the possible length of military service among a people still chiefly made up of farmers obliged to return home often to plough, sow, and reap. By these means Rome in time could put a citizen army of over 300,000 men into the field. Later the Romans *doubled* the size even of this army by enlisting an equal number of troops drawn from the allies. The Mediterranean world had never known an army as large as this.

The Romans, in addition to increasing the size of their armies, improved the use of arms. The spear was now employed by the Romans only as the battle opened, when it was hurled into the ranks of the enemy at short range. After this the Romans fought with short swords, which were much more easily handled at close quarters than long spears.

This figure of a soldier is carved upon a tombstone, erected in his memory by his brother. His fighting weapons are his spear (*pilum*), which he holds in his extended right hand with point upwards, and his heavy short sword (*gladius*), which he wears girded high on his right side. To protect him he has a helmet, a leathern corselet stopping midway between the waist and the knees, and a shield (*scutum*).

A ROMAN SOLDIER OF THE LEGION

For purposes of managing and feeding an army the Romans divided it into *legions*, each containing about four thousand five hundred men, of whom three hundred were cavalry, twelve hundred were light armed troops, and three thousand heavy armed men forming the body of the legion. In battle these heavy armed men were placed in three lines or divisions. Each line was divided into sections called *maniples*, with one hundred and twenty men each. This order of battle was called the phalanx. How the phalanx worked is shown in the following diagram.

The phalanx, as we have said, was placed in three

The Republic of Rome

divisions, one forming the front line, one the middle, and one the rear. The front division was made up of the young and vigorous troops, while the older men were placed in the other two divisions. If the steady old troops behind saw that a gap was being made in the front division, it was the business of a maniple in the second line to advance at once and fill the gap. This was the reason for cutting up the lines into maniples, and the Romans owed much of their success to this idea.

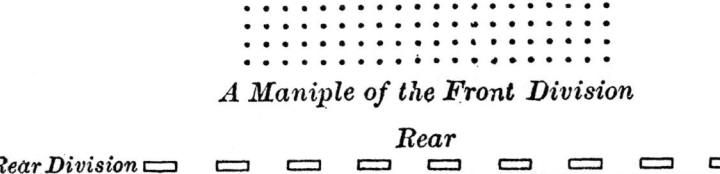

PLAN OF A ROMAN THREEFOLD LINE OF BATTLE WITH DETAIL OF A SINGLE MANIPLE ABOVE IT

In the wars with Carthage they made further improvements in tactics, as these battle arrangements are called. For instance, they moved the second and third lines to different parts of the field to be used as the fighting demanded. Such changes as these in the art of war made the Romans invincible. In discipline the Romans were better than any other people of ancient times, for even among the Greek troops there was great lack of discipline. There is a story of a Roman father who ordered his son to be executed in the presence of the army because the young man had disobeyed orders by fighting single-handed with one of the enemy and killing him.

The Romans had also developed a navy. They had no hope of successfully attacking such a sea-faring nation as Carthage without a strong war fleet. This they did during the First Punic War, and Rome then for the first time became a sea power. The following fragment of a wall-painting at Pompeii shows us a Roman warship, seemingly in battle, for the wreck of another warship is seen on the left.

ROMAN WARSHIP

Notice the two steering *oars* at each side of the stern —a device found on Nile ships three thousand years earlier. The rudder has not yet developed from these steering oars. The Romans ascribed their success, in spite of inexperience, against the Carthaginians to a new boarding grappler, which they invented and called a " crow " (*corvus*). It consisted of a heavy upright timber, which was made to fall over with the end on the enemy's rail, where an iron hook attached to the end of the " crow " grappled and held the opposing craft until the Romans could climb over into it. In the hand-to-hand fighting which followed, the sturdy Romans more than made up for their inexperience in seamanship.

110. Mistress of the East and West

The Republic of Rome, having by means of its fleet and its well-organized armies defeated Carthage and thus become mistress of the western Mediterranean, turned to the east of Italy, and led her wonderful legions to the conquest of Macedonia and Greece in 197 B.C., and the conquest of Asia Minor and Syria in 190 B.C. There was no need to conquer Egypt, because Egypt acknowledged herself a vassal of Rome in 168 B.C. Thus for nearly a century and a half (beginning 264 B.C.) one great war had followed another, and the Roman Republic, beginning these struggles as mistress of Italy only, had in this short space of time (from great-grandfather to great-grandson) become the leader of the world.

The Roman Senate had shown great ability in conducting the great wars, but now, having gained the mastery of the Mediterranean world, Rome was faced with the problem of governing the new lands which had so quickly been conquered. The Romans of the Republic had had no practice in governing far-away possessions, and in this matter they failed. They knew how to govern their districts in Italy because they could keep an eye on all of them. It was a different matter when the country was large and many hundred miles away from Rome. These countries or districts were called " provinces ". A Roman officer was made governor of the province. The people of the province were not allowed to keep an army; they had to pay heavy taxes and to obey the governor in all things. The Roman Senate made careful rules for the government of the provinces, but they were not so careful to see that the governors carried out these rules. Such a governor found himself in a position in which he could do anything he wished. He had as much power as an Eastern prince. He was far from home, with Roman troops at his elbow ready to carry out

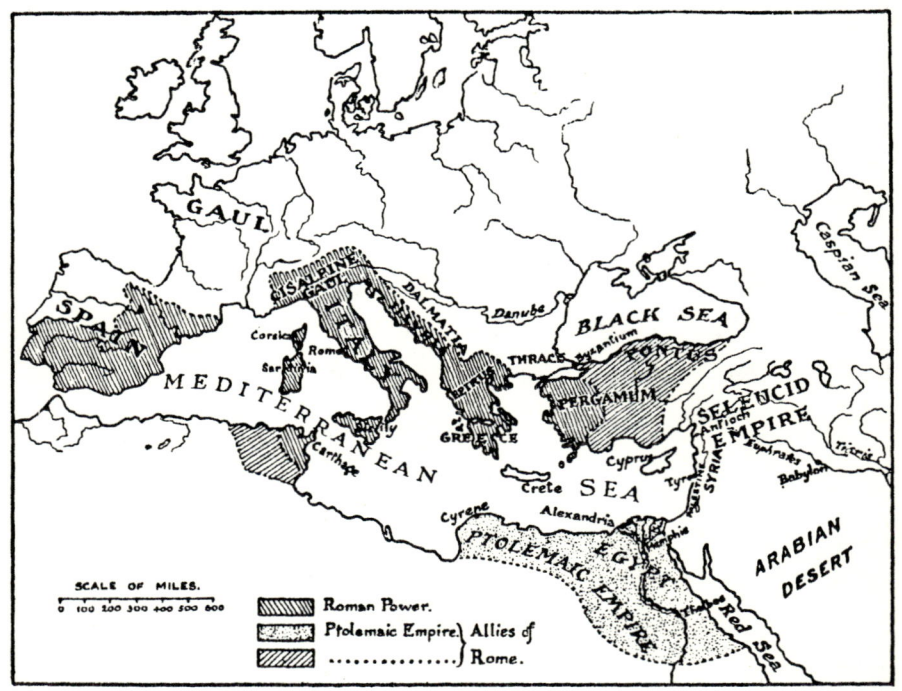

POWER OF ROME SECOND CENTURY B.C.

any order. He had complete control of all the taxes of the province and could take what he wanted from its people to feed his troops and pay his expenses. He had no training in governing a province. Frequently his chief desire was to make a fortune for himself. This he could do because he had wide powers. The Roman Senate passed laws for the punishment of such governors, but these did not seem to have much effect.

The Republic of Rome

What were the effects of these great conquests on Rome itself? We shall see that some of these effects were good and some bad. In the end they brought about the downfall of the Roman Republic and the creation of the Roman Empire. The Empire succeeded where the Republic failed.

III. A Roman House

The enormous conquests of Rome brought about great changes in the city of Rome. With increasing wealth and growing population, there was a great

An Old Roman Atrium-house

increase in the demand for dwellings, and these were being produced on a more comfortable scale than before. This illustration shows us an early form of Roman house. We see that there was no attempt at beautiful architecture, and the bare front showed no adornment whatever. It was built of sun-dried brick, and it had but one room called the "atrium". The opening in the roof which lighted the atrium received the rainfall of a section of the roof sloping towards it, and this water collected in a pool built to receive it on the floor of the atrium below. In this room all the household life centred. The stool and spinning outfit of the wife and the bed of the children were each given a corner, while the kitchen was simply placed in another corner, where the family meals were cooked over an

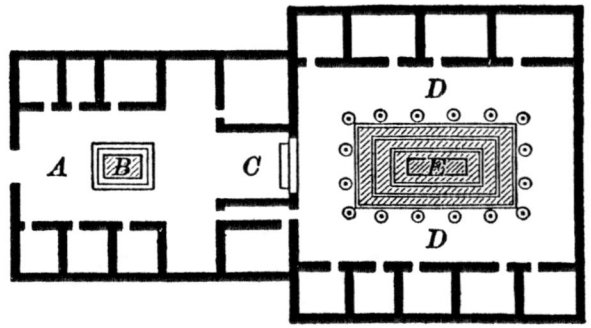

PLAN OF A ROMAN HOUSE WITH PERISTYLE

open fire. There was no chimney, and the smoke passed out of the square hole in the middle of the roof. The whole place was blackened by smoke, and perhaps the word "atrium", by which the room was called, had a connection with the Latin word for "black". Here, then, the family took their meals, here they slept, and here, in full view of pots and kettles, beds and tables, the master of the house received his friends and met his business or official callers.

But the conquests of Rome and the experiences of the Romans in Greece and the East made them very dissatisfied with their old conditions, and we find the simple atrium-house being considerably developed. In the above diagram we see how the atrium-house was added to. It had consisted of the single room, the atrium (*A*), with the pool for the rain-water (*B*). Then a small alcove was erected at the rear (*C*) as a room for the master of the house. Later, the bedrooms on each side of the atrium were added. Finally, under

PERISTYLE OF A POMPEIAN HOUSE

the influence of Greek life, the garden court (*D*), with its surrounding porch and columns, and a fountain in the middle (*E*), was built at the rear. Then a dining-room, sitting-room, and bedrooms were added which opened on this court, and, being without windows, they were lighted from the court through the doors.

In this picture we must imagine ourselves standing with our backs towards the atrium. We look out into the court, the garden of the house. The marble tables and statues and the marble fountain basin in the middle, just as we see them here in this drawing, were all found by the excavators in their places in Pompeii as they were covered by volcanic ashes over eighteen hundred years ago. Here centred the family life, and

BRONZE KITCHEN UTENSILS EXCAVATED AT POMPEII

here the children played about the court, brightened with flowers and the tinkling music of the fountains. As luxury increased, a second story might be added to receive the bedrooms, and perhaps the dining-room also. The atrium then became a large and stately reception hall, where the master of the house could display his wealth in statues, paintings, and other works of art—the trophies of war from the East.

Then many new conveniences were introduced. These were such things as pipes for running water, baths, and sanitary arrangements. The best houses were finally furnished with tile pipes conducting hot air for warming the important rooms, the earliest system of hot-air heating yet found. In the kitchen of the house shown on p. 267 were found beautiful bronze utensils, far better than those commonly found in our own kitchens. The kitchen ware in this illustration used by the cooks of Pompeii was found still lying in the kitchens of the houses as they were uncovered by the excavators. The pieces have been lettered, and the reader will find it interesting to make a list of them by name, indicating their use as far as possible.

112. A Roman Library

Contact with the Greeks brought the Romans to see the glories of Greek literature. Many Greeks who were taken prisoners in the wars became teachers to the Romans. A Greek slave named Andronicus, who had been taken as a lad by the Romans when they captured the Greek city of Tarentum, was given his freedom by his master at Rome. Seeing the interest of the Romans in Greek literature, he translated the *Odyssey* into Latin as a schoolbook for Roman children. For their elders he likewise rendered into Latin the great tragedies that were played in the theatres of Greece, and also a number of Greek comedies. Through his work the materials and the forms of Greek literature began to enter Roman life. Gradually parents began to send their children to the schools which the freed Greek slaves of Rome were beginning to open there. Moreover, there was here and there a household which possessed an educated Greek slave, like Andronicus, who might become the tutor of the children, teaching them to read from the new primer of Andronicus, as we might call his Latin translation of Homer.

Poets and writers of history now arose in Italy, and educated Romans could read of the great deeds of their ancestors in long poems modelled on those of Homer. As the new Latin literature grew, papyrus rolls bearing Latin works were more and more common in Rome. Then publishers in back rooms filled with slave copyists

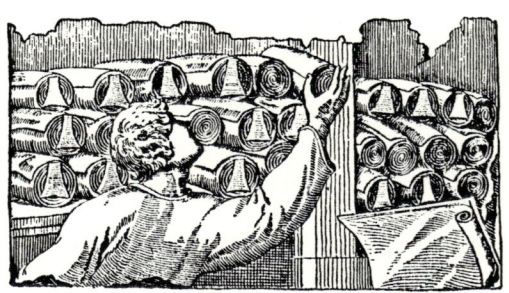

CORNER OF A ROMAN LIBRARY

began to appear in the city. One of the Roman conquerors of Macedon brought back the books of the Macedonian king and founded the first private library in Rome. Wealthy Romans were now providing libraries in their houses, and these were well stocked with Greek and Latin books. The accompanying illustration shows us a sketch of a Roman library. The books are all in the form of rolls, arranged in large pigeon-hole sections like rolls of wallpaper, with the ends pointing outwards, and bearing tags containing the titles of the books. Thus the librarian was quickly able to find a given book, or to return it to its proper place, as he is doing in the picture.

113. THE PEOPLE OF ROME

But the new life of Greek luxury brought with it many evils. Even friends of Greek art were grieved at finding Roman boys in a Greek dancing school, learning strange dances, just as many worthy people among us disapprove of the new dances now widely practised in England. The censors had the power to stop many of the luxurious habits, and they spread terror among the showy young dandies and ladies of fashion in Rome. They passed law after law against expensive habits of many kinds, like the growing love of showy jewellery among the women, or the use of carriages where they formerly went on foot. But such laws could not prevent the Roman people from being spoiled and corrupted. This was especially evident in the lives of the poorer classes, who did not understand Greek civilization, as we can see from the following examples. A historian relates that when the Roman legions were in Greece he saw Roman soldiers playing dice on a wonderful old Greek painting which they had torn down from the wall and spread on the ground like an old piece of canvas. Again, when an educated Roman once thought to gain the votes of the people by arranging a programme of Greek music at a public concert, the audience stopped the performance and shouted to the musicians to throw down their instruments and begin a boxing match!

It was to Roman citizens with such tastes that the leaders of the new age were obliged to turn for votes and for support in order to gain office. Early in the days of the Republic, there had been introduced into Rome an old Etruscan custom of single fights between condemned criminals or slaves, who slew each other to honour the funeral of some great Roman. These fighters came to be called gladiators, from the Latin word *gladius*, meaning "sword". The delight of the Roman people in these bloody displays was such that the officials in charge of the various public feasts, without waiting for a funeral, used to arrange a long programme of such combats in the hope of pleasing the

A BATTLE BETWEEN GLADIATORS AND WILD BEASTS

people, and thus gaining their votes and securing election to further higher offices. These dreadful spectacles took place at first within a temporary circle of seats, which finally became a great stone structure especially built for the purpose. It was called an amphitheatre, because it was formed by placing two (amphi) theatres face to face. The best known example of an amphitheatre is the Colosseum at Rome.

The athletic contests which had so interested the Greeks were far too tame for the appetite of the Roman public, and soon combats between gladiators and wild beasts were introduced. The preceding picture, from a relief found in a Roman amphitheatre, gives us a vivid glimpse of a battle between gladiators and wild beasts, just as the Romans saw it. The gladiators in this combat wore only a tunic and had no defensive armour except a helmet and a shield. Note the expression of pain on the face of the gladiator on the left, whose arm is being torn by the lion. The common people of Rome were thus gradually debased and taught to expect such public spectacles, sometimes lasting for days, as their share of the plunder from the great conquests.

We must add, however, that the chariot race did appeal to the Romans, and they began to build enormous courses surrounded by seats for vast numbers of spectators. These buildings they called circuses.

114. THE LITTLE FARMS

We thus see that the great success of the Republic in war and the wealth war brought in changed considerably the life of the Romans. And the changes were not all to the good. In truth the situation was full of danger. There were dangers at home and abroad. One of the greatest dangers at home was the bad feeling that was growing up between the rich and the poor, and the simple cause of it was that the rich were getting richer and the poor poorer. This was especially true in the country districts.

The Roman citizen farmer had once been the backbone of the State. But the small farmer was now disappearing. The long wars of Rome were the cause of this. Fathers and sons had been absent from home for years, holding their posts in the legion, fighting the battles which brought Rome her great position as mistress of the world. If the soldier returned he often found farm life very dull after the adventures of war, and he would leave the plough for good and rejoin the legion under some great leader whom he loved. Home life was thus broken up. Very often when the soldier did return he found that his family was gone and his little farm, sold for debt, had been bought up by some wealthy Roman of the city and absorbed into a great plantation like those which the Romans had found surrounding Carthage. The neighbours too had disappeared, and their farms had likewise gone to enlarge the rich man's estate. Across the hills he saw the stately villa, the home of the Roman noble, who owned the farms of all the surrounding country. He cursed the wealth which had done all this, and wandered up to the great city to look for free grain from the government, to enjoy the games and circuses, and to increase the poor class already there.

The big estates of the rich were now worked by slaves, for the Roman conquests had brought to Italy great numbers of captives of war, who were sold as slaves. They were treated so badly that in many places they revolted against their masters. This added further to the troubles facing the government of Rome.

115. THE END OF THE REPUBLIC

By the middle of the second century B.C. (about 150 B.C.) we thus find that the Roman people had some difficult problems to solve. The long wars had produced many evils; the cities had become crowded with

GREAT ROMAN VILLA

too many people who were poor and unemployed; the country places were losing their farms and their farmers; Italy and Sicily were flooded with slaves who were unhappy and disheartened; the rich and the poor were becoming real enemies. There were signs that one day nothing but war would settle things between them. In addition to these home troubles there were dangers abroad. Rome was failing to give good government to her new provinces; and, above all, there were tribes of barbarians in the North who were giving more and more trouble on the frontiers.

All these things together looked like breaking the power of Rome to pieces. Rome seemed to be unable to master the dangers. Her government was not strong enough either at home or abroad. The consuls and the Senate and the whole governing system of the Republic were proving a failure. What was to happen? After a hundred years of dreadful civil war and revolution (133–30 B.C.) Rome found an answer to the question. Rome saved herself and her provinces, her frontiers and her civilization, by ceasing to be a Republic and becoming an Empire. Rome changed her system of government, the Senate gave place to the Emperor; the weak rule of many men gave way to the strong rule of one man. In this way peace came to Rome and to Italy, good government came to the provinces, and the frontiers were made so strong that the barbarians were kept out for five hundred years.

The solution was not found in a day. It cost a century of revolution and a great deal of bloodshed. There were some great and famous men in this period. The first were two brothers, Tiberius Gracchus and Gaius Gracchus, who led the people of Rome from about

133 to 121 B.C. These two men tried their best to improve the condition of the farmers and the poor people. They found great fault with the senators and the rich for neglecting the poor, and they brought schemes into the Senate to protect the farmer class. Both Tiberius and Gaius Gracchus were murdered by the senators who hated them.

The next great leader of the people was Marius. He was a man of the people and had once been a ploughboy. He was a brilliant general, and in 102 B.C. he won great victories over the German barbarians who were attacking the frontiers. Thus a man of the people saved Rome from this new danger. But the Senate hated Marius the people's man, and they chose Sulla as their leader. It was now a struggle between Marius and Sulla. First, Sulla marched on Rome and took the city by force. Then Marius captured Rome and murdered the leading senators. Marius died in 86 B.C. In 82 B.C. Sulla became Dictator and murdered the leading men of the people. So the dreadful civil war went on. Sulla died, and the people made their new leader, Pompey, consul in 70 B.C. He was a great soldier and he won many victories for Rome in the East.

At this time, too, there arose the greatest of all the men of this period—indeed perhaps the greatest of all the Romans—Julius Caesar. He was on the side of the people and supported Pompey. Caesar became consul in 59 B.C. He was ambitious and he loved Rome. Above all he wanted good and strong government for Rome and her dominions. He wanted to bring peace to Rome and to end the terrible struggles between the people and the Senate. To bring these changes about, it was necessary for Caesar to have an army. So he was made governor of Gaul, most of which was still unconquered by the Romans. For eight years he showed himself a genius as a soldier in his conquest of Gaul. Feeling strong enough with his wonderful legions to rule Rome, he returned to the capital. The Senate was terrified and chose Pompey as its leader. So it became a struggle between Pompey and Caesar, and Caesar won a great victory over Pompey at Pharsalus, in Thessaly, in 48 B.C. Caesar then made himself master of Egypt and Asia Minor, and by 45 B.C. had obtained complete control of the Roman world.

Caesar did not put an end to the Republic. The forms and offices of the Republic were not done away with. But the power now lay in the hands of one man. The Roman Empire had begun, and Julius Caesar was its first emperor in fact if not in name. Caesar was a great and wise Roman. He had splendid plans for reforming the Senate, the government, and the provinces. He devised schemes for the rebuilding of Rome. He mapped out great new roads to make travel and business easy throughout the Roman territories. But he was not allowed to do more than begin his work. There were people in Rome like Brutus who thought he was too ambitious and that the power of the old Republic should be restored. And these men murdered Caesar in 44 B.C. It was a mistake. Civil war began once more in Italy. Mark Antony, a friend of Caesar, and Octavian, Caesar's grand-nephew and heir, fought and defeated Brutus and his friends. Finally, Octavian mastered all his difficulties, and in 30 B.C. found himself, at the age of twenty-six, the sole lord of the Roman world. The Empire had begun in name and in fact.

CHAPTER XVII

THE ROMAN EMPIRE AND TWO CENTURIES OF PEACE

116. AUGUSTUS

OCTAVIAN, or Augustus, as he was now called, ruled Rome and her possessions for forty-four years, and in doing so he gave the world peace. He wished to maintain the Republic and looked upon himself as its servant. In truth, however, he was the master and not the servant. He held so many of the old offices that no one could refuse to carry out his wishes. He held the command of the army. He had full charge of the most important frontier provinces. He was also a tribune. The Senate gave him the title of " Augustus ", that is, " the august ". The chief name of his office was " Princeps ", that is " the first ", meaning the first of the citizens. Augustus was also a Commander or Imperator, from which our word " emperor " is derived.

The boundaries of the Empire ruled by Augustus were the Sahara in the south, the Atlantic in the west, the Euphrates in the east, the Danube and the Rhine in the north. Thus the great Roman world stretched right round the Mediterranean Sea. Augustus made it his duty to guard strongly the frontiers. To do this he reorganized the army, which now contained about two hundred and twenty-five thousand men, who were chiefly recruited from the provinces. The foreign soldier who entered the ranks became a citizen of Rome in return for his services. Thus the army was still made up of " citizens ". But the tramp of the legions was heard no more in Italy. They were posted far out on the frontiers, and the people at home saw nothing of the troops who defended them.

Augustus also set himself to work on giving good government to the provinces. Under the Republic the governor of a province not only served for a short time but was also without experience. His great power, like that of an Eastern prince, made it impossible for the consuls changing every year at home to control him. The governor of a province was now appointed by the permanent ruler at Rome, and such a governor knew that he was responsible to that ruler for the wise and honest government of his province. He also knew that if he proved successful he could hold his post for years, or be promoted to a better one. There thus grew up under the control of Augustus and his successors a body of provincial governors of experience and efficiency, and Augustus took great care to see that his governors did not use their provinces merely to make their fortunes out of them as the governors under the Republic had done.

PORTRAIT OF AUGUSTUS

Augustus ordered huge census lists to be prepared of the people in the provinces and the amount of property owned. Thus it was easy to work out how much each province should justly pay in taxes. This was a great reform. Augustus used and spent this money well. Much of the money went back to the provinces to pay for roads, bridges, aqueducts, and public buildings. The provinces of the Empire were satisfied with this good order and this era of peace. When Augustus died in A.D. 14, the Senate was so pleased with the wonderful work he had done for the Roman world that it caused to be built in his honour a splendid marble enclosure containing the " Altar of Augustan Peace ".

117. ROME

Augustus paid much attention to the providing of Rome with great public buildings and public improvements. Under him Rome received for the first time organized police, a fire department, a water department, and a government office for the supply of grain. Augustus boasted that he found Rome a city of brick and left it a city of marble. On the Palatine Hill Augustus united several dwelling-houses into a simple palace for his residence. The palace looked down on a splendid group of marble buildings surrounding the ancient Forum or Market-place. The following picture shows us a part of the new Rome of the Empire. The first building Augustus was interested in is marked (E). It is a basilica or business hall which was built by Julius Caesar. It was left unfinished and afterwards damaged by fire. Augustus had it restored and completed. Then he built a new Senate House (G), opposite the basilica. Facing the end of the Forum the emperor built a temple to Caesar. It was called the temple of the Divine Caesar (C). At the other end

THE ROMAN FORUM AND ITS PUBLIC BUILDINGS IN THE EARLY EMPIRE. (After Luckenbach)

of the Forum, facing the temple, Augustus caused to be built a splendid speaker's platform of marble (*H*). In addition to these Augustus built a fine large new Forum, which will be seen (*O*) in the picture on p. 283.

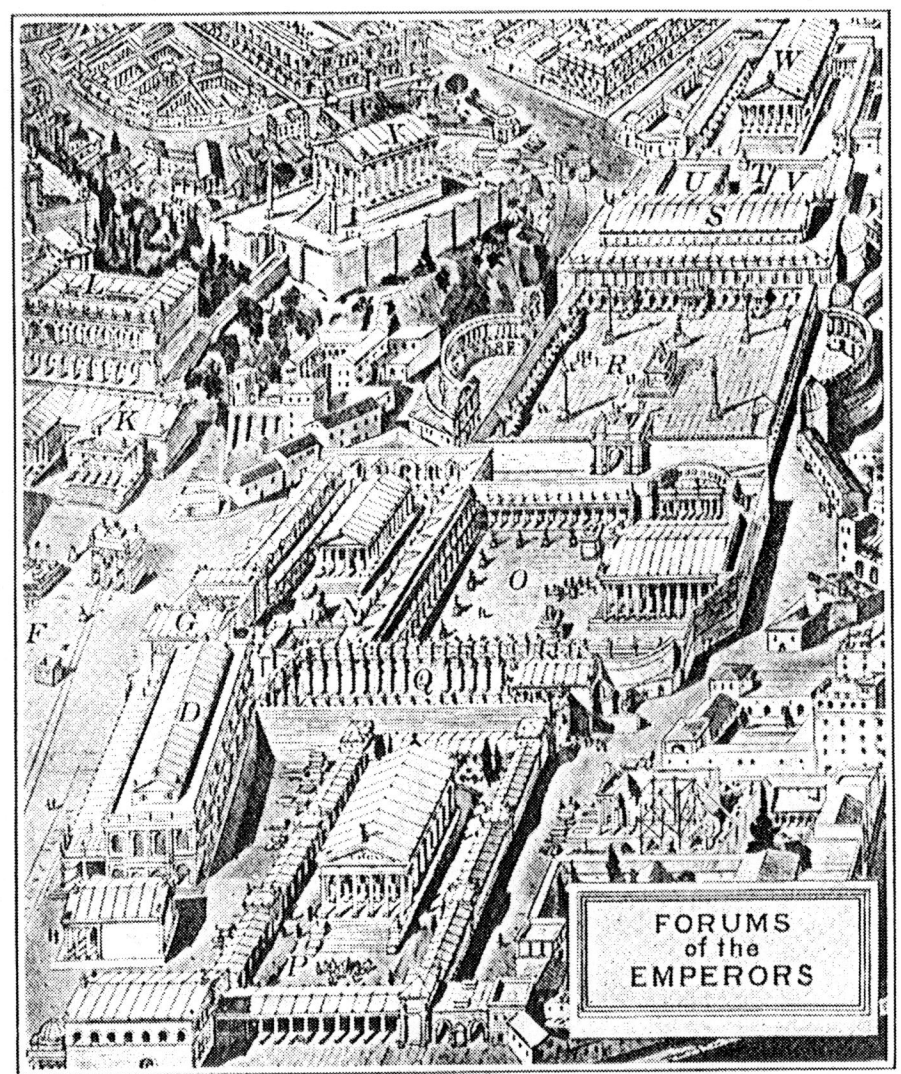

THE FORUMS OF THE EMPERORS CONTINUING THE VIEW OF THE OLD FORUM. After L. Levy (Luckenbach)

The key to the other buildings in the first picture is as follows: *A*, small round temple of Vesta; *B*, Triumphal Arch of Augustus; *D*, Old Basilica (before *E* was built); *E*, Forum—Market-place; *I*, Arch of

A Brief History of Ancient Times

Emperor Severus; *J*, Temple of Saturn; *K*, Temple of Concord; *L*, Public Record Office; *M*, Temple of Jove.

For the sake of convenience we have added on p. 283 a picture of the extensions made in Rome by the emperors who ruled after Augustus. The key to this picture is as follows :

D, Old Basilica.
F, Old Forum.
G, New Senate House.
N, New Forum of Julius Caesar.
O, New Forum of Augustus.
P, New Forum of Peace of Vespasian.
Q, New Forum of Nerva.
R, New Forum of Trajan.
S, New Basilica of Trajan.
U-V, New Libraries of Trajan.
T, Trajan's Column.
W, Temple to Trajan (*by Hadrian*).

In these two pictures we see the most magnificent series of buildings in the ancient world.

118. The Round Arch

The Romans in the Age of Augustus borrowed many ideas from Greece and from the East. This picture

PYRAMID-TOMB OF A ROMAN NOBLE NAMED CESTIUS

shows us the influence of Egypt. Here we see a tomb erected by a Roman on the model of a pyramid. The style of the Greek temples with their beautiful colonnades was much used by the Romans, as we can

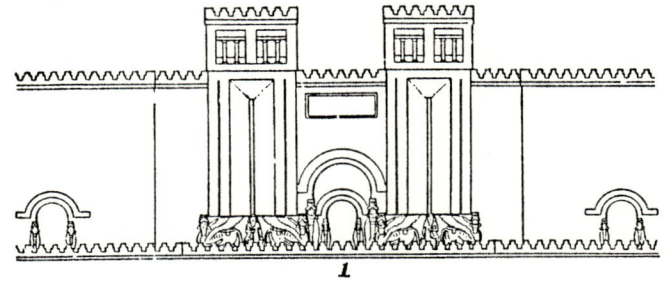

Assyrian Palace Front

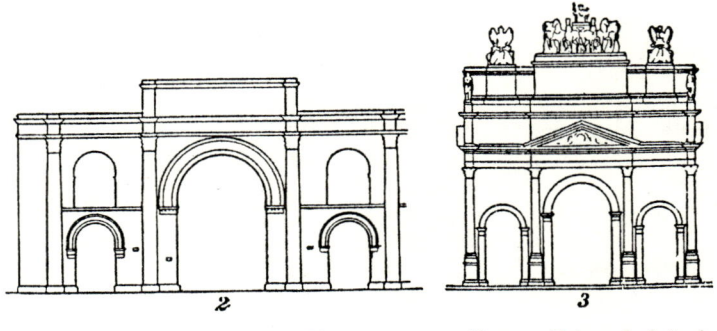

Parthian Palace Front   Roman Triumphal Arch

THE ROMAN TRIUMPHAL ARCH AND ITS ORIENTAL ANCESTORS

see from a study of the Forum buildings on pages 282 and 283. They borrowed from the Near East the idea of the round arch in building. The Romans made magnificent use of this round arch, and through them it has come to be familiar throughout the world. It was a Roman custom to build triumphal arches in memory of great victories in war, and they used the round arch for this purpose. We have already seen in the picture of the Forums the triumphal arches of the Emperors Augustus and Severus

A Brief History of Ancient Times

Many modern cities have built similar arches: for example, Paris, Berlin, London, and New York. The main idea of the triumphal arch is that of a tall arch in the middle with lower arches on each side. We can trace this idea back to the front of an Assyrian palace (Fig. 1, in the preceding diagram). Note that the Assyrian side arches are placed at some distance from the central arch. In Roman times Mesopotamia was occupied by the Parthians, who copied the Assyrian palace front but moved the side arches nearer to the middle arch (Fig. 2). It is easy to see the connection between this Parthian idea and that of the Roman arch (Fig. 3).

119. LITERATURE UNDER AUGUSTUS

While the Romans made progress in architecture, we find that they did not do much to develop sculpture. They could produce beautiful sculpture, but it was all done in the style of the old Greek masters. There were no original sculptors in Rome like those whom we have met in Athens. Nor could the Romans produce any great painters. As in art, so also in science the Romans were borrowers. Rome had no such men as Euclid and Archimedes, and science on the whole

PORTRAIT OF AN UNKNOWN ROMAN

was neglected. But there was a very great interest in literature, especially in the literature of Greece. A cultured Roman was steeped in Greek books and Greek ideas. Public men like Caesar and Cicero, the great orator, had studied in Athens or Rhodes. They knew well the finest works of Greek learning. They spoke Greek every day among themselves, perhaps more than they did Latin. They would read and write books when they were at the wars or in the distant provinces. Caesar wrote a book on Latin grammar while crossing the Alps, when his mind must have been filled with the problems of his great wars in Gaul. This combination of study and practical work produced some of the finest men the world has ever known.

CICERO. (Madrid)

The picture opposite of a bust of an unknown Roman gives us an idea of the kind of man this training in literature and character and public work produced in Rome, especially in the days of Augustus and after.

The greatest Roman writer in the last days of the Republic was Cicero. He was a great master of Latin prose, and was the most cultured man Rome ever produced. His speeches and his essays have influenced the style of speakers and of prose writers in all civilized countries.

Augustus and a number of the leading men about him had known Cicero, and his influence made the time of Augustus a great literary period, often called the Augustan Age. Augustus built two libraries in Rome, and one of them contained the greatest collection of Greek and Latin books in the ancient world. The great writers of the Augustan Age are: *Livy*, who wrote a long history of Rome from the earliest times to the reign of Augustus, a work which cost him forty years of labour; *Horace*, who knew and loved the old songs of Greece, and who wrote of the men and life of his own time in poetry which forms for us an undying picture of the Romans in the days of Augustus; *Virgil*, the greatest poet of Rome, who is famous for beautiful poetry about the country life of Italy, but more especially for the great epic poem, the *Aeneid*, which tells the story of the glorious legends of early Rome, and has ever since been one of the leading schoolbooks of the civilized world, with a lasting influence on the best literature of later times.

120. Water for Rome

The Emperors who followed Augustus were Tiberius, Caligula, Claudius, and Nero.[1] Two of them, Caligula and Nero, were certainly deserving of the contempt in which they are still held, but the other two, Tiberius and Claudius, were in many respects able rulers who did much to improve the government of the Empire as planned by Augustus.

---

[1] Tiberius (A.D. 14–37), Caligula (A.D. 37–41), Claudius (A.D. 41–54), Nero (A.D. 54–68).

The Roman Empire and Two Centuries of Peace

Claudius did much for the Empire and devoted himself to its affairs. He conducted in person a successful campaign in Britain, which had been invaded by Julius Caesar. For the first time Claudius made its southern portion a province of the Empire. At Rome

THE AQUEDUCT OF THE EMPEROR CLAUDIUS

Claudius was greatly interested in buildings and practical improvements. He built two vast new aqueducts, together nearly a hundred miles in length, furnishing Rome with a splendid supply of fresh water from the mountains.

The aqueduct shown in this picture was erected about the middle of the first century A.D. It is over forty miles long. About three-fourths of it is underground, but the last ten miles consists of tall arches of massive masonry, as seen here, supporting the channel in which the water flowed, till it reached the palace of the emperor on the Palatine Hill. Such ancient Roman aqueducts were so well built that four of them are still in use in Rome, and convey to the city a more plentiful supply of water than any other modern city receives.

121. DANGER ON THE DANUBE

The emperors from Augustus to Nero belong to the Julian line. The next emperors belong to the Flavian line.[1] As the period from Augustus to Nero is called the First Century of Peace, so the time from Vespasian to Marcus Aurelius may be called the Second Century of Peace. This second series of emperors brought the Empire to the highest level of prosperity and happiness. One of the big tasks of these emperors was to improve the frontier defences of the Empire. On the south the Empire was protected by the Sahara, and on the west by the Atlantic, but on the north and east it was open to attack. The shifting German tribes constantly threatened the northern frontiers. In fact Mediterranean civilization was in constant danger of being overwhelmed from the north. The great problem of future humanity was whether the Roman emperors would be able to hold off the barbarians until, in course of time, these rude Northerners might gain enough of Mediterranean civilization to respect it, and to preserve at least some of it for mankind in the future

The emperors from Vespasian to Hadrian did much to make the northern frontiers safe. Especially good work was done by the brilliant soldier Trajan, who

---

[1] Vespasian (A.D. 69–79), Titus (A.D. 79–81), Domitian (A.D. 81–96).

After them come Nerva (A.D. 96–98), Trajan (A.D. 98–117), Hadrian (A.D. 117–138), and the Antonines, ending with the death of Marcus Aurelius (A.D. 180).

The Roman Empire and Two Centuries of Peace

followed Nerva as emperor in A.D. 98. He quickly saw that there would be no safety for the Empire along the Danube frontier except by crossing the river and crushing the dangerous power of the growing kingdom of Dacia. Bridging the Danube with boats and hewing

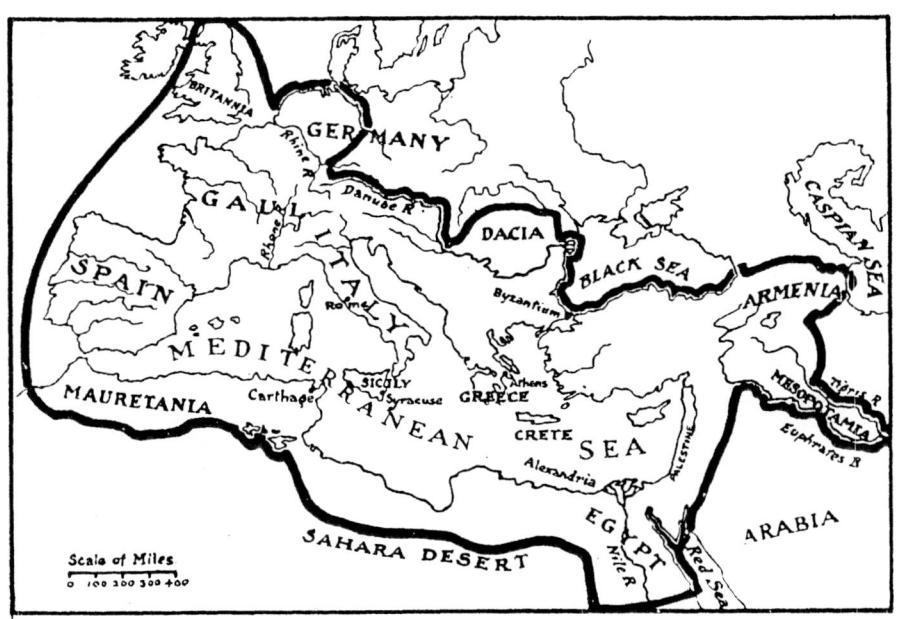

ROMAN EMPIRE AT ITS GREATEST EXTENT

his way through wild forests, Trajan led his army through obstacles never before overcome by Roman troops. He captured one stronghold of the Dacians after another, and in two years finally destroyed their capital. Trajan built a massive stone bridge across the Danube, made Dacia a Roman province, and sprinkled plentiful Roman colonies on the north side of the great river. The descendants of these colonists in the same region still call themselves *Roumanians*, a form of the word " Roman ".

In the background of the following picture we see the heavy stone piers of the bridge, supporting the wooden upper structure, built with strong railings. In the foreground is the altar, towards which the emperor advances from the right with a flat dish in his hand

THE EMPEROR TRAJAN SACRIFICING AT HIS NEW BRIDGE ACROSS THE DANUBE

from which he is pouring a libation upon the altar. At the left of the altar stands a priest naked to the waist, and leading an ox to be slain for the sacrifice. A group of the emperor's officers approach from the left, bearing army standards. The scene is sculptured with many others on the column of Trajan at Rome (see page 294), and is one of the best examples of Roman relief sculpture of the second century.

122. THE COLOSSEUM

While the Flavian emperors and their successors were making the frontiers of the Empire safe, considerable progress was taking place within the Empire, especially in Rome itself, the great controlling centre of the Mediterranean world. The visitor in Rome at the close of the reign of Hadrian found it the most magnificent monumental city in the world of that day. It had by that time quite surpassed Alexandria in the size and in the number and splendour of its public buildings. At the eastern end of the Forum, Vespasian erected a vast amphitheatre for gladiatorial combats, now known as the Colosseum. It was completed and dedicated by his son Titus, who arranged a series of bloody spectacles lasting a hundred days.

This enormous building, the Colosseum, one of the greatest in the world, was an oval arena surrounded by rising tiers of seats accommodating nearly fifty thousand people. Although now much damaged, it is still one of the most famous buildings in the world.

It was especially in and alongside the old Forum that the grandest buildings of the Empire had thus grown up. The business of the great world capital led Vespasian and Nerva to erect two more magnificent forums, as we have already seen (page 283). These two, with the two of Caesar and Augustus, formed a group of four new forums along the north side of the old Forum. At the north-west end of this group of four, Trajan built another, a fifth new forum, which surpassed in magnificence anything which the Mediterranean world had ever seen before. On one side was a vast new business basilica, and beyond this rose the mighty column of Trajan.

The Trajan column is of Parian marble and stands a hundred feet high. Round it winds a spiral band of one hundred and fifty-four relief scenes picturing

Trajan's brilliant frontier campaigns. The band passes twenty-two times round the shaft. This band contains two thousand five hundred human figures, and if it could be unrolled it would be over six hundred and

THE COLUMN OF TRAJAN

fifty feet long. An examination of one of these reliefs (see page 292) shows us that they are very interesting works of art, wrought with much skill. On each side of the column was erected a library, one for Greek and one for Latin literature. The column still stands beside one of the busy streets of modern Rome, but little of the other magnificent buildings has survived.

123. CONCRETE

In the buildings of Hadrian and Trajan the architecture of Rome reached its highest level both of splendour and beauty and also of workmanship.

INTERIOR VIEW OF THE DOME OF THE PANTHEON BUILT AT ROME BY AGRIPPA AND HADRIAN

Sometime in the Hellenistic Age architects had begun to employ cement concrete, though it is still uncertain where or by whom the hardening properties of cement were discovered. Under Hadrian and his successors the Roman builders completely mastered the art of making huge casts of concrete. The domed roof of Hadrian's Pantheon is a single enormous concrete cast, over one hundred and forty feet across. The Romans, therefore, eighteen hundred years ago, were employing concrete on a scale which we have only recently learned to imitate, and after all this lapse of time the roof of the Pantheon seems to be as safe as it was when Hadrian's architects first knocked away the posts which supported the wooden form for the great cast. The Pantheon, as seen in the picture, is one of the most beautiful and impressive domed interiors ever designed. The circular hole in the ceiling is 30 feet across; it is 142 feet above the pavement, and the diameter of the huge dome is also 142 feet. This is the only ancient building in Rome which is still standing with walls and roof in a perfectly preserved state. It is thus a remarkable example of Roman skill in the use of concrete.

124. Walls and Barracks

While these arts of peace were developing, the military glory of Rome, which had declined since the days of Caesar, returned in splendour, as we have seen, under the great soldier emperors Trajan and Hadrian. Hadrian retained Dacia and strengthened the whole northern frontier, especially the long barrier reaching from the Rhine to the Danube, where the completion of a continuous wall was largely due to him. He built a similar wall along the northern boundary across Britain. The line of both these walls is still visible.

This masonry wall, some 300 miles long, protected the northern boundary of the Roman Empire between the upper Rhine and the upper Danube, where it was most exposed to German attack. At short intervals there were blockhouses along the wall, and at points of

The Roman Empire and Two Centuries of Peace

RESTORATION OF THE ROMAN FORTIFIED WALL ON THE GERMAN FRONTIER

GLIMPSES OF A ROMAN FRONTIER STRONGHOLD
(Restored after Waltze-Schulze)

great danger strongholds and barracks for the shelter of the garrisons.

The preceding picture shows us glimpses of a Roman frontier stronghold. Above, on the left, we see the main gate of the fort; the other three views show the barracks. When not on sentry duty, the soldier lived with his comrades in one of these large garrisons, with fine barracks and living quarters for officers and men. The discipline necessary to keep the troops always ready to meet the barbarians outside the walls was never relaxed. Besides regular drill, the troops were also employed in making roads, building bridges, aqueducts, and public buildings, or in repairing the frontier walls.

125. A Soldier's Letter

Under Trajan and Hadrian the Roman army was the greatest and most skilfully managed organization of the kind the ancient world had ever seen. Drawn from all parts of the Empire, the army now consisted of many nationalities, like the British army in the Great War. A legion of Spaniards might be stationed on the Euphrates, or a group of youths from the Nile might spend many years on sentry duty on the wall that barred out the Germans. Although far from home, such young men were enabled to communicate easily with their friends by a very efficient military postal system covering the whole Empire like a network. We are still able to hold in our hands the actual letter written from a northern post by a young Egyptian recruit in the Roman army to his father and sister in a distant little village on the Nile. This Egyptian youth, Apion, having enlisted in the Roman army in company with other boys from his little village in Egypt, bade his family good-bye and embarked on a great government ship from Alexandria for Italy. After a dangerous voyage he arrived safely at Misenum, the Roman war harbour near Naples, and hastened ashore in his new uniform to have a small portrait of himself painted, and to send his father the letter shown in the picture overleaf.

It was written for him in Greek on papyrus in a beautiful hand by a hired public letter-writer, and reads as follows (with the present author's explanations in brackets):

Apion to Epimachos his father and lord, many good wishes! First of all I hope you are in good health, and that all goes well with you and my sister and her daughter and my brother always. I thank the lord Serapis [a great Egyptian god] that he saved me at once when I was in danger of the sea. When I arrived at Misenum, I received from the emperor three gold pieces [about three pounds] as road money, and I am getting on fine. I beg of you, my lord father, write me a line, first about your own well-being, second about that of my brother and sister, and third in order that I may devotedly greet your hand, because you brought me up well and I may therefore hope for rapid promotion, the gods willing. Give my regards to Capiton [some friend], and my brother and sister, and Serenilla and my friends. I send you by Euktemon my little portrait. My [new Roman] name is Antonius Maximus. I hope that it may go well with you.

On the left margin, where we see two vertical lines inserted, just as we are accustomed to insert them, Apion's chums (the other village boys who enlisted with him) sent home their regards. Folded and sealed, the letter went by the great Roman military post, arrived safely, and was read by the young soldier's

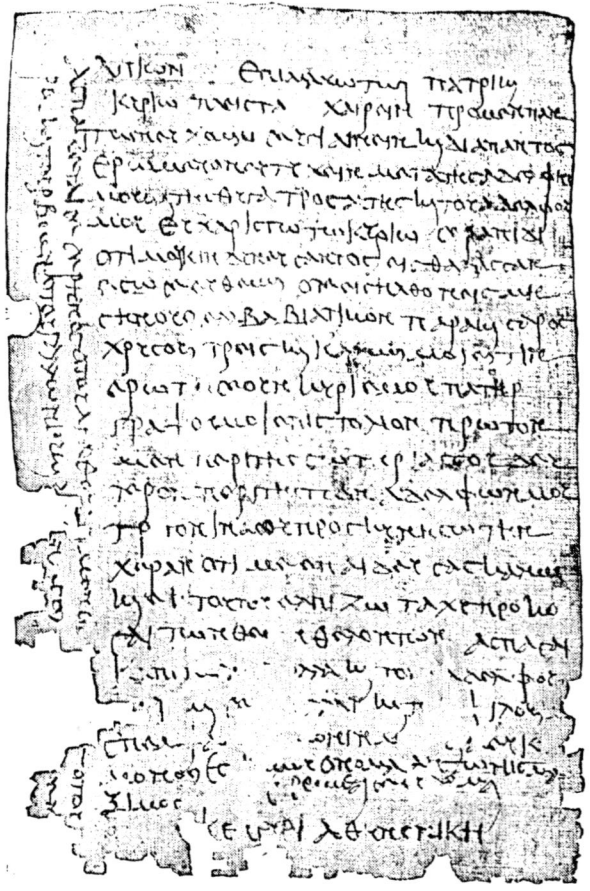

Letter of Apion, a young Soldier in the Roman Army, to his Father, Epimachos, in Egypt

waiting father and family in the little village on the Nile over seventeen hundred years ago.

126. Pompeii

Let us now consider the people who made up the Roman Empire. In Africa were the Moors, North

Africans, and Egyptians; in the Eastern background, Arabs, Jews, Phoenicians, Syrians, Armenians, and Hittites; in Europe, Greeks, Italians, Gauls, and Iberians (Spaniards); while north of these were the Britons and some Germans within the frontier lines.

A STREET IN ANCIENT POMPEII AS IT APPEARS TO-DAY

All these people were of course very different from one another in native manners, clothing, and customs, but they all enjoyed Roman protection and rejoiced in the far-reaching Roman peace. For the most part they lived in cities, and the life of the age was chiefly a city life, even though many of the cities were small.

Fortunately, one of the provincial cities has been preserved to us with much that we might have seen there if we could have visited it nearly two thousand years ago. The little city of Pompeii, covered with volcanic ashes in the brief reign of Titus (A.D. 79), still shows us the very streets and houses, the forum and the public buildings, the shops and the markets, and a host of other things very much as we might have found them if we had been able to visit the place before the disaster. We can look down long streets where the chariot wheels have worn deep ruts in the pavement.

In the preceding picture we note that the roadway and pavements are in perfect condition as when they were first covered by the falling ashes. At the left is a public fountain, and in the foreground is a street crossing. Of the buildings in this street only a half-story still stands, except at the top left, where we see the entrance of two shops, with the tops of the doors in position and the walls preserved to the level of the second floor above. We can look into kitchens with the cookery utensils (see page 268) still scattered about and the cooking hearth in perfect order for building another fire. We can look into the baker's shop with the charred bread still in the ovens and the flour mills standing silent and deserted.

In a court beside the bakery we see the mills for grinding the baker's flour. Each mill is an hourglass-shaped stone, which is hollow, the upper part forming a funnel-shaped hopper, into which the grain was poured. The lower part of the stone is an inverted funnel placed over a cone-shaped stone inside it. The grain drops between the inner stone and the outer, and when the outer stone is turned by a long timber inserted in its side, the grain is ground between the two. Thus the very life of the people in the early Roman Empire seems to rise before us as we tread the now silent streets of this wonderfully preserved place.

127. ON A ROMAN ROAD

Throughout the Empire the splendid Roman roads, strongly paved with smooth stone like a town street, led straight over the hills and across the rivers by fine bridges. Some of these bridges still stand and are of use to-day. Near the cities there was much traffic on these highways. One met the ponderous coach of the Roman governor, perhaps returning from his province to Rome. The curtains are drawn and the great man is comfortably reading or dictating to his secretary. Behind him trots a pedlar on a donkey, which he quickly draws to one side to make room for a cohort of Roman legionaries marching with swinging stride, their weapons gleaming through a cloud of dust. Following them rides an officer accompanied by a shackled prisoner going up to Rome for trial. He is perhaps a Christian named Paul. A young dandy, showing the paces of his fine horse to two ladies riding in a palanquin, grudgingly gives place on the road to a rider of the imperial post who comes clattering down the next hill at high speed. Often the road is filled with long lines of donkeys laden with bales of goods or caravans of heavy waggons creaking and groaning under their heavy loads of merchandise—the goods trains of the Roman Empire. As for passenger trains, the traveller must use the horse coach or small special carriage or ride his own horse. The speed of travel was fully as high as that maintained in Europe over a century ago, before the introduction of the steam railway, and the roads were better.

Both business and pleasure now made travel very common. The educated Roman citizen made his tour of the Mediterranean much as the modern sight-seer does. Having arrived in the provincial town, however, he found no good hotels, and if he did not sleep in his own roomy coach or a tent carried by his servants, he was obliged to pass the night in untidy rooms over some shop, the keeper of which entertained travellers. More often, however, the traveller of birth and means brought with him letters of introduction which procured him entertainment at some wealthy private house.

Even in the provincial town the traveller found a group of successful men of business and public affairs who had gained wealth and had been given the rank of Roman knights. Among them now and then was one of special prominence who had been given senatorial rank by the emperor. Below the senators and knights there were merchants, shopkeepers, artisans, and craftsmen. These men were organized into numerous guilds, societies, and clubs, each trade or calling by itself. These societies were in some ways like our trade unions. They were chiefly intended for mutual benefit of the members in their occupations; some of them also aided in social life, in the celebration of popular holidays, and they paid the funeral expenses when a member died, just as some societies among us do. Often the richest and most important man of the place was a freedman, that is a man who had once been a slave. There was in every large town a great number of freedmen, and they carried on a large share of the business of the Empire.

The Roman Empire and Two Centuries of Peace

As the traveller walked about such a town in the Roman Empire he found everywhere traces of the citizens' interest in their town. There were fountains, theatres, music halls, baths, gymnasiums, and schools, erected by wealthy men and given to the community. The boys and girls of these towns found open to them schools with teachers paid by the government. The boy who turned to business could engage a stenographer to teach him shorthand, and the young man who wished higher instruction could still find university teachers at Alexandria and Athens, and also a number of younger universities in both East and West, especially the new university established by Hadrian at Rome and called the Athenaeum.

Here is an interesting relic of some schoolboys in the days of the Empire. In passing a brickyard, these boys of seventeen hundred years ago amused themselves in scribbling school exercises *in Greek* on the soft clay bricks before they were baked. At the top a little boy who was still making capitals wrote the capital letter S (Greek Σ) ten times, and under it the similar letter K, also ten times. These he followed by the words "turtle" (ΧΕΛΩΝΑ), "mill" (ΜΥΛΑ), and "pail" (ΚΑΔΟΣ), all in capitals. Then an older boy, who could do more than write capitals, has pushed the little chap aside and showed him his superiority by writing in two lines an exercise in tongue gymnastics (like "Peter Piper picked a peck of pickled peppers", etc.), which in our letters is as follows :

Nai neai nea naia neoi temon, hōs neoi ha naus.

This means, "Boys cut new planks for a new ship, that the ship might float". A third boy then added two lines at the bottom. The brick illustrates the spread of Greek as well as provincial education under the Roman Empire.

SCRIBBLINGS OF SICILIAN SCHOOLBOYS ON A BRICK IN THE DAYS OF THE ROMAN EMPIRE

128. THE FAR-FLUNG REMAINS

A Roman once said, "Wherever a Roman has conquered, there he also lives". This was especially true of the West. Roman merchants and Roman officials were everywhere, and many of the cities were Roman colonies. The civilized language of all the West was Latin, the language of Rome, whereas east of Sicily the traveller heard only Greek. In this age western Europe was building cities under the guidance of Roman architects, and their buildings looked like those of Rome. In north Africa, between the desert and the sea, west of Carthage, the ruins of whole cities with magnificent public buildings still survive to show us how Roman

The Roman Empire and Two Centuries of Peace

civilization reclaimed regions little better than barbarous before the Roman conquest.

This picture is of a Roman amphitheatre seen across the huts of a modern North African village. The town which once supported a public place of amusement like this has given way to a poor village, and the whole region west of Carthage has to a large extent sunk back

ROMAN AMPHITHEATRE SEEN ACROSS THE HUTS OF A MODERN NORTH AFRICAN VILLAGE

into barbarism. Similar imposing Roman remains survive in western Europe, especially in southern France. We can still visit and study massive bridges, spacious theatres, great public monuments, rich villas, and luxurious public baths—a line of ruins stretching from Britain through southern France and Germany to the northern Balkans.

The structure shown overleaf was built by the Romans about A.D. 20 to supply the Roman colony of Nemausus (now called Nîmes) in southern France with water from two excellent springs twenty-five miles distant. It is nearly 900 feet long and 160 feet high, and carried the

ROMAN BRIDGE AND AQUEDUCT AT NÎMES, FRANCE

water over the valley of the river Gard. The channel for the water is at the very top, and one can still walk

RUINS OF ROMAN BATHS AT BATH

through it. The miles of aqueduct on either side of this bridge and leading to it have almost disappeared.

The Roman Empire and Two Centuries of Peace

There are hot springs at Bath, and here the Roman colonists in Britain developed a fashionable watering-place. In recent years the soils and rubbish which, through the centuries, had collected over the old Roman buildings have been removed, and we can get some idea of how they were arranged. The preceding picture represents a model of a part of the ruins. To the right is a large quadrangular pool, 83 by 40 feet in size, and to the left a circular bath. Over the whole a fine hall was built, with recesses on either side of the big pool, where one might sit and talk with friends.

129. The Commerce of the Empire

Sailing and shipping made great progress under the Roman Empire. From the splendid harbour laid out at the mouth of the Tiber by Claudius, the traveller could take a large and comfortable ship for Spain and land there in a week. The Roman whose son was studying in Athens could send a bank-note for the youth's university expenses, and a week later the boy could be spending the money. A Roman merchant could send a letter to his agent in Alexandria in ten days. The huge government corn ships that plied regularly between the Roman harbours and Alexandria were stately vessels carrying several thousand tons. They could carry an Egyptian obelisk weighing from three to four hundred tons which the emperor desired to erect in Rome, besides a large cargo of grain and several hundred passengers. Good harbours had everywhere been equipped with docks, and lighthouses modelled on that at Alexandria guided the mariners into every harbour.

Thus business flourished as never before. The good roads led merchants to trade beyond the frontiers and to find new markets. Goods found their way from Italy even to the northern shores of Europe and Britain, whence great quantities of tin passed up the Seine and down the Rhone to Marseilles. At the other end of the Empire the discovery of the seasonal winds in the Indian Ocean led to a great increase of trade with India, and there was a fleet of a hundred and twenty ships sailing regularly across the Indian Ocean between the Red Sea and the harbours of India. The goods which they brought crossed the desert by caravan from the Red Sea to the Nile and were then shipped west from the docks of Alexandria, which still remained the greatest commercial city on the Mediterranean, the Liverpool of the Roman Empire. It shipped beside East Indian luxuries Egyptian paper (papyrus), linen, rich embroideries, the finest of glassware, great quantities of grain for Rome, and a host of other things. There was a proverb that you could get everything at Alexandria except snow. Along the northern roads of the Eastern world was the caravan connection with China which continued to bring silk goods to the Mediterranean.

Rome was thus the centre of a wonderful world stretching from Britain to the Orient. The outward life in Rome, the houses and the costumes of the wealthy were, on the whole, not much changed from that which we found towards the close of the Republic. Luxury and display had somewhat increased, and in this direction rare things from the East now played a noticeable part. Roman ladies were decked with diamonds, pearls, and rubies from India, and they dressed themselves in shining silks from China. The tables of the rich were bright with peaches and apricots, now appearing for the first time in the Roman world. Roman cooks learned to prepare rice, formerly a delicacy required only by the sick. Instead of sweetening their dishes with honey as formerly, Roman households began to find a new product in the market-place known as "sakari"; for so the report of a venturesome Oriental sailor of the first century A.D. calls the syrup of the sugar-cane, which he brought by water from India into the Mediterranean for the first time. This is the earliest mention of sugar in history. These new things from the Orient were beginning to appear in Roman life just as the potatoes, tobacco, and Indian corn of America found their way into Europe after the voyages of Columbus had disclosed a new Western world.

130. CHRISTIANITY FROM THE EAST

The old Roman religion had been mostly given up, and new faiths from the East, especially from Egypt, became popular in Rome. Among all these faiths of the East, the common people were more and more inclined towards one, whose teachers told how their Master, Jesus, a Hebrew, was born in Palestine, the land of the Jews, in the days of Augustus. Everywhere they told the people of His vision of human brotherhood and divine fatherhood, surpassing that which the Hebrew prophets had once described. This faith He had preached for a few years in the Aramaic language of His countrymen—till He incurred their hatred, and in the reign of Tiberius, they had put Him to death.

A Jewish tentmaker of Tarsus named Paul, a man of fine eloquence and deep love for his Master, passed far and wide through the cities of Asia Minor and Greece, and even to Rome, proclaiming his Master's teaching. He left behind him a line of devoted churches stretching from Palestine to Rome. Certain letters which he wrote in Greek to his followers were circulated widely among them and were read with eagerness. At the same time a narrative of the Master's life had also been written in Aramaic, the language in which He had preached. This perished, but Greek accounts drawing upon the Aramaic narrative also appeared, and were now widely read by the common people. There were finally *four* leading biographies of Jesus in Greek, which came to be regarded as genuine, and these we now call the four Gospels. Along with the letters of Paul and some other writings they were later put together in a Greek book, now known in the English translation as the New Testament.

The other Eastern faiths could not offer to their followers the fellowship of a life so beautiful, so full of brotherly appeal as that of the new Hebrew Teacher. In the hearts of the toiling millions of the Roman Empire His simple summons, " Come unto Me all ye that labour and are heavy laden ", proved a mightier power than all the commands of the Roman emperors. The slave and the freedman, the artisan and craftsman, the humble and the despised in the huge barracks which sheltered the poor in Rome, listened to this new " mystery " from the East, as they thought it to be, and as time passed, multitudes responded and found joy in the hopes which it awakened. At first the " Christians " were persecuted, but their numbers steadily grew, and in the second century of peace Christianity was rapidly becoming the most important religion of the Roman Empire. The God of Israel and Christ were becoming the holy ones of Rome.

131. THE END OF THE EMPIRE

The two great centuries of peace which we have been describing ended in the time of the emperor Marcus Aurelius (A.D. 161–180). He was a great man and a philosopher, but in his day the Roman Empire was entering into trouble and decay. A new century of revolution begins. The Roman armies were getting out of hand. They were composed of men of many different nationalities. They were posted far away from Rome, the centre. Discipline became weaker. The rough soldiers began to fear the authority of Rome less and less. They even began to elect the emperors themselves. There was no law in Rome that stated how emperors were to be chosen. In A.D. 212 Roman citizenship was granted to all freemen within the Empire, and the various provinces felt that they had as much right as Italy to determine who should be their ruler.

All this caused great confusion and disorder. In one period of ninety years as many as eighty rulers of the Empire were chosen out of the class of rough and barbarous soldiers. Thus there was a century of revolution from about A.D. 180 to 280. Civilization collapsed. For at least fifty years there was no public order, as the plundering troops passed the sceptre of Rome from one soldier emperor to another. Life and property were nowhere safe, robbery and murder were everywhere, business was ruined. The Roman Empire became bankrupt. The Roman army lost its strength in civil war.

The northern barbarians took prompt advantage of the weakness of the Empire. They crossed the frontiers wherever they chose and penetrated far into Greece and Italy. In the West they poured into Gaul and Spain, and some of them even reached Africa. In addition a new power and danger arose in the East. The Parthians who had held Mesopotamia were overthrown in A.D. 226 by a new Persian power, the Sassanids, who made Persia a very dangerous rival of Rome. Their capital was Ctesiphon on the Tigris. Rome had now to concentrate on the East.

The emperor Diocletian (A.D. 284–305) had to wage such continued war with the new Persia of the Sassanids that he lived most of his time, not in Rome, but in Asia Minor. In order to look after Rome and the West, Diocletian appointed another emperor to rule jointly with him. It was not his intention to divide the Empire into two parts, but from this time the eastern and the western portions of the Roman Empire began to drift apart.

From the struggles after the death of Diocletian there arose a strong emperor in the person of Constantine the Great (A.D. 324–337). He is famous for two things in particular: (1) he was the first important Christian emperor, and (2) he determined to establish a new Rome in the eastern half of the Empire. He chose the old Greek town of Byzantium on the Bosporus. He made a magnificent new town of it and called it Constantinople. There were now two capitals, Rome and Constantinople. Thus the Empire was in practice divided in two, and usually thereafter there was one emperor in Italy and one in Constantinople. Then the barbarians from the North overwhelmed the western half of the Empire, and thus we come to what is really the end of Rome as a State.

The eastern part of the Roman Empire with Constantinople as its capital survived for another thousand years—until 1453, but the western part collapsed between A.D. 400 and 500. In A.D. 476 the last of the western emperors appeared and disappeared. Let us now consider briefly the people who were invading the Roman Empire and helping to break it up.

132. THE GERMANS

On the northern boundaries of the Empire lived many different tribes of the Teutonic race. We call them generally the Germans. They were a fair-haired, blue-eyed race of men of great stature and strength. In their native forests of the North each German people or nation occupied a very small area, probably not over forty miles across, and in numbers such a people had not usually more than twenty-five or thirty thousand persons. They lived in villages, each of about a hundred families, and there was a head man over each village. Their homes were but slight huts, easily moved. They had little interest in farming the fringe of fields around the village, much preferring their cattle, and they shifted their houses often. They had no writing and very little in the way of industries or commerce. They were hardened to wind and weather in their raw northern climate. Their love of war and plunder often led them to wander, followed by their wives and families in heavy waggons. A whole people might consist of some fifty villages, but each village group remained together, protected by its body of about a hundred warriors, the heads of the village families. These hundreds together made up an army of five to six thousand men.

In spite of lack of discipline these fighting groups of a hundred men, united by ties of blood and daily work, formed battle units as terrible as any ever seen in the ancient world. These German groups had for a long time been accustomed to wander *within* the borders of the Roman Empire. Hopeless of being able to drive them back (especially now that the carefully disciplined Roman legions which had gained for Rome the leadership of the world were no more), the emperors had allowed them to settle within the frontiers. Indeed the lack of men for the Roman army had long since led the emperors to hire the Germans as soldiers. Later on *entire* German peoples were allowed to live within the Empire in their accustomed manner. The men were received into the Roman army, but they remained under their own German leaders and they fought in their old village units.

Barbarian life, customs, and manners were thus introduced into the Empire. The customs and manners of the Empire also had an effect on the barbarians, who thus not only became familiar with the Roman civilization, but showed much respect for it. The barbarian leaders were given high office under the Roman government. They had friends among the noblest of the Romans. They married educated Roman women of rank. Some of them were converted to Christianity. Chief among these barbarians were the Franks along

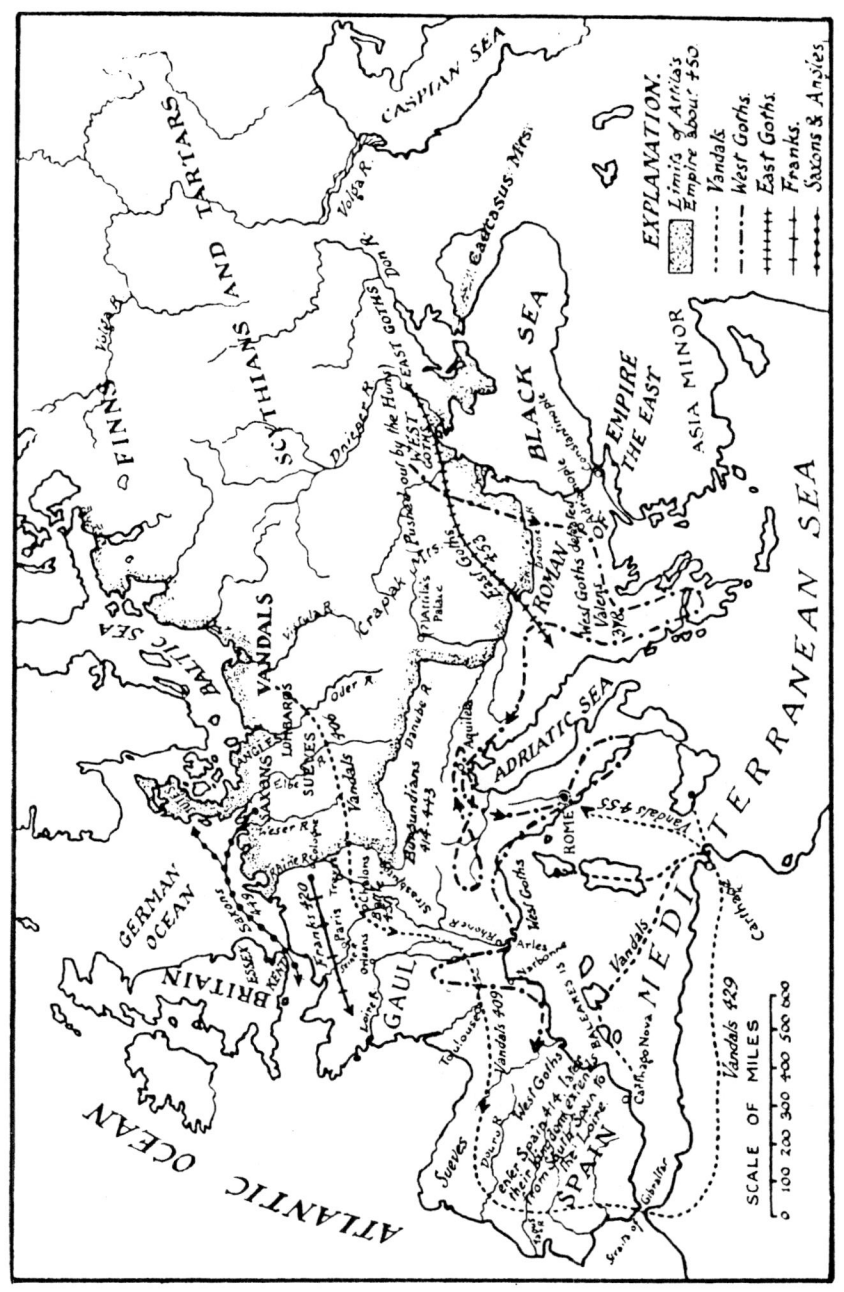

THE MIGRATION OF THE GERMANS IN THE FIFTH CENTURY

the lower Rhine, the Vandals near the Baltic, the Alemanni near the frontiers, and the Goths on the Danube. About the year A.D. 400 all these peoples were on the move towards the Empire that was weakening more and more.

Then a very fierce people called the Huns, who were not Germans, began to push the Goths from the lower Danube. This made the pressure upon the Empire much more serious. Thus the fifth century became a time of continuous migration in which the western part of the Empire was slowly absorbed by the barbarians and broken up into German kingdoms. We can trace on the map overleaf the great movements that took place in Europe in the fifth century. The Roman Empire we have known passed away. It continued in a shrunken form in Greece and Asia Minor with Constantinople as its capital until the fifteenth century. But the grandeur of the Rome of the Caesars had disappeared.

Out of the fragments of the Roman Empire and the newly formed nations of the North, the nations of Modern Europe came forth. In France, Spain, and Italy, Latin speech survived among the people to become French, Spanish, and Italian. In the island of Britain the German language spoken by the invading Angles and Saxons mingled later with much Latin and French to form our own English speech, written with Roman letters inherited from Greece, Phoenicia, and Egypt.

133. The Legacy of Rome

The Roman Empire passed away, but much of the Roman civilization remained in Europe. Rome left her stamp on the peoples of Europe, still evident, not only in the languages they use, but also in many other important matters of life, and especially in law and government. Roman law was the great creation of the Roman genius. It is still a power in modern government, and it has affected the later world more than any other Roman institution.

Another great work done by Rome was to preserve and to spread throughout the Empire that civilization which the Greeks had brought forth under contact with the Orient. Rome gave to that civilization the splendid order and organization of empire which under the Greeks it had lacked. Rome and her emperors preserved that civilization for five centuries. Through Rome the wonderful culture of Greece has come down to us. Finally Rome handed on Christianity to later Europe in the form of an organized Church. The barbarians were tamed no longer by the Roman legions but by the legions of Christ. And by means of these legions and the Church the great gifts of Greece and Rome were passed on to the new peoples and helped to make them also great.

134. Looking Back

While Mediterranean civilization was thus steadily declining, it nevertheless slowly spread northward, especially under the influence of the Church, till it completely changed the ruder life of the North. At this point, then, we have returned to the region of western and northern Europe where we first took up the career of man, and there among the crumbling ruins of the Stone Age Christian Churches began to rise.

A Brief History of Ancient Times

Books and good government and everything that we mean by the word civilization, once found only along the Mediterranean, were now reaching the northern shores of Europe.

We have looked at the stages in the early growth of this *our* civilization. Its long story we have sketched in this book. We have examined some of the things that reveal the fascinating trail along which our ancestors came. Let us recount the steps: the stone fist hatchets lie deep in the river gravels of France; the furniture of the pile villages sleeps at the bottom of the Swiss lakes; the pyramids and temples announcing the dawn of civilization rise along the Nile; by the Tigris and Euphrates the silent and deserted city-mounds still shelter their countless clay tablets and records of earliest business; the fallen palaces of Crete look out towards the sea they once ruled; the noble temples of Greece still proclaim the new world of beauty and freedom first revealed by the Greeks; the splendid Roman roads and aqueducts assert the organized control of Rome; and finally, the Christian Church-spires proclaim the new ideal of human brotherhood. These are the chapters in the great human story which we call Ancient History.

THE END

ALL AUDIO AND VIDEO TAPES AVAILABLE NOW • CALL 1 (800) 952-LOST FOR OUR FREE CATALOG

ANCIENT MYSTERIES OF NORTH AMERICA, by Tédd St. Rain. This in-depth slide presentations, which is based on his forthcoming book *Mystery of America*, outlines some of the most perplexing ancient mysteries and other anomalies that have been found in North America. Explore the evidence for Arabian, Celtic, Chinese, Egyptian, Greco-Roman, Hindu, Irish, Mesopotamian, Minoan, Nordic, Pacific Islander, Phoenician, Viking, Welsh, and West African voyages to the New World. Other topics include runestones and tablets found in the East; prehistoric mines near Lake Superior; Roman relics found in Arizona; enigmatic beehive structures, ancient coins unearthed in the Midwest; elephant slabs found in New Mexico; ground and rock petroglyphs in the Southwest; Egyptian hieroglyphics and Chinese characters; ancient footprints fossilized in rock; a 14-inch mummy found in Wyoming; human teeth found in coal deposits; red-headed giants that lived in Nevada; underground cities in the Grand Canyon; evidence for an advanced civilization; and many more anomalous finds discovered in North America. AMNA-01a • 110 min Audio Tape • $12.00 / AMNA-01 • 110 min VHS Video Tape • $19.95 Inquire on availability of other videos in St. Rain's *"Mystery of the World"* series.

REMOTE VIEWING TRAINING SESSIONS

REMOTE VIEWING TRAINING SESSIONS: DISCOVERING YOUR INTUITION, with Prudence Calabrese and TransDimensional Systems. Prudence Calabrese is the Director of TransDimensional Systems, www.largeruniverse.com, which provides information solutions to government, corporations and individuals using an array of services including remote viewing, knosomatics, intuitive counseling, technology transfer, consciousness mapping, physical profiling and other techniques. This seven-part, 13 hour, video program includes training in Basic Remote Viewing and Knosomatics, the Collector, Use of the Matrix and Advanced Post-Matrix Exercises. Included as a bonus is a discussion and explanation of techniques in Remote Healing and use of Remote Viewing for everyday purposes and career choices. Actual in-class results are shared, sessions are examined and the entire process is revealed. Join Prudence Calabrese and her staff as she leads another class into the unknown world and the Larger Universe. RVT-00a • 13 Hours on 7 Audio Tapes • $60.00 postpaid / RVT-00 • 13 Hours on 7 VHS Video Tapes • $110.00 postpaid / Introduction only • RVT-01 • 2 hour VHS Video Tape • $19.95

NEW SCIENCE / ANCIENT WISDOM - 2000 CONFERENCE

THE COSMIC ORIGINS OF MAN, with Father Charles Moore. Father Charles Moore graduated from Stanford University with a degree in law, was admitted to the California Bar and then was elected District Attorney of Santa Cruz County in 1954. He was ordained a Roman Catholic Priest in 1964. Father Charlie is a local spiritual leader, historian and scholar who speaks about our history, spirituality, ancient cultures and modern society. His broad grasp on human nature, our origins, organized religions, legends and myths make this presentation a fascinating and informative exposé of our ancient political and religious practices. With his incredible knowledge he gives new dimensions and deeper understandings to topics we thought we already knew. He has traveled extensively in search of the roots of religious practice. His quest has taken him to Britain, Europe, Hawaii, Alaska, Mexico, and India. He shares with us his highly unconventional views about human genetic, religious and cultural origins. BACN-01a • 105 min Audio Tape • $12.00 / BACN-01 • 105 min VHS Video Tape • $19.95

21ST CENTURY VISIONS OF NOSTRADAMUS, with Dolores Cannon. Dolores Cannon is an internationally known specialist in the recovery and cataloging of "lost" knowledge through regression. In thisr lecture, she focuses on the 21st century visions of Nostradamus. Dolores Cannon has written several books on the prophecies of Nostradamus. Working through several different subjects, Dolores was able to establish communication with the living Michel De Notredame better known as the prophet, Nostradamus. His revelations and their impact on our own time provide a fascinating look into a rarely discussed subject. BACN-02a • 105 min Audio Tape • $12.00 / BACN-02 • 105 min VHS Video Tape • $19.95

HUMAN RELATIONSHIPS WITH ETS, with Barbara Lamb. Barbara Lamb, a regular at our conferences and one of the nation's most experienced therapists working with UFO experiencers, suggests that either the numbers of experiencers are rising rapidly or more people are willing to talk publicly about such encounters. Her stellar achievements have made her an asset to humanity and her qualities and standards should be considered beyond reproach. This tape describes her experiences in hypnotherapy and ongoing human relationships with ETs and shows slides that she has just recently compiled. BACN-03a • 60 min Audio Tape • $12.00 / BACN-03 • 60 min VHS Video Tape • $19.95

ET RELATIONSHIPS PANEL, with Barbara Lamb, Pamela Stonebrooke, Eve Lorgen and Dolores Cannon. Barbara Lamb, a regular at our conferences and one of the nation's most experienced therapists working with UFO experiencers, suggests that either the numbers of experiencers are rising rapidly or more people are willing to talk publicly about such encounters. Pamela Stonebrooke is a professional singer in the Los Angeles area, is writing the story of her alien encounters. Eve Lorgen provides insights from her recent book, which explores how alien beings may be orchestrating human love dramas for their own ends. Dolores Cannon has also written several books on the prophecies of Nostradamus. Cannon is a regressive hypnotist specializing in past life recall, and she is fascinated by the details of history which are revealed by many of her subjects. These experts have gathered to discuss the relationships between ETs and humans. BACN-04a • 90 min Audio Tape • $12.00 / BACN-04 • 90 min VHS Video Tape • $19.95

SCIENCE, POLITICS AND THE NEW MILLENNIUM, with Dr. Nick Begich. Best selling author and lecturer Dr. Nick Begich presents an overview of the HAARP (High Frequency Active Auroral Research Program) transmitter and antenna in Alaska. His countless years of research help to provide a glimpse of new technological achievements that can help better the environment and reshape mankind in the future. Pulling from an array of extensive documentation from government, academic and media sources, Begich is able explain the big picture in terms that anyone can understand. On the eve of the 2000 presidential election, Nick discussed science and politics in the new millennium. He discussed differences between the two major parties and what is going behind the scenes. He also gave an update on the latest research activities including new technologies, health and earth science related issues. BACN-05a • 120 min Audio Tape • $12.00 / BACN-05 • 120 min VHS Video Tape • $19.95

MUSIC OF THE SPHERES, with Randy Masters. Randy Masters, a musician, composer and recording artist, has delved deeply into the study of sacred geometry, harmony and resonance, searching for the true knowledge of the music of the spheres. He has been a musician and educator about the science of music for many years. He has a unique understanding of the harmonic mathematics, and teaches about the ancient knowledge of Pythagoras and esoteric teachings. He has released numerous recordings of multi-national jazz music and composed several feature-length movie scores. He specializes in spiritual teaching and harmonic attunements using special tuning forks designed from his research, color and essential oils. Randy explains how sound could be the key to unlocking and opening monuments such as the Hall of Records under the Sphinx, which contain information about advanced civilizations before Egypt. Randy also reveals how our bodies contain the microcosm of these codes that can be ignited through sound to explore these ancient structures. BACN-06a • 90 min Audio Tape • $12.00 / BACN-06 • 90 min VHS Video Tape • $19.95

TECHNOLOGY OF THE GODS, with David Hatcher Childress. David Hatcher Childress is a real-life Indiana Jones. He has written a series of books about his journeys and research into lost cities and ancient mysteries of Africa, Arabia, China, Central Asia, India, South America Ancient Lemuria, Central America, Atlantis, Europe, as well as other locations. He is recognized as an expert not only on ancient civilizations and technology, but also on free energy, anti-gravity and UFOs. In his lecture, he presents fascinating information on the advanced technology and anomalous architecture of our predecessors from around the globe. David Hatcher Childress provides a qualified presentation about his search for Atlantis, megalithic cultures and ancient technology. In this presentation, Childress explores the massive cities high in the Andes and their links to Atlantis and Mu. A full two hours with over 200 slides from his travels around the world. Visit www.wexclub.com for more info. BACN-07a • 120 min Audio Tape • $12.00 / BACN-07 • 120 min VHS Video Tape • $19.95

ANCIENT WISDOM / NEW SCIENCE 2001 CONFERENCE

BIGFOOT / UFO CONNECTION, with Jack "Kewaunee" Lapseritis.. Kewaunee Lapseritis is a social scientist, applied anthropologist and health care professional who has thoroughly researched the Bigfoot/Sasquatch phenomenon for the last 45 years. In 1979, Kewaunee received the shock of his life when both a Bigfoot and ET simultaneously communicated with him telepathically. Since that time, he has documented 95 percipients, including a college professor, a government administrator and a whole array of people who have had similar psychic close encounters. Unlike many researchers looking for hard evidence of this elusive creature, Lapseritis has concentrated more on documenting the "experience" of the phenomenon, and gathering first-hand accounts of contacts. That is, after hearing dozens of accounts of Sasquatch contact from witnesses who tell similar stories it is impossible for him not to accept the truth of these experiences. His findings are chronicled in his book, The Psychic Sasquatch and Their UFO Connection. BACN-08a • 105 min Audio Tape • $12.00 / BACN-08 • 105 min VHS Video Tape • $19.95

OUT-OF-BODY ADVENTURES, with Albert Taylor. Al Taylor, Ph.D., left behind nearly two decades of work as an aeronautical engineer/scientist to become a metaphysical researcher, teacher, lecturer and artist. Taylor describes his Out-of-Body (OBEs) with great insight and humor. Taylor reveals how these paranormal events have impacted his personal growth and relationships. After a myriad of paranormal events, and as a result of a spiritual awakening, Taylor left behind nearly two decades of work as an aeronautical engineer/scientist, to author and publish his book, Soul Traveler. Author of the Los Angeles Times #1 bestseller SOUL TRAVELER: A Guide to Out-Of-Body Experiences and the Wonders Beyond, he is an active member of International Association of Near Death Studies (IANDS) and a participant in the Monroe Institute's Voyagers program. With his characteristic wit, he reveals how paranormal events have impacted his personal growth and explain step-by-step how you can also have an OBE. BACN-09a • 90 min Audio Tape • $12.00 / BACN-09 • 90 min VHS Video Tape • $19.95

EGYPTIAN MYSTERIES, with Karena Bryan. Karena Bryan is a dynamic healer, writer, teacher and practitioner of the matriarchal Egyptian mysteries. She is a lifelong student of ancient and modern spiritual practice, with particular emphasis on social, cultural, and political anthropology as it applies to the Divine Feminine. Her training includes thirteen years of study and practice of core and region specific shamanic divination and healing. Among her many achievements, This tape describes her travels and experience in and with the people of Egypt, and how their ancient mysteries touch even our modern society. Karena's training includes over ten years of study and practice of shamanic healing. In her presentation she provides a visual map of the role of the goddess and the sacred teachings of procreative alchemy. BACN-10a • 90 min Audio Tape • $12.00 / BACN-10 • 90 min VHS Video Tape • $19.95

UFOS AND RELIGION PANEL, with Stella Harder-Kucera, Moderator and Ted Peters, Jose Tirado and Matthew Fox, Panelists. Stella Harder-Kucera is a Filipina journalist, independent filmmaker and spiritual director who took a special reading course on UFOs with Dr. Ted Peters while pursuing the Master of Divinity/Master of Arts degree. She does pastoral counseling and spiritual direction with experiencers of anomalous trauma. Matthew Fox is a creation spirituality theologian who has been an ordained priest since 1967. He offers his insights on the phenomenon of UFOs, and how spirituality can be helpful in handling unexplained and unexpected experiences. Ted Peters is Professor of Systematic Theology at Pacific Lutheran Theological Seminary, in Berkeley, CA. He has a longstanding theological interest in the possibility of extraterrestrial life in the universe. Jose Tirado is a Chaplain and Clinical Pastoral Education Supervisory Candidate at California Pacific Medical Center's Institute for Health and Healing. José is ordained as a Pastoral Care Minister in the Nalandabodhi Buddhist Community. BACN-11a • 90 min Audio Tape • $12.00 / BACN-11 • 90 min VHS Video Tape • $19.95

PARADIGM POLITICS, with Daniel Sheehan. Daniel Sheehan is a social activist who has spent virtually his entire life working on progressive social programs and initiatives. As the Legal Counsel on such nationally-recognized investigative cases involving government as The Karen Silkwood Case, The Iran/Contra Case, The Pentagon Papers Case, The Watergate Burglary Case, and The American Sanctuary Movement Case, Dan brings to the issue of Extraterrestrial Intelligence and the UFO Phenomenon a unique background in investigating and exposing the world of American governmental covert operations, "black budget" operations, mind control programs, government disinformation projects, covert warfare and clandestine operations. Recently Daniel served as Director of "The Strategic Initiative to Identify the New Paradigm" for the State of the World Forum. He currently teaches World Politics at UC Santa Cruz and acts as General Counsel to Dr. Stephen Greer's Disclosure Project. BACN-12a • 120 min Audio Tape • $12.00 / BACN-12 • 120 min VHS Video Tape • $19.95

INTUITIVE ANIMAL COMMUNICATION, with Raphaela Pope. Raphaela Pope was a critical care nurse for many years before becoming a telepathic animal communicator. She has made her living for many years by talking to animals about life and death, about health and behavior problems, asking their opinions and discovering their desires. Her journey is described in her book, Wisdom of Animals: Communication Between Animals and the People Who Love Them, which she co-wrote with Elizabeth Morrison. She helps people locate lost pets, solve behavior problems, diagnose illnesses and even simply find out what their pets are thinking. In her presentation she shares some simple techniques with the audience. BACN-13a • 90 min Audio Tape • $12.00 / BACN-13 • 90 min VHS Video Tape • $19.95

ALL AUDIO AND VIDEO TAPES AVAILABLE NOW • CALL 1 (800) 952-LOST FOR OUR FREE CATALOG

FORBIDDEN ARCHAEOLOGY, with Michael Cremo. Michael Cremo is on the cutting edge of science and culture issues. In the course of a few months' time he might be found on pilgrimage to sacred sites in India, appearing on a national television show, lecturing at a mainstream science conference, or speaking to an alternative science gathering. As he crosses disciplinary and cultural boundaries, he presents to his various audiences a compelling case for negotiating a new consensus on the nature of reality. In his talk, Michael shows some of the more spectacular examples of what have been called out-of-place artifacts and outlines the extreme antiquity of humanity. He also explains how he was inspired by the ancient Sanskrit writings of India and other wisdom traditions. BACN-14a • 120 min Audio Tape • $12.00 / BACN-14 • 120 min VHS Video Tape • $19.95

ANCIENT WISDOM / NEW SCIENCE 2002 CONFERENCE

TALKING TO THE OTHER SIDE, with Mark Macy. Mark Macy was an agnostic until a brush with colon cancer set him on a spiritual search in the 1980s. Then he learned about the miracles of Instrumental TransCommunication (ITC): personal letters planted mysteriously in computers by invisible hands, images from other realms flashing across TV screens, and actual phone calls from angels. These researchers use contemporary electronic technology – from audio and video recorders to personal computers – for documenting what they claim are communications from their friends and associates on "the other side." His mission is simple: to present graphic evidence that the worlds of the dead and the living are coming closer together. BACN-15a • 105 min Audio Tape • $12.00 / BACN-15 • 105 min VHS Video Tape • $19.95

NEW PARADIGMS FOR LOVE, with Deborah Taj Anapol. Deborah Taj Anapol attended Barnard College, graduated Phi Beta Kappa from UC Berkeley and received her Ph.D. in Clinical Psychology from the University of Washington in 1981. She is the author of Polyamory: The New Love Without Limits, co-founder of Loving More magazine and producer of the Pelvic-Heart Integration videos. Compersion: Using Jealousy as a Path to Unconditional Love is now available in Xerox pamphlet form, and she is currently at work on a book about balancing feminine and masculine energies. She currently works with individuals, couples and moresomes who are exploring New Paradigm relating and leads workshops nationwide on tantra, sexual healing, and polyamory with her tantric lover, Victor Gold. BACN-16a • 60 min Audio Tape • $12.00 / BACN-16 • 60 min VHS Video Tape • $19.95

MEDIA COVER-UPS, with Terry Hansen. Terry Hansen is an independent journalist with an interest in scientific controversies and the politics of mass media. He is author of The Missing Times: News Media Complicity in the UFO Cover-up. He has organized and moderated two symposiums about the science and politics of UFO research for the Science Museum of Minnesota. Hansen holds a bachelor's degree in biology and a master's degree in science journalism, both from the University of Minnesota. BACN-17a • 90 min Audio Tape • $12.00 / BACN-17 • 90 min VHS Video Tape • $19.95

MEDIA PANEL ON UFO'S: Lucia August, Moderator; Ralph Steiner, Leslie Kean, and Terry Hansen as Panelists. Lucia August is a Licensed Marriage and Family Therapist and Certified Hypnotherapist with a diverse private practice in Fremont, CA. Ralph Steiner is an independent producer and science journalist affiliated with KPFA and the Pacifica Radio Network. Leslie Kean is an investigative reporter, author and producer for Pacifica Radio. In May 2000, she published an investigative feature for the Boston Globe about the French report by high level military and space officials called "UFOs and Defense: What are We Prepared for?" Terry Hansen is an independent journalist with an interest in scientific controversies and the politics of mass media. He has organized and moderated two symposia about the science and politics of UFO research for the Science Museum of Minnesota. BACN-18a • 75 min Audio Tape • $12.00 / BACN-18 • 75 min VHS Video Tape • $19.95

THE TRUTH ABOUT 9-11, with Carol Brouillet. Carol Brouillet is a Co-Founder of the International Media Project, which produces Making Contact, a half-hour radio program now heard on over 165 stations, primarily in the U.S. and Canada. Carol also helped found the Who's Counting Project, which promotes the film Who's Counting? Marilyn Waring on Sex, Lies & Global Economics. Both non-profits seek to connect people, vital ideas and important information to nurture healthy social change, economic justice and ecological sustainability. A passionate advocate of local currencies to raise consciousness, nurture community, and increase local self-reliance, her paper Reinventing Money, Restoring the Earth, Reweaving the Web of Life has won an honourable mention from the Millennium Institute as one of the best ideas for the 21st Century. BACN-19a • 120 min Audio Tape • $12.00 / BACN-19 • 120 min VHS Video Tape • $19.95

ANCIENT EGYPTIAN HI-TECH, with Christopher Dunn. Christopher Dunn has an extensive background as a master craftsman, starting as a journeyman lathe turner in his hometown of Manchester, England. Recruited by an American aerospace company, he immigrated to the United States in 1969. The author's pyramid odyssey began in 1977 when he read Peter Tompkins' book Secrets of the Great Pyramid. His immediate reaction to the Giza Pyramid's schematics was that this edifice was a gigantic machine. Discovering the purpose of this machine and documenting his case has taken the better part of twenty years of research. BACN-20a • 120 min Audio Tape • $12.00 / BACN-20 • 120 min VHS Video Tape • $19.95

NEW SCIENCE BREAKTHROUGHS, with Joe Firmage. Joe Firmage founded his first company, Serius, at age 18, embarking on a career in science and technology research, which has included everything from Internet consulting to investigating JFK's UFO intelligence files. Currently chairman of Motion Sciences Organization, he will explain how physics can advance technologies for nonpolluting energy generation and land, sea, air and space transportation systems. BACN-21a • 90 min Audio Tape • $12.00 / BACN-21 • 90 min VHS Video Tape • $19.95

THE AZTEC UFO 2002 SYMPOSIUM

THE INTERCEPTION: Roswell Crash Site Metal Recovery with Dennis Balthaser. Dennis Balthaser, concentrates his research on the 1947 Roswell Incident, Area 51 and Underground Bases. At the 2002 Aztec Symposium he will talk about his Interception experience. While still affiliated with the International UFO Museum in Roswell, NM, in 1997 as the UFO investigator, he was contacted by a gentleman in Oklahoma claiming his father had been a military policeman at the Roswell crash site and had a piece of the metal from the crashed vehicle. In this lecture Balthaser gives a detailed account of the events that transpired from the original phone call through the current investigation, which is still on-going. Aztec-01a • 2 Hour Audio Tape • $12.00 / Aztec-01 • 2 Hour VHS Video Tape • $19.95

MYSTERIOUS UFO INCIDENT IN PENNSYLVANIA AND BIG FOOT, with Stan Gordon. This presentation includes a detailed account of the 1965 UFO crash incident near Kecksburg, PA, and the bizarre 1973 UFO/Bigfoot outbreak in the state. Stan's interest in UFO's and other unusual happenings began at age 10. Since 1965, Stan has been conducting investigations into thousands of UFO and other strange encounters reported across Pennsylvania. During the late 1960's, Stan acted as a telephone report sighting coordinator for the UFO Research Institute of Pittsburgh. Stan has been internationally recognized as an authority on the subject of the UFO and Bigfoot phenomena. Due to copyright restrictions this tape does not include the slides. Aztec-02a • 2 Hour Audio Tape • $12.00 / Aztec-02 • 2 Hour VHS Video Tape • $19.95

UFOS: THE TECHNOLOGY ISSUE with John Schuessler. John Schuessler is a founding member of the Mutual UFO Network, Inc., and is currently the MUFON International Director and a member of the Board of Directors. He first became active in UFO research in 1965 when he joined the Aerial Phenomena Research Organization. John is an aerospace consultant specializing in space commercialization and space tourism. Prior to his retirement from Boeing he was involved engineering for most human space flight programs including Gemini, Skylab, Space Shuttle and the International Space Station. On his last major project, he was Program Manager for the design and construction of the new NASA Neutral Buoyancy Laboratory and in 1997, he received the NASA Public Service Medal for his leadership on the project. Aztec-03a • 2 Hour Audio Tape • $12.00 / Aztec-03 • 2 Hour VHS Video Tape • $19.95

THE DAY AFTER ROSWELL: Revelations from Beyond the Grave with Karl Pflock. Karl Pflock, author, consultant, and UFO researcher, is the author of numerous works of fiction and nonfiction. He has written and ghostwritten several nonfiction books and has been a consulting senior editor for Arlington House Publishers, editor of Libertarian Review, a senior editor at the American Enterprise Institute, contributing editor to Reason, and science columnist for Eternity Science Fiction. Mr. Pflock's interest in UFOs is virtually lifelong, and his investigations have left no doubt in his mind that UFOs are real. In the late 1960s and early 1970s he served as a member and chairman of the National Capital Area [investigations] Subcommittee of the National Investigations Committee on Aerial Phenomena (NICAP), then the world's largest private UFO research organization. Aztec-04a • 2 Hour Audio Tape • $12.00 / Aztec-04 • 2 Hour VHS Video Tape • $19.95

CRITIQUE OF THE ROSWELL CRITICS with Stanton Friedman. Stanton T. Friedman was born in New Jersey on July 29, 1934. He was named valedictorian of his 1951 Linden, New Jersey, high school class and spent two years at Rutgers University in New Brunswick, New Jersey before switching to the University of Chicago in 1953. He received BS and MS degrees in Physics from UC in 1955 and 1956, where Carl Sagan was a classmate. Since 1967 he has lectured on the topic Flying Saucers Are Real at more than 600 colleges and over 100 professional groups in fifty states, and nine Canadian provinces. Stan is the original civilian investigator of the Roswell Incident, who co-authored Crash at Corona and instigated the Unsolved Mysteries Roswell program. Aztec-05a • 2 Hour Audio Tape • $12.00 / Aztec-05 • 2 Hour VHS Video Tape • $19.95

AZTEC 1949-1950: New Information on the Aztec UFO Crash with Linda Moulton Howe. Linda Moulton Howe, Emmy Award-winning TV producer, investigative reporter and writer, will present eyewitness accounts and documents about a "dog fight" of silver discs in the sky over Aztec followed by a crash and retrieval of one disc from Hart Canyon in March 1949; multiple disc flyovers by the hundreds the next year on March 17, 1950 reported in The Denver Post and The Farmington Daily Times; and alleged government knowledge and cover-up of the Aztec disc crash and subsequent disc flyovers. Linda Moulton Howe is a graduate of Stanford University with a Masters Degree in Communication. She has devoted her documentary film, television and radio career to productions concerning science, medicine and the environment. She also produces, writes and reports for television segments. Aztec-06a • 2 Hour Audio Tape • $12.00 / Aztec-06 • 2 Hour VHS Video Tape • $19.95

HOW THE WAR ON TERROR INTERRUPTED ET CONTACT, with Jim Marrs. A native of Fort Worth, Texas, Mr. Marrs has worked for several Texas newspapers, including the Fort Worth Star-Telegram, where beginning in 1968 he served as police reporter. Since 1980, Mr. Marrs has been a freelance writer and public relations consultant. Since 1976, Mr. Marrs has taught a course on the assassination of President John F. Kennedy at the University of Texas at Arlington. In 1989, his book, , was published to critical acclaim and within three years had gone into an eighth printing in both hardbound and softbound editions. Crossfire reached the New York Times Paperback Non-Fiction Best Seller list in mid-February 1992 and remained there for more than six weeks. Aztec-07a • 2 Hour Audio Tape • $12.00 / Aztec-07 • 2 Hour VHS Video Tape • $19.95

EGYPT AND THE SCIENCE OF IMMORTALITY: Parts 1 and 2, with John Anthony West. Ancient Egypt was a one-issue civilization - its energies were entirely devoted to expressing and furthering its doctrine of Immortality. The number symbolism, the geometry of the temples, the fabulous architecture, art and sculpture, even the gods themselves, all played a role in this astonishing doctrine that fused science, art, religion and philosophy into a single, coherent Wisdom Teaching. Mere lectures do not allow enough time to broach this broad subject, but this 3-hour Institute provides a golden opportunity to explore Ancient Egypt's major aspects in depth, along with my latest research into how that system actually performed. This presentation is his Friday afternoon workshop. SIGNS-01a & 02a • 2 90 min Audios • $22.00 / SIGNS-01 and 02 • 2 90 min Videos • $39.95

THE GREAT SPHINX AND THE QUEST TO REWRITE HISTORY, with John Anthony West. A writer, scholar and Pythagorean from New York, John Anthony West is the author of "The Traveler's Key to Ancient Egypt" and "Serpent in the Sky: The High Wisdom of Ancient Egypt." The ancient Egyptians attributed their wisdom to an earlier age going back 36,000 years. John set out to test whether the Sphinx is older than its recognized date of 2,500 B.C. John Anthony West won an Emmy Award for his 1993 NBC Special Documentary, "The Mystery of the Sphinx," hosted by Charlton Heston. This presentation is his Saturday evening keynote address. For more information visit www.jawest.com SIGNS-03a • 2 70 min Audios • $19.95 / SIGNS-03 • 139 min Video • $24.95

THE CROP CIRCLES PRIMARY MESSAGE, with Drunvalo Melchizedek. As a celebrated mystic and teacher, Drunvalo Melchizedek's life experience reads like and encyclopedia of breakthroughs in human endeavor. After having taking physics and art at UC Berkeley, he ventured out, and over the last 25 years has studied with over 70 masters from all belief systems and religious backgrounds. An accomplished speaker, he instinctively communicates what's in this heart, his personal warmth, his love for life in all forms and his deep compassion for humanity. An expert on Sacred Geometry, he has studied how Crop Circles manifest these ancient forms for a decade. For more information visit www.floweroflife.com SIGNS-04a • 2 hour Audio • $12.00 / SIGNS-04 • 2 hour Video • $19.95

SACRED GEOMETRY WORKSHOP, with Drunvalo Melchizedek. Drunvalo's 2 hour workshop on sacred geometry. SIGNS-05a • 2 hour Audio • $12.00 / SIGNS-05 • 2 hour Video • $19.95

CHECK YOUR FAVORITE BOOKSELLER FOR AVAILABILITY OR CALL 1 (800) 952-LOST FOR OUR FREE CATALOG

ALL BOOKS ARE 6 X 9 AND TRADE PAPER

STAGE MAGIC AND TRICKS

AFTER-DINNER SLEIGHTS AND POCKET TRICKS, by C. Lang Neil. ISBN 1-59016-011-8 • 92 pages • illustrated • GB£7.95 • US$11.95

BOOK OF TRICKS AND MAGIC: Containing a Choice Selection of Tricks and Games for Parlor Entertainment, edited by Professor Svengarro. ISBN 1-59016-079-7 • 88 + 12 pages • illustrated • GB£7.95 • US$11.95

FIFTY NEW CARD TRICKS: A Comprehensive Description of the Continuous Front and Back Hand Palm with Cards, by Howard Thurston. ISBN 1-59016-239-0 • 83 + 12 pages • illustrated • GB£7.95 • US$11.95

GILBERT COIN TRICKS FOR BOYS AND GIRLS, by Alfred C. Gilbert. ISBN 1-59016-283-8 • 60 + 42 pages • illustrated • GB£7.95 • US$11.95

MAGIC FOR HOME AND STAGE, by the Shrewesbury Publishing Company. ISBN 1-59016-502-0 • 150 pages • illustrated • GB£9.95 • US$14.95

MODERN CARD EFFECTS AND HOW TO PERFORM THEM, by George DeLawrence and James "Kater" Thompson. ISBN 1-59016-523-3 • 80 + 12 pages • illustrated • GB£7.95 • US$11.95

MODERN CARD TRICKS WITHOUT APPARATUS, by Will Goldston. ISBN 1-59016-524-1 • 109 pages • illustrated • GB£7.95 • US$11.95

NEW BOOK OF COIN TRICKS, by Professor Svengarro. ISBN 1-59016-557-8 • 92 pages • illustrated • GB£7.95 • US$11.95

NEW BOOK OF PARLOR TRICKS AND MAGIC, by Hernandez. ISBN 1-59016- 558-6 • 61 + 47 pages • illustrated • GB£8.95 • US$12.95

PARLOR BOOK OF MAGIC AND DRAWING ROOM ENTERTAINMENTS, edited by Signor Blitz. ISBN 1-59016-638-8 • 214 pages • illustrated • GB£12.95 • US$17.95

PROFESSIONAL MAGIC TRICKS REVEALED, by George Milburn. ISBN 1-59016-679-5 • 64 + 44 pages • illustrated • GB£7.95 • US$11.95

THE SECRETS OF HOUDINI, by J. C. Cannell. ISBN 1-59016-759-7 • 279 pages • illustrated • GB£15.95 • US$20.95

TRAGIC MAGIC: Compromising Magical Sketches and a Number of Original Tricks, by Harry Leat. ISBN 1-59016-860-7 • 122 pages • illustrated • GB£8.95 • US$12.95

TRICKS WITH CARDS, by Professor Hoffman. ISBN 1-59016-866-6 • 145 pages • illustrated • GB£9.95 • US$13.95

TRICKS AND MAGIC MADE EASY, by Edward Summers Squier. ISBN 1-59016- 867-4 • 188 pages • illustrated • GB£11.95 • US$15.95

TRIX AND CHATTER, by W. Dornfeld. ISBN 1-59016-864-X • 286 pages • illustrated • GB£15.95 • US$21.95

TWENTY MAGICAL NOVELTIES, by Bagshawe. ISBN 1-59016-875-5 • 80 pages • illustrated • GB£7.95 • US$11.95

FOLKLORE AND MYTHOLOGY

BOOK OF RUSTEM: Retold From the Shah Nameh of Firdausi, by E.M. Wilmot-Buxon. ISBN 1-59016-077-0 • 240 + xii + 10 illustrated pages • illustrated • GB£13.95 • US$19.95

CLASSIC MYTH-LORE IN RHYME, by Cary Blair McKenzie. ISBN 1-59016-125-4 • 104 + ii pages • illustrated • GB£7.95 • US$11.95

CLASSIC MYTHS IN ENGLISH LITERATURE AND IN ART: Volume One, by Charles Mills Gayley. ISBN 1-59016-126-2 • 276 + xxxxiv + 10 illustrated pages • illustrated • GB£17.95 • US$23.95

CLASSIC MYTHS IN ENGLISH LITERATURE AND IN ART: Volume Two, by Charles Mills Gayley. ISBN 1-59016- 127-0 • 319 + iv + 7 illustrated pages • illustrated • GB£17.95 • US$23.95

DICTIONARY OF MYTHOLOGY: Of Characters Found in Grecian and Roman Mythology, by John H. Bechtel. ISBN 1-59016-167-X • 221 pages • illustrated • GB£12.95 • US$17.95

FOLK TALES FROM THE FAR EAST, by Charles H. Meeker. ISBN 1-59016-251-X • 254 + xii pages • illustrated • GB£14.95 • US$19.95

FRIDTHJOF'S SAGA: A Norse Romance, by Esaias Tegnér. Translated from Swedish. ISBN 1-59016-257-9 • 213 + viii pages • GB£15.95 • US$12.95

FORTY MODERN FABLES, by George Ade. ISBN 1-59016-253-6 • 303 + viii pages • GB£16.95 • US$22.95

GREEK AND ROMAN MYTHOLOGY, by Jessie M. Tatlock. ISBN 1-59016-292-7 • 370 + xxxiv pages • heavily illustrated • GB£20.95 • US$26.95

ON THE TRACK OF ULYSSES, by W. J. Stillman. ISBN 1-59016-611-6 • 106 + xii pages • illustrated • GB£8.95 • US$12.95

PAN AND HIS PIPES AND OTHER TALES FOR CHILDREN, by Katherine Dunlap Cather. ISBN 1-59016-635-3 • 84 pages • illustrated • GB£7.95 • US$11.95

STORIES OF NORSE GODS AND HEROES, by Annie Klinggensmith. ISBN 1-59016-782-1 • 101 + ii pages • illustrated • GB£7.95 • US$11.95

THE STUDENT'S MYTHOLOGY, by C. A. White. ISBN 1-59016-814-3 • 315 + iv pages • GB£16.95 • US$22.95

WINE, WOMEN AND SONG, by John Addington Symonds. ISBN 1-59016-918-2 • 180 + viii pages • GB£11.95 • US$15.95

THE YOUNG FOLK'S BOOK OF MYTHS, by Amy Cruse. ISBN 1-59016-965-4 • 265 + xiv + 42 illustrated pages • heavily illustrated • GB£16.95 • US$22.95

ARCHAEOLOGY

THE ROMANCE OF EXCAVATION, by David Masters. ISBN 1-59016-736-8 • 191 + xiv + 25 illustrated pages • illustrated • GB£12.95 • US$17.95

ARCHAEOLOGY OF THE DELAWARE RIVER VALLEY, by Max Schrabisch. ISBN 1-59016-037-1 • 181 + viii pages • illustrated • GB£11.95 • US$16.95

MAGIC SPADES, by R. V. D. Magoffin and Emily C. Davis. ISBN 1-59016-504-7 • 348 + xiv pages • illustrated • GB£18.95 • US$24.95

THE STONE, BRONZE AND IRON AGES, by John Hunter-Duvar. ISBN 1-59016-778-3 • 285 +xvi pages • illustrated • GB£15.95 • US$21.95

SUSSEX ARCHAEOLOGICAL COLLECTIONS, compiled by the Sussex Archaeological Society. ISBN 1-59016-819-4 • 215 + vi + 16 illustrated pages • illustrated • GB£13.95 • US$18.95

ANCIENT HISTORY

THE BIBLICAL STORY OF CREATION, by Giorgio Bartoli. ISBN 1-59016-064-9 • 155 + iv + 2 illustrated pages • illustrated • GB£9.95 • US$14.95

A BRIEF HISTORY OF ANCIENT TIMES, by James Henry Breasted. ISBN 1-59016-083-5 • 320 pages • illustrated • GB£16.95 • US$22.95

DARIUS THE GREAT: Ancient Ruler of the Persian Empire, by Jacob Abbott. ISBN 1-59016-152-1 • 286 pages • illustrated • GB£15.95 • US$20.95

THE DAWN OF HISTORY: An Introduction to Pre-Historic Study. Edited by Charles Francis Keary. ISBN 1-59016-155-6 • 240 + viii pages • illustrated • GB£13.95 • US$18.95

AN ANCIENT HISTORY FOR BEGINNERS, by George Willis Botsford. ISBN 1-59016-029-0 • 492 + xxii + 36 maps/illustrated pages • illustrated • GB£25.95 • US$34.95

HEROES AND CRISES OF EARLY HEBREW HISTORY, by Charles Foster Kent. ISBN 1-59016-309-5 • 251 + xvi pages • GB£14.95 • US$19.95

OUTPOSTS OF CIVILIZATION, by W. A. Chalfant. ISBN 1-59016-623-X • 193 pages • GB£11.95 • US$16.95

RASSELAS: PRINCE OF ABYSSINIA, by Samuel Johnson. ISBN 1-59016-704-X • 263 + iv pages • GB£14.95 • US$19.95

STORIES FROM THE EARLY WORLD, by R. M. Fleming. ISBN 1-59016-779-1 • 162 + xii + 11 illustrated pages • illustrated • GB£11.95 • US$15.95

THE UPANISHADS: Translated into English with a Preamble and Arguments by G.R.S. Mead and Jagadisha Chandra Chattopâdhyâya. ISBN 1-59016-883-6 • 137 pages • illustrated • GB£9.95 • US$13.95

MESOPOTAMIAN RELIGION

ASSYRIA: Its Princes, Priests and People, by Archibald Henry Sayce. ISBN 1-59016-047-9 • 166 pages • illustrated • GB£10.95 • US$14.95

THE RELIGION OF BABYLONIA AND ASSYRIA, by Theophilus G. Pinches. ISBN 1-59016-708-2 • 126 pages • illustrated • GB£8.95 • US$13.95

RELIGIOUS AND MORAL IDEAS IN BABYLONIA AND ASSYRIA, by Samuel A. B. Mercer. ISBN 1-59016-711-2 • 129 + xiv pages • illustrated • GB£9.95 • US$13.95

MESOPOTAMIAN HISTORY

ANCIENT ASSYRIA, by C. H. W. Johns. ISBN 1-59016-025-8 • 175 + 2 illustrated pages • illustrated • GB£10.95 • US$15.95

ANCIENT BABYLONIA, by C. H. W. Johns. ISBN 1-59016-026-6 • 148 pages • illustrated • GB£9.95 • US$14.95

THE ANCIENT EMPIRES OF THE EAST, by Archibald Henry Sayce. ISBN 1-59016-032-0 • 303 + xxiv illustrated pages • illustrated • GB£16.95 • US$23.95

BABYLONIAN LIFE AND HISTORY, by Ernest Alfred Thompson Wallis Budge. ISBN 1-59016-054-1 • 168 pages • illustrated • GB£10.95 • US$15.95

BOOK OF HISTORY: Volume IV, The Middle East: India, Ceylon, Burma, Siam and Central Asia, by W. M. Flinders Petrie, et al. ISBN 1-59016-074-6 • 434 + vi pages • illustrated • GB£21.95 • US$28.95

THE CIVILIZATION OF BABYLONIA AND ASSYRIA: Volume One, by Morris Jastrow, Jr. ISBN 1-59016-120-3 • 236 + xx + 31 illustrated pages • illustrated • GB£15.95 • US$21.95

THE CIVILIZATION OF BABYLONIA AND ASSYRIA: Volume Two, by Morris Jastrow, Jr. ISBN 1-59016-121-1 • 277 + xx + 45 illustrated pages • illustrated • GB£17.95 • US$23.95

HISTORY OF BABYLONIA, by George Smith. ISBN 1-59016-320-6 • 192 pages • illustrated • GB£11.95 • US$16.95

HISTORY OF BABYLONIA AND ASSYRIA, by Hugo Winkler. ISBN 1-59016-321-4 • 352 + xii pages • illustrated • GB£18.95 • US$24.95

A HISTORY OF BABYLONIA AND ASSYRIA: Volume One, by Robert William Rogers. ISBN 1-59016-316-8 • 429 + xx + 2 illustrated pages • illustrated • GB£21.95 • US$29.95

A HISTORY OF BABYLONIA AND ASSYRIA: Volume Two, by Robert William Rogers. ISBN 1-59016-317-6 • 418 + xvii pages • illustrated • GB£21.95 • US$28.95

HISTORY OF EGYPT, CHALDEA, SYRIA, BABYLONIA AND ASSYRIA: Volume Six, by Gaston Maspero. ISBN 1-59016-324-9 • 446 + xiv pages • illustrated • GB£22.95 • US$29.95

CHECK YOUR FAVORITE BOOKSELLER FOR AVAILABILITY OR CALL 1 (800) 952-LOST FOR OUR FREE CATALOG

LIFE IN ANCIENT EGYPT AND ASSYRIA, by Sir Gaston Camille Charles Maspero. ISBN 1-59016-463-6 • 374 +xviii pages • illustrated • GB£19.95 • US$26.95
MESOPOTAMIA: The Babylonian and Assyrian Civilization, by L. Delaporte. ISBN 1-59016-516-0 • 369 + xxii pages • illustrated • GB£19.95 • US$26.95
MESOPOTAMIAN ARCHAEOLOGY, by Percy S. P. Handcock. ISBN 1-59016-518-7 • 421 + xxii + 31 illustrated pages • illustrated • GB£22.95 • US$30.95
MYTHS AND LEGENDS OF BABYLONIA AND ASSYRIA, by Lewis Spence. ISBN 1-59016-547-0 • 410 + 22 illustrated pages • illustrated • GB£21.95 • US$28.95
POPULAR DICTIONARY OF ASSYRIAN AND BABYLONIAN TERMINOLOGY, by F. C. Norton. ISBN 1-59016-655-8 • 201 pages • illustrated • GB£11.95 • US$16.95
A SMALLER ANCIENT HISTORY OF THE EAST, by Philip Smith. ISBN 1-59016-766-X • 316 pages • illustrated • GB£16.95 • US$22.95
STORIES OF ANCIENT PEOPLES, by Emma J. Arnold. ISBN 1-59016-784-8 • 232 + ii illustrated pages • illustrated • US$18.95
THE STORY OF CHALDEA, by Zénaïde A. Ragozin. ISBN 1-59016-787-2 • 381 + xxii pages • 56 illustrations • GB£20.95 • US$26.95
THE STORY OF EXTINCT CIVILIZATIONS OF THE EAST by Robert E. Anderson. ISBN 1-59016-790-2 • 213 pages • illustrated • GB£12.95 • US$17.95
THE SUMERIANS: A Civilization in 3,500 B.C., by C. Leonard Woolley. ISBN 1-59016-818-6 • 198 + x + 24 illustrated pages • illustrated • GB£12.95 • US$18.95
VOICES OF THE PAST: From Assyria and Babylonia, by Henry S. Roberton. ISBN 1-59016-892-5 • 219 + 24 illustrated pages • illustrated • GB£14.95 • US$19.95

TRANSLATIONS FROM THE PAST

ARMENIAN LITERATURE, with a Special Introduction by Robert Arnot. ISBN 1-59016-038-X • 142 + x + 1 illustrated pages • illustrated • GB£9.95 • US$14.95
ASSYRIAN AND BABYLONIAN LITERATURE, with Critical Introduction by Robert Francis Harper. ISBN 1-59016-044-4 • 480 + lxxxvi + 4 illustrated pages • illustrated • GB£26.95 • US$35.95
BABYLONIAN LITERATURE, with a Special Introduction by Epiphanius Wilson. ISBN 1-59016-055-X • 309 + viii + 3 illustrated pages • illustrated • GB£16.95 • US$22.95

EGYPTIAN HISTORY

ANCIENT EGYPT FROM THE RECORDS, by M. E. Monckton Jones. ISBN 1-59016-028-2 • 244 + x + 13 illustrated pages • illustrated • GB£14.95 • US$19.95
EGYPTIAN HISTORY AND ART, by A. A. Quibell. ISBN 1-59016-203-X • 178 + xii + 15 illustrated pages • illustrated • GB£11.95 • US$16.95
EGYPTIANS OF LONG AGO, by Louise Mohr. ISBN 1-59016-204-8 • 154 pages • illustrated • GB£9.95 • US$14.95
AN EXCURSION IN THE LEVANT: 1903 by Colonel Thomas Innes. ISBN 1-59016-222-6 • 82 + 31 illustrated pages • illustrated • GB£8.95 • US$12.95
KINGS AND GODS OF EGYPT, by Alexandre Moret. ISBN 1-59016-438-5 • 290 + xii + 16 illustrated pages • illustrated • GB£16.95 • US$22.95
OUR INHERITANCE IN THE GREAT PYRAMID: Volume One, by Piazzi Smyth. ISBN 1-59016-614-0 • 296 + xviii + 23 illustrated pages • illustrated • GB£17.95 • US$23.95
OUR INHERITANCE IN THE GREAT PYRAMID: Volume Two, by Piazzi Smyth. ISBN 1-59016-615-9 • 328 + vi pages • illustrated • GB£17.95 • US$23.95
TUTANKHAMEN AND THE DISCOVERY OF HIS TOMB, by G. Elliot Smith. ISBN 1-59016-870-4 • 133 pages • illustrated • GB£8.95 • US$13.95

GREEK HISTORY

EPOCHS OF ANCIENT HISTORY: The Greeks and The Persians, by G. W. Cox. ISBN 1-59016-214-5 • 218 + xxii + 4 illustrated pages • illustrated • GB£13.95 • US$18.95
GREEK ARCHITECTURE AND SCULPTURE, by T. Roger Smith and George Redford. ISBN 1-59016-294-3 • 145 pages • illustrated • GB£9.95 • US$13.95
GREEK TRAGEDY, by J. T. Sheppard. ISBN 1-59016-296-X • 160 + viii pages • illustrated • GB£10.95 • US$14.95
THE HEROES OR GREEK FAIRY TALES, by Charles Kingsley. ISBN 1-59016-310-9 • 208 pages • GB£10.95 • US$15.95
HISTORY OF THE SCIENCES IN GRECO-ROMAN ANTIQUITY, by Arnold Reymond. ISBN 1-59016-330-3 • 245 + x pages • illustrated • GB£13.95 • US$19.95
OLD GREEK LIFE, by J. P. Mahaffy. ISBN 1-59016-596-9 • 101 pages • illustrated • GB£7.95 • US$11.95
POMPEI: ITS LIFE AND ART, by August Mau. ISBN 1-59016-652-3 • 558 + xxii + 18 illustrated pages • illustrated • GB£26.95 • US$35.95
THE STORY OF THE GREEKS, by H. A. Guerber. ISBN 1-59016-804-6 • 288 pages • illustrated • GB£15.95 • US$21.95

ROMAN HISTORY

HISTORY OF NERO, by Jacob Abbott. ISBN 1-59016-328-1 • 321 pages • 12 illustrations • GB£16.95 • US$22.95

ANCIENT ROME: From The Earliest Times Down to 476 A.D., compiled by R. F. Pennell. ISBN 1-59016-031-2 • 206 + iv pages • illustrated • GB£12.95 • US$17.95
HISTORICAL TALES: ROMAN TIMES, by Charles Morris. ISBN 1-59016-312-5 • 340 + ii + 11 illustrated pages • illustrated • GB£18.95 • US$24.95
AN INTRODUCTION TO ROMAN HISTORY LITERATURE AND ANTIQUITIES, by A. Petrie. ISBN 1-59016-370-2 • 126 pages • illustrated • GB£8.95 • US$12.95
RAMBLES IN ROME, by S. Russell Forbes. ISBN 1-59016-702-3 • 368 + xxx pages • illustrated • GB£20.95 • US$26.95
A SHORT HISTORY OF ROME AND ITALY, by Mary Platt Parmele. ISBN 1-59016-763-5 • 276 + xvi pages • GB£15.95 • US$21.95
STORIES IN STONE FROM THE ROMAN FORUM, by Isabel Lovell. ISBN 1-59016-781-3 • 258 + x + 14 illustrated pages • illustrated • GB£15.95 • US$20.95

HISTORY OF THE AMERICAS

AMERICA NOT DISCOVERED BY COLUMBUS, by Rasmus B. Anderson. ISBN 1-59016-018-5 • 164 pages • illustrated • GB£10.95 • US$14.95
THE STORY OF EXTINCT CIVILIZATIONS OF THE WEST, by Robert E. Anderson. ISBN 1-59016-791-0 • 195 pages • illustrated • GB£11.95 • US$16.95
ANCIENT CIVILIZATIONS OF MEXICO AND CENTRAL AMERICA, by Herbert J. Spinden. ISBN 1-59016-027-4 • 270 pages • illustrated • GB£14.95 • US$20.95
AZTECS AND MAYAS, by Thomas J. Diven. ISBN 1-59016-049-5 • 248 pages • illustrated • GB£13.95 • US$19.95
DISCOVERIES OF AMERICA TO 1525, by Arthur James Weise. ISBN 1-59016-170-X • 378 + xiv + 21 illustrated pages • illustrated • GB£20.95 • US$27.95
HISTORY OF LATIN AMERICA, by Hutton Webster. ISBN 1-59016-326-5 • 243 + xiv + 36 illustrated pages • GB£15.95 • US$21.95
THE SPANISH CONQUERORS, by Irving Berdine Richman. ISBN 1-59016-771-6 • 238 + iv pages • GB£13.95 • US$18.95
THE STORY OF THE PANAMA CANAL, by Logan Marshall. ISBN 1-59016-808-9 • 286 + 72 illustrated pages • illustrated • GB£18.95 • US$24.95

AMERICAN HISTORY

THE CONSTITUTION OF THE UNITED STATES: A Historical Survey of Its Formation, by Robert Livingston Schuyler. ISBN 1-59016-141-6 • 211 + viii pages • GB£12.95 • US$17.95
HISTORIC SHRINES OF AMERICA, by John T. Faris. ISBN 1-59016-314-1 • 419 + 40 illustrated pages • GB£21.95 • US$29.95
HISTORY OF CALIFORNIA, by Helen Elliott Bandini. ISBN 1-59016-323-0 • 302 pages • GB£15.95 • US$21.95
THE HISTORY OF THE UNITED STATES, by John Clark Ridpath. ISBN 1-59016-332-X • 218 + viii + 9 illustrated pages • illustrated • GB£13.95 • US$18.95
ONE HUNDRED YEARS OF THE MONROE DOCTRINE, by Robert Glass Cleland. ISBN 1-59016-607-8 • 127 pages • GB£8.95 • US$12.95
THE SOUTHERN MOUNTAINEERS, by Samuel Tyndale Wilson. ISBN 1-59016-770-8 • 202 + xiv pages • GB£12.95 • US$17.95
THE STORY OF THE CONSTITUTION, prepared by Sol Bloo. ISBN 1-59016-802-X • 192 pages • illustrated • GB£11.95 • US$16.95
THE TRANSFORMATION OF JOB: A Tale of the High Sierras, by Frederick Vining Fisher. ISBN 1-59016-865-8 • 214 + xviii pages • heavily illustrated • GB£12.95 • US$18.95
THE WAR MYTH IN THE UNITED STATES, by C. H. Hamlin. ISBN 1-59016-902-6 • 92 + iv pages • GB£7.95 • US$11.95

EUROPEAN HISTORY

THE GREAT HISTORIANS, by Kenneth Bell and G. M. Morgan. ISBN 1-59016-288-9 • 349 + xvi pages • GB£18.95 • US$24.95
A PRIMER OF HERALDRY FOR AMERICANS, by Edward S. Holden. ISBN 1-59016-676-0 • 106 + x + 24 illustrated pages • illustrated • GB£9.95 • US$13.95
THE QUEST OF THE COLONIAL, by Robert and Elizabeth Shackleton. ISBN 1-59016-691-4 • 443 + xv pages • illustrated • GB£21.95 • US$28.95
TEN FRENCHMEN OF THE NINETEENTH CENTURY, by F. M. Warren. ISBN 1-59016-832-1 • 265 + vi + 9 illustrated pages • illustrated • GB£15.95 • US$20.95

GENERAL HISTORY

EPOCHS OF MODERN HISTORY, by William Stubbs. ISBN 1-59016-215-3 • 300 + viii + 2 illustrated pages • illustrated • GB£16.95 • US$22.95
ICE AGES: The Story of the Earth's Revolutions, by Joseph McCabe. ISBN 1-59016-352-4 • 134 + x + 4 illustrated pages • illustrated • GB£9.95 • US$14.95
THE LOST CITIES OF CEYLON, G. E. Mitton. ISBN 1-59016-482-2 • 256 + xiv + 34 illustrated pages • illustrated • GB£15.95 • US$21.95
THE REVOLUTIONARY SPIRIT PRECEDING THE FRENCH REVOLUTION, by Félix Rocquain. ISBN 1-59016-717-1 • 186 + xii pages • GB£11.95 • US$16.95

CHECK YOUR FAVORITE BOOKSELLER FOR AVAILABILITY OR CALL 1 (800) 952-LOST FOR OUR FREE CATALOG

WORLD HISTORY

HENRY VIII AND HIS COURT, Herbert Beerbohm Tree. ISBN 1-59016-308-7 • 117 + vi pages • illustrated • GB£8.95 • US$12.95
EVENTFUL DATES IN THE HISTORY OF THE WORLD, by Felix Berol. ISBN 1-59016-220-X • 176 pages • GB£11.95 • US$15.95
THE FIFTEEN DECISIVE BATTLES OF THE WORLD: From Marathon to Waterloo, by E. S. Creasy. ISBN 1-59016-238-2 • 364 pages • GB£18.95 • US$24.95
THE WORLD'S REVOLUTIONS, by Ernest Untermann. ISBN 1-59016-933-6 • 176 + ii pages • GB£10.95 • US$15.95

MEDIEVAL HISTORY

TALES OF THE CRUSADERS, by Anonymous. ISBN 1-59016-829-1 • 327 pages • illustrated • GB£17.95 • US$23.95
SCOTTISH CHIEFS: The Life Story of Sir William Wallace, by Jane Porter. ISBN 1-59016-758-9 • 350 + iv pages • GB£18.95 • US$24.95
THE HOLY GRAIL: SIX KINDRED ADDRESSES AND ESSAYS, by James A. B. Scherer. ISBN 1-59016-338-9 • 210 pages • GB£11.95 • US$16.95
KING ARTHUR AND HIS KNIGHTS, by Maude L. Radford. ISBN 1-59016-435-0 • 268 pages • illustrated • GB£14.95 • US$19.95
KING ARTHUR AND THE KNIGHTS OF THE ROUND TABLE, by Charles Morris. ISBN 1-59016-436-9 • 255 + vi + 5 illustrated pages • illustrated • GB£14.95 • US$19.95
A SYLLABUS OF MEDIEVAL HISTORY, by Dana Carleton Munro and George Clarke Sellery. ISBN 1-59016-824-0 • 148 + viii + (42 + iv) pages • GB£11.95 • US$16.95

ANTHROPOLOGY

PEASANTS & POTTERS, by Harold Peake and Herbert John Fleure. ISBN 1-59016-644-2 • 152 + vi pages • illustrated • GB£10.95 • US$14.95
THE CHAIN OF LIFE, by Lucretia Perry Osborn. ISBN 1-59016-112-2 • 189 + xiv + 14 illustrated pages • illustrated • GB£12.95 • US$17.95
THE FRUIT OF THE FAMILY TREE by Albert Edward Wiggam. ISBN 1-59016-262-5 • 389 + xiv pages • GB£20.95 • US$26.95
OUR PREHISTORIC ANCESTORS, by Herdman Fitzgerald Cleland. ISBN 1-59016-618-3 • 377 + xii pages • illustrated • GB£19.95 • US$26.95
PREHISTORIC MAN, by Joseph McCabe. ISBN 1-59016-670-1 • 128 + vi + 6 illustrated pages • illustrated • GB£9.95 • US$13.95
THE RISE OF MAN, by Paul Carus. ISBN 1-59016-728-7 • 103 + vi pages • illustrated • GB£8.95 • US$12.95
THE STORY OF AB, by Stanely Waterloo. ISBN 1-59016-786-4 • 292 + viii pages • GB£15.95 • US$21.95
THE STORY OF MANKIND, by Hendrik Van Loon. ISBN 1-59016-795-3 • 488 + xxxii + 16 illustrated pages • heavily illustrated • GB£24.95 • US$32.95

PALEONTOLOGY AND PREHISTORIC WORLD

ANIMALS OF THE PAST, by Frederic A. Lucas. ISBN 1-59016-034-7 • 207 + xii pages • illustrated • GB£12.95 • US$17.95
PREHISTORIC SUSSEX, by E. Cecil Curwen. ISBN 1-59016-671-X • 172 + x + 31 illustrated pages • illustrated • GB£12.95 • US$17.95
STORIES OF THE UNIVERSE: The Earth in Past Ages, by H. G. Seeley. ISBN 1-59016-783-X • 190 pages • illustrated • GB£11.95 • US$17.95

STORY OF LANGUAGE

THE STORY OF THE ALPHABET, by Edward Clodd. ISBN 1-59016-800-3 • 209 pages • illustrated • GB£12.95 • US$17.95
THE LIFE AND GROWTH OF LANGUAGE, by William Dwight Whitney. ISBN 1-59016-461-X • 327 + x pages • illustrated • GB£17.95 • US$23.95
THE SCIENCE OF ETYMOLOGY, by Walter W. Skeat. ISBN 1-59016-756-2 • 242 + xx pages • GB£14.95 • US$19.95

WRITING AND AUTHORSHIP

WRITING THE SHORT STORY, by Joseph Berg Esenwein. ISBN 1-59016-942-5 • 441 + xvi pages • illustrated • GB£22.95 • US$29.95
BRIEF BUSINESS ENGLISH AND BUSINESS LETTERS, by Benjamin J. Campbell and Bruce L. Vass. ISBN 1-59016-084-3 • 192 + viii pages • GB£11.95 • US$16.95
THE CENTURY HANDBOOK OF WRITING, by Garland Greever and Easley S. Jones. ISBN 1-59016-110-6 • 228 + xiv pages • GB£13.95 • US$18.95
ELEMENTARY COMPOSITION AND RHETORIC, by William Edward Mead. ISBN 1-59016-209-9 • 286 pages • GB£15.95 • US$20.95
THE HAND BOOK OF CONVERSATION: Its Faults and Graces, compiled by Andrew P. Peabody. ISBN 1-59016-302-8 • 152 pages • GB£9.95 • US$14.95
THE PREPARATION OF MANUSCRIPTS FOR THE PRINTER, by Frank H. Viztelly. ISBN 1-59016-673-6 • 148 + vi pages • illustrated • GB£9.95 • US$14.95
TECHNICAL WRITING, by T. A. Richard. ISBN 1-59016-831-3 • 178 + vi pages • GB£10.95 • US$15.95

ACTING AND CINEMATOGRAPHY

A CONDENSED COURSE IN MOTION PICTURE PHOTOGRAPHY, by the New York Institute of Photography. ISBN 1-59016-139-4 • 382 + 100 illustrated pages • illustrated • GB£22.95 • US$30.95
FILM FOLK, by Rob Wagner. ISBN 1-59016-241-2 • 356 + x pages • illustrated • GB£19.95 • US$26.95
SCREEN ACTING: Its Requirements and Rewards, by Inez and Helen Klumph. ISBN 1-59016-760-0 • 243 pages • illustrated • GB£13.95 • $18.95
THE ART OF MAKE-UP, by Helena Chalmers. ISBN 1-59016-039-8 • 159 + viii pages • illustrated • GB£10.95 • US$14.95
STAGE SCENERY AND LIGHTING, by Samuel Seldon and Hunton D. Sellman. ISBN 1-59016-772-4 • 433 + xiv pages • illustrated • GB£22.95 • US$29.95

THEATER AND DRAMA

THE ART OF PLAY PRODUCTION, by John Dolman, Jr. ISBN 1-59016-040-1 • 464 + xviii + 12 illustrated page • illustrated • GB£22.95 • US$30.95
BRITISH DRAMA, by Allardyce Nicoll. ISBN 1-59016086-X • 496+ viii + 16 illustrated pages • illustrated • GB£24.95 • US$32.95
THE COMIC SPIRIT IN RESTORATION DRAMA, by Anonymous. ISBN 1-59016-133-5 • 148 + viii pages • GB£9.95 • US$14.95
THE DEVELOPMENT OF THE DRAMA, by Branders Matthews. ISBN 1-59016-163-7 • 351 + vi pages • GB£18.95 • US$24.95
DRAMA AND MANKIND, by Halcott Glover. ISBN 1-59016-180-7 • 192 pages • GB£11.95 • US$16.95
THE DRAMA: Its Law and Its Technique, by Elisabeth Woodbridge. ISBN 1-59016-181-5 • 181 + xvi pages • GB£11.95 • US$16.95
HISTORIC COSTUME, by Katherine Morris Lester. ISBN 1-59016-313-3 • 244 pages • illustrated • GB£13.95 • US$18.95
HOW TO PRODUCE PLAYS AND PAGEANTS, by Mary M. Russell. ISBN 1-59016-346-X • 219 + 10 illustrated pages • illustrated • GB£12.95 • US$17.95
ON THE ART OF THE THEATRE, by Edward Gordon. ISBN 1-59016-610-8 • 296 + xxii + 14 illustrated pages • illustrated • GB£17.95 • US$23.95
THE POPULAR THEATRE, by George Jean Nathan. ISBN 1-59016-657-4 • 236 pages • GB£13.95 • US$18.95
RHYTHMIC ACTION PLAYS AND DANCES, by Irene E. Phillips Moses. ISBN 1-59016-722-8 • 164 + vi pages • illustrated • GB£10.95 • US$15.95
SCENES AND MACHINES OF THE ENGLISH STAGE DURING THE RENAISSANCE, by Lily B. Campbell. ISBN 1-59016-751-1 • 302 + x + 8 illustrated pages • illustrated • GB£169.95 • US$22.95
THE STORY OF THE THEATER, by Glenn Hughes. ISBN 1-59016-809-7 • 421 + x + 28 illustrated pages • illustrated • GB£22.95 • US$29.95
STUDIES IN STAGECRAFT, by Clayton Hamilton. ISBN 1-59016-815-1 • 298 + vi pages • GB£15.95 • US$21.95
THEATRON: An Illustrated Record of Twentieth Century Theater, by Clarence Stratton. ISBN 1-59016-838-0 • 260 + ii pages • illustrated • GB£16.95 • US$22.95
THE TWENTIETH CENTURY THEATRE, by William Lyon Phelps. ISBN 1-59016-873-9 • 147 + vi pages • GB£9.95 • US$14.95

SCIENCE AND TECHNOLOGY

THE ABCS OF WIRELESS RADIO, by Edward Trevert. ISBN 1-59016-004-5 • 116 pages • illustrated • GB£8.95 • US$12.95
THE EINSTEIN THEORY OF RELATIVITY, by Garrett P. Serviss. ISBN 1-59016-207-2 • 108 pages • illustrated • GB£7.95 • US$11.95
ABCS OF THE TELEPHONE, by James E Homans. ISBN 1-59016-002-9 • 347 + xxiv pages • illustrated • GB£19.95 • US$25.95
THE AGE OF INVENTION, by Holland Thompson. ISBN 1-59016-012-6 • 267 + x pages • GB£14.95 • US$20.95
DREAMS OF AN ASTRONOMER, by Camille Flammarion. ISBN 1-59016-187-4 • 223 pages • GB£12.95 • US$17.95
ELEMENTS OF GENERAL SCIENCE, by Otis William Caldwell and William Lewis Eikenberry. ISBN 1-59016-210-2 • 402 + xviii pages • illustrated • GB£20.95 • US$27.95
THE FAIRYLAND OF SCIENCE, by Arabella B. Buckley. ISBN 1-59016-228-5 • 266 pages • illustrated • GB£15.95 • US$19.95
A LABORATORY MANUAL IN PHYSICS, by N. Henry Black. ISBN 1-59016-451-2 • 115 + x pages • illustrated • GB£8.95 • US$12.95
MAKER'S OF PROGRESS, by William L. and Stella H. Nida. ISBN 1-59016-506-3 • 208 + vi pages • illustrated • GB£12.95 • US$17.95
MARVELS OF MODERN MECHANICS, by Harold T. Wilkins. ISBN 1-59016-508-X • 280 + xii + 15 illustrated pages • illustrated • GB£16.95 • US$22.95
TELSA, NIKOLA: Various Articles, Patents and Lectures - Coming Soon, Call 1 (800) 952-LOST for our current catalog.

CHECK YOUR FAVORITE BOOKSELLER FOR AVAILABILITY OR CALL 1 (800) 952-LOST FOR OUR FREE CATALOG

NINETEENTH CENTURY PHOTOGRAPHY: Anthony's Annual International Photographic Bulletin, June 1891. ISBN 1-59016-569-1 • 468 + xxii + 14 illustrated pages • illustrated • GB£24.95 • US$32.95
PRINCIPLES OF BACTERIOLOGY, by Arthur A. Eisenberg. ISBN 1-59016-678-7 • 198 pages • illustrated • GB£11.95 • US$16.95
ROBINSON'S MANUAL OF RADIO TELEGRAPHY AND TELEPHONY, by Captain S. S. Robinson, U.S. Navy. ISBN 1-59016-732-5 • 307 + vi illustrated pages • illustrated • GB£16.95 • US$22.95
STEAM, STEEL AND ELECTRICITY, by James W. Steele. ISBN 1-59016-777-5 • 240 + viii pages • illustrated • GB£13.95 • US$18.95
THE STORY OF INVENTION, by Hendrik Van Loon. ISBN 1-59016-793-7 • 252 pages • heavily illustrated • GB£13.95 • US$19.95
THE STORY OF THE ART OF BUILDING, by P. Leslie Waterhouse. ISBN 1-59016-801-1 • 215 pages • illustrated • GB£12.95 • US$17.95
THE WONDERS OF SCIENCE IN MODERN LIFE, by Henry Smith Williams and Edward H. Williams. ISBN 1-59016-922-0 • 191 + viii + 8 illustrated pages • illustrated • GB£11.95 • US$16.95

GAMES, ENTERTAINMENT, HUMOR

THE AMERICAN CHECKER PLAYER'S HAND BOOK, by Erroll A. Smith. ISBN 1-59016-020-7 • 160 pages • illustrated • GB£9.95 • US$14.95
CHESS FOR BEGINNERS, by E. E. Cunnington. ISBN 1-59016-114-9 • 112 pages • illustrated • GB£8.95 • US$12.95
A COMIC HISTORY OF THE UNITED STATES, by Livingston Hopkins. ISBN 1-59016-132-7 • 223 pages • illustrated • GB£12.95 • US$17.95
COMMON SENSE IN CHESS, by Emanuel Lasker. ISBN 1-59016-136-X • 139 pages • illustrated • GB£9.95 • US$13.95
DANCES, DRILLS AND STORY PLAYS: For Every Day and Holidays, by Nina B. Lamkin. ISBN 1-59016-151-3 • 117 pages • GB£8.95 • US$12.95
DICK'S GAMES OF PATIENCE: SOLITAIRE WITH CARDS, edited by William B. Dick. ISBN 1-59016-166-1 • 154 + ii pages • GB£9.95 • US$14.95
FUN WITH CARDS, by Dean Bryden. ISBN 1-59016-266-8 • 165 + viii pages • GB£10.95 • US$15.95
FUN WITH PAPER FOLDING, by William D. Murray and Francis J. Rigney. ISBN 1-59016-267-6 • 95 + ii pages • illustrated • GB£7.95 • US$11.95
GAMES FOR THE PLAYGROUND, HOME, SCHOOL AND GYMNASIUM, by Jessie H. Bancroft. ISBN 1-59016-276-5 • 454 + viii + 22 illustrated pages • illustrated • GB£22.95 • US$30.95
THE GENTLEMEN'S HAND-BOOK ON POKER, by Florence. ISBN 1-59016-278-1 • 195 + viii pages • illustrated • GB£11.95 • US$16.95
HOW TO PLAY CHESS, by E. E. Cunnington. ISBN 1-59016-345-1 • 88 pages • GB£7.95 • US$11.95
MR. PUNCH'S AFTER DINNER STORIES, edited by J. A. Hammerton. ISBN 1-59016-683-3 • 192 + ii pages • illustrated • GB£11.95 • US$16.95
SONGS FOR LITTLE CHILDREN, composed and arranged by Eleanor Smith. ISBN 1-59016-769-4 • 213 + viii pages • illustrated with musical score • GB£12.95 • US$17.95

CRAFTWORK AND HOBBIES

THE GLAZER'S CLAY BOOK AND HOW TO USE IT, by E. L. Raes. ISBN 1-59016-285-4 • 137 + ii pages • tables • GB£9.95 • US$13.95
HOME TANNING AND LEATHER MAKING GUIDE, by Albert B. Farnham. ISBN 1-59016-340-0 • 176 pages • GB£10.95 • US$15.95
THE INDUSTRIAL ARTS IN SPAIN, by Juan F. Riaño. ISBN 1-59016-358-3 • 276 + vi pages • illustrated • GB£15.95 • US$20.95
INSTRUCTIONAL UNITS IN WOOD FINISHING, by R. A. McGee and Arthur G. Brown. ISBN 1-59016-363-X • 128 pages • illustrated • GB£8.95 • US$13.95
THE STAMP COLLECTOR, by Stanely C. Johnson. ISBN 1-59016-775-9 • 317 + 31 illustrated pages • illustrated • GB£17.95 • US$24.95
SWOOPE'S LESSONS IN PRACTICAL ELECTRICITY: Volume One, by Erich Hausmann. ISBN 1-59016-822-4 • 344 + xii pages • heavily illustrated • GB£18.95 • US$24.95
SWOOPE'S LESSONS IN PRACTICAL ELECTRICITY: Volume Two, by Erich Hausmann. ISBN 1-59016-823-2 • 348 + x pages • heavily illustrated • GB£18.95 • US$24.95

MUSIC STUDIES

CARUSO AND THE ART OF SINGING, by Salvatore Fucito and Barnet J. Beyer. ISBN 1-59016-104-1 • 219 + x + 12 illustrated pages • illustrated • GB£13.95 • US$18.95
THE THEORY AND PRACTICE OF MUSICAL FORM, by J. H. Cornell. ISBN 1-59016-836-4 • 214 + xviii pages • heavily illustrated • GB£14.95 • US$19.95
HOW TO LISTEN TO MUSIC, by Henry Edward Krehbiel. ISBN 1-59016-344-3 • 361 + xiv pages • illustrated • GB£18.95 • US$24.95
INTRODUCTORY TO MUSIC, by Thaddeus P. Giddings, Will Earhart, Ralph Baldwin and Elbridge Newton. ISBN 1-59016-372-9 • 176 + ii pages • GB£10.95 • US$15.95
LESSONS IN MUSICAL HISTORY, by John Comfort Fillmore. ISBN 1-59016-457-1 • 183 + xviii + 37 chronology pages • GB£13.95 • US$18.95
LISTENING LESSONS IN MUSIC, by Agnes Moore Fryberger. ISBN 1-59016-468-7 • 264 + xiv pages • GB£14.95 • US$20.95
MUSIC CLUB PROGRAMS FROM ALL NATIONS, by Arthur Elson. ISBN 1-59016-541-1 • 185 + x + 9 illustrated pages • illustrated • GB£11.95 • US$16.95
MUSICAL HARMONY SIMPLIFIED, by F. H. Shepard. ISBN 1-59016-545-4 • 242 + viii pages • heavily illustrated • GB£13.95 • US$19.95
THE NEW EDUCATIONAL MUSIC COURSE, by James M. McLaughlin. ISBN 1-59016-561-6 • 130 + viii pages • GB£9.95 • US$13.95
OUTLINES OF MUSIC HISTORY, by Clarence G. Hamilton. ISBN 1-59016-621-3 • 308 + xxxvi pages • illustrated • GB£17.95 • US$23.95
PRACTICAL GUIDE TO THE IDEAL HOME MUSIC LIBRARY, by Albert E. Wier. ISBN 1-59016-662-0 • 113 + viii pages • illustrated • GB£8.95 • US$12.95
STANDARD HISTORY OF MUSIC, by James Francis Cooke. ISBN 1-59016-776-7 • 260 + ii pages • heavily illustrated • GB£18.95 • US$19.95

SONG BOOKS

BEETON'S BOOK OF SONGS, edited by Ward, Lock & Co. ISBN 1-59016-059-2 • 162 + xiv pages • illustrated • GB£10.95 • US$15.95
FROM SONG TO SYMPHONY, by Daniel Gregory Mason. ISBN 1-59016-259-5 • 243 + vi pages • illustrated • GB£13.95 • US$19.95
GLEE AND CHORUS BOOK, by J. E. NeCollins. ISBN 1-59016-286-2 • 208 + ii pages • illustrated with musical score • GB£12.95 • US$17.95
THE IDEAL HOME MUSIC LIBRARY: Volume IX, Sentimental Music, compiled and edited by Albert E. Wier. ISBN 1-59016-355-9 • 256 + ii pages • illustrated with musical score • GB£14.95 • US$19.95
THE IDEAL HOME MUSIC LIBRARY: Volume X, Favorite Home Songs, compiled and edited by Albert E. Wier. ISBN 1-59016-356-7 • 336 + ii pages • illustrated with musical score • GB£17.95 • US$23.95
JUNIOR MUSIC, by Thaddeus P. Giddings, Will Earhart, Ralph L. Baldwin and Elbridge W. Newton. ISBN 1-59016-395-8 • 256 + ii pages • illustrated • GB£14.95 • US$19.95
LAUREL GLEE BOOK FOR MALE VOICES, by M. Teresa Armitage. ISBN 1-59016-455-5 • 126 + iv pages • illustrated with musical score • GB£8.95 • US$13.95
OUR FAMILIAR SONGS AND THEIR AUTHORS: Volume One, by Helen Kendrick Johnson. ISBN 1-59016-612-4 • 290 + x pages • GB£15.95 • US$21.95
OUR FAMILIAR SONGS AND THEIR AUTHORS: Volume Two, by Helen Kendrick Johnson. ISBN 1-59016-613-2 • 368 + viii pages • GB£18.95 • US$25.95
SONG AND LEGEND FROM THE MIDDLE AGES, selected and arranged by William D. McClintock and Porter Lander McClintock. ISBN 1-59016-767-8 • 141 + ii pages • GB£9.95 • US$13.95
SONG TREASURY: 20th Century Americana, compiled and edited by Harriet Garton Cartwright. ISBN 1-59016-768-6 • 214 + xviii pages • illustrated with musical score • GB£12.95 • US$18.95

PAINTING AND DRAWING

AIMS AND IDEALS OF REPRESENTATIVE AMERICAN PAINTERS, written and arranged by John Rummell and E. M. Berlin. ISBN 1-59016-014-2 • 114 pages • GB£8.95 • US$12.95
ANATOMY AND DRAWING, by Victor Perard. ISBN 1-59016-024-X • 175 + xx pages • illustrated • GB£11.95 • US$16.95
APPLIED DRAWING, by Harold Haven Brown. ISBN 1-59016-036-3 • 266 + vi pages • illustrated • GB£14.95 • US$20.95
ART STUDIES FOR SCHOOLS, by Anna M. Von Rydingsvärd. ISBN 1-59016-043-6 • 185 + ii pages • heavily illustrated • GB£11.95 • US$15.95
DRAWING MADE EASY, by Joseph Cummings Chase. ISBN 1-59016-183-1 • 146 pages • GB£9.95 • US$13.95
ELECTRICAL DRAFTING and Design, by Calvin C. Bishop. ISBN 1-59016-208-0 • 165 + vi pages • illustrated • GB£10.95 • US$15.95
LETTERS AND LETTERING: A Treatise with Two Hundred Examples, by Frank Chouteau Brown. ISBN 1-59016-459-8 • 214 + xviii pages • heavily illustrated • GB£12.95 • US$18.95
PAINTERS, PICTURES AND THE PEOPLE, by Eugene Neuhaus. ISBN 1-59016-631-0 • 224 + x + 31 illustrated pages • illustrated • GB£14.95 • US$19.95
PAINTING AND DECORATING WORKING METHODS, produced under the direction of Painting and Decorating Contractors of America. ISBN 1-59016-633-7 • 294 + xiv pages • illustrated • GB£16.95 • US$22.95
THE PRACTICE OF OIL PAINTING AND OF DRAWING, by Solomon J. Soloman. ISBN 1-59016-667-1 • 278 pages • illustrated • GB£14.95 • US$20.95
THE STORY OF DUTCH PAINTING, by Charles H. Caffin. ISBN 1-59016-789-9 • 210 + viii + 31 illustrated pages • illustrated • GB£13.95 • US$19.95

CHECK YOUR FAVORITE BOOKSELLER FOR AVAILABILITY OR CALL 1 (800) 952-LOST FOR OUR FREE CATALOG

THE STORY OF FRENCH PAINTING, by Charles H. Caffin. ISBN 1-59016-792-9 • 232 + xii + 40 illustrated pages • illustrated • GB£15.95 • US$20.95
TOPOGRAPHICAL MAPS AND SKETCH MAPPING, by J. K. Finch. ISBN 1-59016-851-8 • 175 + xiv + 3 illustrated pages • heavily illustrated • GB£11.95 • US$16.95

FAMOUS PEOPLE
ABRAHAM LINCOLN: Volume One, by Carl Sandburg. ISBN 1-59016-007-X • 298 + x pages • GB£16.95 • US$22.95
ABRAHAM LINCOLN: Volume Two, by Carl Sandburg. ISBN 1-59016-008-8 • 304 + iv pages • GB£16.95 • US$22.95
BENJAMIN FRANKLIN: American Statesman, by John T. Morse, Jr. ISBN 1-59016-061-4 • 442 + xxii + 2 illustrated pages • illustrated • GB£22.95 • US$30.95
CELEBRATED FEMALE SOVEREIGNS, by Anna B. Jameson. ISBN 1-59016-109-2 • 245 pages • illustrated • GB£13.95 • US$18.95
FAMOUS WOMEN, by Joseph Adelman. ISBN 1-59016-231-5 • 328 + x pages • illustrated • GB£17.95 • US$23.95
THE LIFE OF BENJAMIN FRANKLIN, by M. L. Weems. ISBN 1-59016-466-0 • 239 + 5 illustrated pages • illustrated • GB£13.95 • US$18.95
MACAULAY'S LIFE OF SAMUEL JOHNSON, edited by Albert Perry Walker. ISBN 1-59016-501-2 • 92 + xxxii + 6 illustrated pages • illustrated • GB£8.95 • US$13.95
MEMORABLE ADDRESSES BY AMERICAN PATRIOTS, from a collection by John Clark Ridpath. ISBN 1-59016-513-6 • 112 + ii pages • GB£8.95 • US$12.95
MESSER MARCO POLO, by Donn Byrne. ISBN 1-59016-521-7 • 147 + iv pages • GB£9.95 • US$14.95
THE POCKET UNIVERSITY: Famous Explorers, edited by George Iles. ISBN 1-59016-648-5 • 171 + x pages • GB£10.95 • US$15.95

QUESTIONS AND ANSWERS
ANSWER THIS ONE: QUESTIONS FOR EVERYONE, compiled by Franklin P. Adams and Harry Hansen. ISBN 1-59016-035-5 • 192 pages • illustrated • GB£11.95 • US$16.95
ONE THOUSAND AND ONE RIDDLES, compiled by David McKay. ISBN 1-59016-609-4 • 203 + iv pages • GB£11.95 • US$16.95
THE QUESTION BOOK FOR YOUNG FOLKS, compiled by Sylvia Weil and Rosetta C. Goldsmith. ISBN 1-59016-688-4 • 95 pages • illustrated • GB£7.95 • US$11.95
WHAT'S THE ANSWER? edited by John A. Bassett. ISBN 1-59016-910-7 • 111 + iv pages • GB£8.95 • US$12.95

GEOLOGY AND MINERALS
DIAMONDS AND OTHER GEMS, by John Clyde Ferguson. ISBN 1-59016-164-5 • 160 pages • illustrated • GB£9.95 • US$14.95
THE TRAGEDY OF PELEÉ, by George Kennan. ISBN 1-59016-859-3 • 257 + 14 illustrated pages • illustrated • GB£14.95 • US$20.95
FIELD BOOK OF COMMON ROCKS AND MINERALS, by Frederic Brewster Loomis. ISBN 1-59016-236-6 • 278 + xvi + 73 illustrated pages • illustrated • GB£18.95 • US$24.95
A FIRST BOOK IN GEOLOGY, by N. S. Shaler. ISBN 1-59016-245-5 • 255 + xx pages • illustrated • GB£14.95 • US$20.95
GEOGRAPHIC INFLUENCES IN AMERICAN HISTORY, by Albert Perry Brigham. ISBN 1-59016-280-3 • 285 + x pages • illustrated • GB£15.95 • US$21.95
GEOGRAPHY OF CALIFORNIA, by Harold W. Fairbanks. ISBN 1-59016-281-1 • 239 + ii + 2 illustrated pages • illustrated • GB£13.95 • US$18.95
MINERAL TABLES FOR THE DETERMINATION OF MINERALS BY THEIR PHYSICAL PROPERTIES, by Arthur S. Eakle. ISBN 1-59016-522-5 • 73 + iv pages • tables • GB£7.95 • US$11.95
SAN FRANCISCO'S GREAT DISASTER, by Anonymous. ISBN 1-59016-746-5 • 422 pages • heavily illustrated • GB£20.95 • US$27.95
STORIES IN STONE, by Willis T. Lee. ISBN 1-59016-780-5 • 226 + x + 49 illustrated pages • illustrated • GB£15.95 • US$21.95

NATURAL HISTORY
MARVELS OF NATURAL HISTORY, by Henry Davenport Northrop. ISBN 1-59016-509-8 • 360 + 12 illustrated pages • heavily illustrated • GB£18.95 • US$24.95
NATURE'S PROGRAM, by Gaylord Johnson. ISBN 1-59016-554-3 • 181 + vi pages • GB£11.95 • US$15.95
THE POCKET UNIVERSITY: The Earth Around Us, edited by George Iles. ISBN 1-59016-649-3 • 191 + xxii pages • GB£12.95 • US$17.95

BIOLOGY
SEX SECRETS, by Robert B. Armitage, M.D. ISBN 1-59016-761-9 • 317 + ii pages • heavily illustrated • GB£16.95 • US$22.95
THE SEXUAL LIFE, by C. W. Malchow, M.D. ISBN 1-59016-762-7 • 317 pages • GB£16.95 • US$22.95

MISCELLANEOUS
THE ART OF THINKING, by Ernest Dimnet. ISBN 1-59016-042-8 • 221 + xii pages • GB£13.95 • US$18.95

CHARACTER READING THROUGH ANALYSIS OF THE FEATURES, by Gerald Elton Fosbroke. ISBN 1-59016-113-0 • 193 + xii + 56 illustrated pages • heavily illustrated • GB£14.95 • US$19.95

HEALTH AND NUTRITION
STRENGTH FROM EATING, by Bernarr MacFadden. ISBN 1-59016-812-7 • 194 pages • illustrated • GB£11.95 • US$16.95
A COMPEND OF MATERIA MEDICA AND THERAPEUTICS, by Samuel O. L. Potter. ISBN 1-59016-137-8 • 147 pages • GB£9.95 • US$13.95
DRUG ENCYCLOPEDIA, compiled by Brunswig Drug Company, circa 1908. ISBN 1-59016-190-4 • 241 pages • illustrated • GB£13.95 • US$18.95

EDUCATION AND SCHOOLING
COLLEGE: WHAT'S THE USE? by Herbert E. Hawkes. ISBN 1-59016-130-0 • 143 + vi pages • illustrated • GB£9.95 • US$14.95
A JUNIOR CLASS HISTORY OF THE UNITED STATES, by John J. Anderson. ISBN 1-59016-393-1 • 242 pages • illustrated • GB£13.95 • US$18.95
POISE: HOW TO ATTAIN IT, by D. Starke. ISBN 1-59016-650-7 • 159 pages • illustrated • GB£9.95 • US$14.95

COURSEWORK AND STUDY GUIDES
A COURSE IN PILOTING SEAMANSHIP AND SMALL BOAT HANDLING, by Charles F. Chapman. ISBN 1-59016-144-0 • 120 pages • illustrated • GB£8.95 • US$12.95
A COURSE IN WOOD TURNING, by Archie S. Milton and Otto K. Wohlers. ISBN 1-59016-145-9 • 200 pages • GB£11.95 • US$16.95

MONEY AND BUSINESS
THE THEORY AND HISTORY OF BANKING, by Charles F. Dunbar. ISBN 1-59016-835-6 • 199 + vi pages • illustrated • GB£11.95 • US$16.95
MONEY & INVESTMENTS, by Montgomery Rollins. ISBN 1-59016-525-X • 493 + xxii + 22 misc pages • graphs • GB£24.95 • US$33.95
PATENT OFFICE PRACTICE, by Archie R. McCrady. ISBN 1-59016-640-X • 385 + xx pages • illustrated • GB£20.95 • US$26.95
THE ROMANCE OF BUSINESS, by W. Cameron Forbes. ISBN 1-59016-734-1 • 258 + viii + 3 illustrated pages • illustrated • GB£14.95 • US$20.95

DICTIONARIES AND REFERENCE
A DESK-BOOK OF IDIOMS AND IDIOMATIC PHRASES, by Frank H. Vizetelly and Leander J. DeBekker. ISBN 1-59016-161-0 • 496 + x pages • GB£23.95 • US$31.95
THE ENGLISH DICTIONARIE OF 1623, by Henry Cockeram. ISBN 1-59016-212-9 • 197 + xxii pages • GB£12.95 • US$17.95
HANDY DICTIONARY OF ENGLISH SYNONYMS, by Thomas Fenby. ISBN 1-59016-305-2 • 268 + xii pages • GB£14.95 • US$20.95
A HANDY DICTIONARY OF SYNONYMS, by H. C. Faulkner. ISBN 1-59016-306-0 • 217 pages • GB£12.95 • US$17.95
THE NUTTALL DICTIONARY OF ANAGRAMS, A. R. Ball. ISBN 1-59016-584-5 • 120 pages • GB£8.95 • US$12.95
PRACTICAL SYNONYMS, by John H. Bechtel. ISBN 1-59016-664-7 • 226 + ii pages • GB£12.95 • US$17.95
PRONUNCIATION DICTIONARY, by John H. Bechtel. ISBN 1-59016-609-9 • 143 + ii pages • GB£9.95 • US$13.95
THE REPORTER'S WORD BOOK, by Anonymous. ISBN 1-59016-715-5 • 155 + iv pages • GB£9.95 • US$14.95
THE STORY KEY TO GEOGRAPHIC NAMES, by O. D. Von Engeln and Jane McKelway Urquhart. ISBN 1-59016-785-6 • 279 + xiv pages • GB£15.95 • US$21.95
WORDS: THEIR SPELLING, PRONUNCIATION, DEFINITION AND APPLICATION, compiled by Rupert P. SoRelle and Charles W. Kitt. ISBN 1-59016-925-5 • 127 + ii pages • tables • GB£8.95 • US$13.95
THE WRITER'S BLUEBOOK, by Leigh H. Irvine. ISBN 1-59016-938-7 • 82 pages • GB£7.95 • US$11.95

QUOTATIONS
THE BOOK OF FAMILIAR QUOTATIONS, compiled from Various Authors. ISBN 1-59016-070-3 • 503 + viii pages • GB£23.95 • US$32.95
THE WORLD'S BEST EPIGRAMS, by J. Gilchrist Lawson. ISBN 1-59016-931-X • 231 pages • GB£12.95 • US$17.95

BOOKS ON BOOKS
A BOOK FOR ALL READERS, by Ainsworth Rand Spofford. ISBN 1-59016-068-1 • 507 + vi pages • GB£24.95 • US$32.95
HOW TO FORM A LIBRARY, by H. B. Wheatley. ISBN 1-59016-343-5 • 248 + viii pages • GB£13.95 • US$18.95
THE STORY OF LIBRARIES AND BOOK COLLECTING, by Ernest A. Savage. ISBN 1-59016-794-5 • 230 + vi pages • GB£13.95 • US$18.95
WHAT I KNOW ABOUT BOOKS, by George C. Lorimer. ISBN 1-59016-908-5 • 110 pages • GB£8.95 • US$11.95
WHO WROTE IT? by William A. Wheller. ISBN 1-59016-915-8 • 174 + iv pages • illustrated • GB£10.95 • US$15.95

NOVELTY BOOKS
THE AMERICAN POETS BIRTHDAY BOOK, by Various Poets. ISBN 1-59016-022-3 • 183 pages • illustrated • GB£11.95 • US$15.95
BEASLEY'S CHRISTMAS PARTY, by Booth Tarkington. ISBN 1-59016-058-4 • 100 + iv pages • illustrated • GB£7.95 • US$11.95

CHECK YOUR FAVORITE BOOKSELLER FOR AVAILABILITY OR CALL 1 (800) 952-LOST FOR OUR FREE CATALOG

A CAMPFIRE GIRL'S FIRST COUNCIL FIRE, by Jane L. Stewart. ISBN 1-59016-103-3 • 246 pages • illustrated • GB£13.95 • US$18.95
THE CHRISTMAS STORY FROM DAVID HARUM, by Edward Noyes Westcott. ISBN 1-59016-118-1 • 107 + x pages • GB£8.95 • US$12.95
CUPID'S CYCLOPEDIA, compiled by Oliver Herford and John Cecil Clay. ISBN 1-59016-148-3 • 100 pages • illustrated • GB£7.95 • US$11.95

Furniture and Decorating
DECORATIVE STYLES AND PERIODS IN THE HOME: Furnishings of the Nineteenth Century, by Helen Churchill Candee. ISBN 1-59016-159-9 • 297 + xx + 100 illustrated pages • illustrated • GB£20.95 • US$27.95
ENGLISH FURNITURE OF THE CABRIOLE PERIOD, by H. Avray Tipping. ISBN 1-59016-213-7 • 79 + vi + 32 illustrated pages • GB£8.95 • US$12.95
FURNITURE OF THE NINETEENTH CENTURY, compiled by the Century Furniture Company. ISBN 1-59016-270-6 • 156 pages • illustrated • GB£11.95 • US$14.95
INSIDE OF ONE HUNDRED HOMES, by William Martin Johnson. ISBN 1-59016-360-5 • 140 pages • illustrated • GB£9.95 • US$13.95
INSIDE THE HOUSE OF GOOD TASTE, edited by Richardson Wright. ISBN 1-59016-361-3 • 155 + x pages • illustrated • GB£9.95 • US$10.95
OLD GLASS: European and American, by N. Hudson Moore. ISBN 1-59016-594-2 • 389 + xx pages • illustrated • GB£20.95 • US$27.95

Cooking and Household
AUNT MARTHA'S CORNER CUPBOARD: Stories about Tea, Coffee, Sugar and Rice, by Mary and Elizabeth Kirby. ISBN 1-59016-046-0 • 144 pages • 32 illustrations • GB£9.95 • US$14.95
CHAFING DISH POSSIBILITIES, by Fannie Merritt Farmer. ISBN 1-59016-111-4 • 161 pages • GB£9.95 • US$14.95
ONE HUNDRED TESTED RECEIPTS, compiled by Jennie C. Benedict. ISBN 1-59016-606-X • 88 + ii pages • GB£7.95 • US$11.95
THE RUMFORD COMPLETE COOK BOOK, by Lily Haxworth Wallace. ISBN 1-59016-741-4 • 236 + xvii pages • GB£13.95 • US$19.95
THE SAGINAW COOK BOOK, compiled by the Women's Society of the First Congregational Church. ISBN 1-59016-744-9 • 247 + ii pages • GB£13.95 • US$18.95
THE SKANEATELES COOK BOOK, issued by the Women's Village Improvement Association. ISBN 1-59016-765-1 • 113 pages • GB£8.95 • US$12.95
THE TIDIOUTE COOK BOOK, compiled and arranged by Ladies from Tidioute, Pennsylvania. ISBN 1-59016-845-3 • 238 + ii pages • heavily illustrated • GB£13.95 • US$18.95

Children's Books
CHILDREN OF HISTORY, by Mary S. Hancock. ISBN 1-59016-116-5 • 192 + ii pages • illustrated • GB£11.95 • US$16.95
CHILDREN'S SAYINGS: Early Life at Home, by Caroline Hadley. ISBN 1-59016-117-3 • 160 pages • illustrated • GB£9.95 • US$14.95
MAGIC STORIES, by Frank N. Freeman, Grace E. Storm, Eleanor M. Johnson and W. C. French. ISBN 1-59016-505-5 • 288 + ii pages • illustrated • GB£15.95 • US$21.95
MOTHER HUBBARD'S MELODIES, with illustrations by Gordon Browne, R. Marriott Watson, L.L. Weedon and Others. ISBN 1-59016-527-6 • 146 + xiv pages • heavily illustrated • GB£9.95 • US$14.95
TOP OF THE WORLD STORIES FOR BOYS AND GIRLS, by Emilie Poulsson and Laura E. Poulsson. ISBN 1-59016-850-X • 206 + ii + 15 illustrated pages • illustrated • GB£12.95 • US$17.95

Travel and Adventure
ADVENTURES BY LAND AND SEA, by Various Authors. ISBN 1-59016-010-X • 127 + x + 2 illustrated pages • illustrated • GB£9.95 • US$13.95
HOW THE WORLD TRAVELS, by A. A. Methley. ISBN 1-59016-342-7 • 127 + x + 2 illustrated pages • illustrated • GB£9.95 • US$13.95
LITTLE JOURNEYS TO THE HOMES OF GREAT REFORMERS, by Elbert Hubbard. ISBN 1-59016-472-5 • 170 + vi + 10 illustrated pages • illustrated • GB£11.95 • US$15.95
SCENES FROM EVERY LAND, by Gilbert H. Grosvenor. ISBN 1-59016-753-8 • 216 pages • heavily illustrated • GB£12.95 • US$17.95
SINBAD AND HIS FRIENDS, by Simeon Strunsky. ISBN 1-59016-764-3 • 261 + viii pages • GB£14.95 • US$20.95
WORLD CRUISE OF THE NORTHERN AND SOUTHERN HEMISPHERES, by Thomas Cook & Son. ISBN 1-59016-928-X • 103 pages • illustrated • GB£7.95 • US$11.95

Short Stories
AMONG THE CAMPS: Young People's Stories of the Civil War, by Thomas Nelson Page. ISBN 1-59016-023-1 • 163 pages • illustrated • GB£10.95 • US$15.95
A LITTLE BOOK OF PROFITABLE TALES, by Eugene Field. ISBN 1-59016-470-9 • 243 pages • illustrated • GB£13.95 • US$19.95

Sports and Athletics
SWIMMING SCIENTIFICALLY TAUGHT: A Practical Manual for Young and Old, by Frank Eugen Dalton. ISBN 1-59016-943-3 • 247 pages • illustrated • GB£13.95 • US$18.95
GREEK ATHLETICS, by F. A. Wright. ISBN 1-59016-295-1 • 123 + 8 illustrated pages • illustrated • GB£9.95 • US$13.95
PHYSICAL TRAINING MANUAL, by Sargent Arthur W. Wallander. ISBN 1-59016-646-9 • 159 pages • illustrated • GB£9.95 • US$14.95

TUMBLING, PYRAMID BUILDING AND STUNTS FOR MEN AND WOMEN, by Bonnie and Donnie Cotteral. ISBN 1-59016-868-2 • 143 + vi + 11 illustrated pages • illustrated • GB£9.95 • US$14.95

FBI Files Revealed
EINSTEIN, ALBERT: FBI Files Revealed - Coming Soon, Call 1 (800) 952-LOST for our current catalog.
TESLA, NIKOLA: FBI Files Revealed. ISBN 1-59016-833-X • 276 pages • GB£14.95 • US$19.95

Audio and Video Tapes (VHS NTSC)
REMOTE VIEWING TRAINING SESSIONS: Discovering Your Intuition, with Prudence Calabrese and TransDimensional Systems. RVT-00a • 13 Hours on 7 Audio Tapes • $60.00 postpaid / RVT-00 • 13 Hours on 7 VHS Video Tapes • $110.00 postpaid / Introductory tape only • RVT-01 • 2 hour Video • $19.95 • Other tapes available individually. Visit www.largeruniverse.com for more information.
ANCIENT MYSTERIES OF NORTH AMERICA with Tedd St. Rain. AMNA-01a • 110 min Audio • $12.00 / AMNA-01 • 110 min Video • $19.95
THE COSMIC ORIGINS OF MAN with Father Charles Moore. BACN-01a • 105 min Audio • $12.00 / BACN-01 • 105 min Video • $19.95
21ST CENTURY VISIONS OF NOSTRADAMUS with Dolores Cannon. BACN-02a • 105 min Audio • $12.00 / BACN-02 • 105 min Video • $19.95
HUMAN RELATIONSHIPS WITH ETS with Barbara Lamb. BACN-03a • 60 min Audio • $12.00 / BACN-03 • 60 min Video • $19.95
ET RELATIONSHIPS PANEL with Barbara Lamb, Pamela Stonebrooke, Eve Lorgen and Dolores Cannon. BACN-04a • 90 min Audio • $12.00 / BACN-04 • 90 min Video • $19.95
SCIENCE, POLITICS AND THE NEW MILLENNIUM with Dr. Nick Begich. BACN-05a • 2 hour Audio • $12.00 / BACN-05 • 2 hour Video • $19.95
MUSIC OF THE SPHERES with Randy Masters. BACN-06a • 90 min Audio • $12.00 / BACN-06 • 90 min Video • $19.95
TECHNOLOGY OF THE GODS with David Hatcher Childress. BACN-07a • 2 hour Audio • $12.00 / BACN-07 • 2 hour Video • $19.95
BIGFOOT / UFO CONNECTION with Jack "Kewaunee" Lapseritis. BACN-08a • 105 min Audio • $12.00 / BACN-08 • 105 min Video • $19.95
OUT-OF-BODY ADVENTURES with Albert Taylor. BACN-09a • 90 min Audio • $12.00 / BACN-09 • 90 min Video • $19.95
EGYPTIAN MYSTERIES with Karena Bryan. BACN-10a • 90 min Audio • $12.00 / BACN-10 • 90 min Video • $19.95
UFOS AND RELIGION PANEL with Stella Harder-Kucera, Moderator and Ted Peters, Jose Tirado and Matthew Fox, Panelists. BACN-11a • 90 min Audio • $12.00 / BACN-11 • 90 min Video • $19.95
PARADIGM POLITICS with Daniel Sheehan. BACN-12a • 2 hour Audio • $12.00 / BACN-12 • 2 hour Video • $19.95
INTUITIVE ANIMAL COMMUNICATION with Raphaela Pope. BACN-13a • 90 min Audio • $12.00 / BACN-13 • 90 min Video • $19.95
FORBIDDEN ARCHEOLOGY with Michael Cremo. BACN-14a • 2 hour Audio • $12.00 / BACN-14 • 2 hour Video • $19.95
TALKING TO THE OTHER SIDE, with Mark Macy. BACN-15a • 105 min Audio • $12.00 / BACN-15 • 90 min Video • $19.95
NEW PARADIGMS FOR LOVE, with Deborah Taj Anapol. BACN-16a • 90 min Audio • $12.00 / BACN-16 • 60 min Video • $19.95
NEWS MEDIA DECEPTIONS, with Terry Hansen. BACN-17a • 90 min Audio • $12.00 / BACN-17 • 90 min Video • $19.95
MEDIA PANEL ON UFO'S – Lucia August, Moderator; Panelists Ralph Steiner, Leslie Kean, and Terry Hansen. BACN-18a • 75 min Audio • $12.00 / BACN-18 • 75 min Video • $19.95
THE TRUTH ABOUT 9-11, with Carol Brouillet. BACN-19a • 105 min Audio • $12.00 / BACN-19 • 105 min Video • $19.95
ANCIENT EGYPTIAN HI-TECH, with Christopher Dunn. BACN-20a • 105 min Audio • $12.00 / BACN-20 • 105 min Video • $19.95
NEW SCIENCE BREAKTHROUGHS, with Joe Firmage. BACN-21a • 90 min Audio • $12.00 / BACN-21 • 90 min Video • $19.95
THE INTERCEPTION: Roswell Crash Site Metal Recovery with Dennis Balthaser. Aztec-01a • 2 hour Audio • $12.00 / Aztec-01 • 2 hour Video • $19.95
MYSTERIOUS UFO INCIDENT IN PENNSYLVANIA AND BIG FOOT, with Stan Gordon. Aztec-02a • 2 hour Audio • $12.00 / Aztec-02 • 2 hour Video • $19.95
UFOS: THE TECHNOLOGY ISSUE, with John Schuessler. Aztec-03a • 2 hour Audio • $12.00 / Aztec-03 • 2 hour Video • $19.95
THE DAY AFTER ROSWELL: Revelations from Beyond the Grave, with Karl Pflock. Aztec-04a • 2 hour Audio • $12.00 / Aztec-04 • 2 hour Video • $19.95
CRITIQUE OF THE ROSWELL CRITICS, with Stanton Friedman. Aztec-05a • 2 hour Audio • $12.00 / Aztec-05 • 2 hour Video • $19.95
AZTEC 1949-1950: New Information on the Aztec UFO Crash, with Linda Moulton Howe. Aztec-06a • 2 hour Audio • $12.00 / Aztec-06 • 2 hour Video • $19.95
HOW THE WAR ON TERROR INTERRUPTED ET CONTACT, with Jim Marrs. Aztec-07a • 2 hour Audio • $12.00 / Aztec-07 • 2 hour Video • $19.95

ALL AUDIO AND VIDEO TAPES AVAILABLE NOW • CALL 1 (800) 952-LOST FOR OUR FREE CATALOG

AUDIO AND VIDEO TAPES (CONTINUED)

UFOS AND REALITY TRANSFORMATION, with Chris Styles. MUFON-01a • 76 min Audio • $12.00 / MUFON-01 • 76 min Video • $19.95

THE DAY AFTER PHIL CORSO, with William J. Birnes. MUFON-02a • 82 min Audio • $12.00 / MUFON-02 • 82 min Video • $19.95

SCIENTIFIC CONNECTIONS IN PHOTO/VIDEO UFOLOGY, with Jeff Sainio. MUFON-03a • 68 min Audio • $12.00 / MUFON-03 • 68 min Video • $19.95

THE LIMITS OF SCIENCE IN UFO RESEARCH, with Richard Dolan. MUFON-04a • 70 min Audio • $12.00 / MUFON-04 • 70 min Video • $19.95

IN SEARCH OF EBE'S, with William Hamilton. MUFON-05a • 75 min Audio • $12.00 / MUFON-05 • 75 min Video • $19.95

FIVE THEMES ON UFO ABDUCTION, with Dan Wright. MUFON-06a • 73 min Audio • $12.00 / MUFON-06 • 73 min Video • $19.95

BUILDING A PROFESSIONAL COMMUNITY, with David Jacobs. MUFON-07a • 73 min Audio • $12.00 / MUFON-07 • 73 min Video • $19.95

CONFLICTING INTEREST IN THE CONTROL OF EXTRATERRESTRIAL INTELLIGENCE, with Timothy Good. MUFON-08a • 77 min Audio • $12.00 / MUFON-08 • 77 min Video • $19.95

AIR TRAFFIC CONTROL ZONES, PILOTS, AIRCRAFT AND UFOS, with Don Ledger. MUFON-09a • 78 min Audio • $12.00 / MUFON-09 • 78 min Video • $19.95

THE ABDUCTION PHENOMENON - Where We Are Now? with Budd Hopkins. MUFON-10a • 72 min Audio • $12.00 / MUFON-10 • 72 min Video • $19.95

AN AMERICAN IN SUFFOLK: The Rendlesham Forest UFO Incident, with Peter Robbins. MUFON-11a • 90 min Audio • $12.00 / MUFON-11 • 90 min Video • $19.95

MIRACLES: UFO CONTACT, with Betty Hill. MUFON-12a • 68 Min Audio • $12.00 / MUFON-12 • 68 Min Video • $19.95

ARE THERE UFOS ON MARS? with Richard Thieme. MUFON-13a • 49 min Audio • $12.00 / MUFON-13 • 49 min Video • $19.95

TURKISH UFO INVESTIGATION, with Esen Sekerkarar. MUFON-14a • 79 min Audio • $12.00 / MUFON-14 • 79 min Video • $19.95

MUFON FIELD INVESTIGATOR TRAINING, with Dan Wright. MUFON-15a • 115 min Audio • $12.00 / MUFON-15 • 115 min Video • $19.95

EGYPT AND THE SCIENCE OF IMMORTALITY: Parts 1 and 2, with John Anthony West. SIGNS-01a & 02a • 2 92 min Audios • $19.95 / SIGNS-01 and 02 • 2 92 min Videos • $39.95

THE GREAT SPHINX AND THE QUEST TO REWRITE HISTORY, with John Anthony West. SIGNS-03a • 2 70 min Audios • $19.95 / SIGNS-03 •139 min Video • $24.95

THE CROP CIRCLES PRIMARY MESSAGE, with Drunvalo Melchizedek. SIGNS-04a • 2 hour Audio • $12.00 / SIGNS-04 • 2 hour Video • $19.95

SACRED GEOMETRY WORKSHOP, with Drunvalo Melchizedek. SIGNS-05a • 2 hour Audio • $12.00 / SIGNS-05 • 2 hour Video • $19.95

THE IMPORTANCE OF WHERE AND HOW THE CROP CIRCLE PHENOMENON BEGAN, with Colin Andrews. SIGNS-06a • 92 min Audio • $12.00 / SIGNS-06 • 92 min Video • $19.95

THERMAL PLASMAS OF UNKNOWN ORIGIN: Hessdalen 2002, with Linda Moulton Howe. SIGNS-07a • 60 min Audio • $12.00 / SIGNS-07 • 60 min Video • $19.95

THE CIRCLES, THE SCIENCE AND AN EYEWITNESS ACCOUNT, with Nancy Talbott. SIGNS-08a • 92 min Audio • $12.00 / SIGNS-08 • 92 min Video • $19.95

SCIENTIFIC ANALYSIS OF CROP CIRCLES: A Practical Guide, with Nancy Talbott. SIGNS-09a • 108 min Audio • $12.00 / SIGNS-09 • 108 min Video • $19.95

FIELD OF DREAMS: Crop Circles in Canada, with Paul Anderson. SIGNS-10a • 68 min Audio • $12.00 / SIGNS-10 • 68 min Video • $19.95

GROWING CROP CIRCLE SEEDS FOR FOOD, with Steve Purkable. SIGNS-11a • 26 min Audio • $12.00 / SIGNS-11 • 26 min Video • $19.95

ENGLAND'S CROP CIRCLES OF 2002, with Francine Blake. SIGNS-12a • 115 min Audio • $12.00 / SIGNS-12 • 115 min Video • $19.95

CROP CIRCLES IN GERMANY: Amazing Recent Developments, with Andreas Mueller. SIGNS-13a • 85 min Audio • $12.00 / SIGNS-13 • 85 min Video • $19.95

CROP CIRCLES REVEALED: A Spiritual Perspective, with Barbara Lamb. SIGNS-14a • 89 min Audio • $12.00 / SIGNS-14 • 89 min Video • $19.95

CROP CIRLCES 2001-2002: A Year of Surprises, with Dr. Chet Snow. SIGNS-15a • 53 min Audio • $12.00 / SIGNS-15 • 53 min Video • $19.95

For Audio/Video Tapes Only: To order individual tapes add $5.00 shipping and handling for the first item and $1.00 for each additional item. Send your check or money order to (CA residents add 8.25% sales tax): LOST ARTS MEDIA, POST OFFICE BOX 15026, LONG BEACH, CA 90815. Visit WWW.LOSTARTSMEDIA.COM or to order by credit card call 1 (800) 952-LOST or 1 (562) 596-ARTS.

NEWS AND INFORMATION

NEXUS MAGAZINE is an international bi-monthly alternative news magazine, covering the fields of Suppressed Science, Earth's Ancient Past, Alternative Health, UFOs, the Unexplained and much more. For subscription information visit www.nexusmagazine.com or call 1 (888) 909-7474.

ATLANTIS RISING MAGAZINE: One of the best magazines on Atlantis, ancient mysteries, lost continents, cryptozoology, and a whole host of other related subjects. For subscription information visit www.atlantisrising.com or call 1 (800) 228-8381.

STEAMSHOVEL PRESS is a zine that is dedicated to exposing the secrets behind the conspiracies that have shaped history. For subscription information visit www.steamshovelpress.com

PARANOIA – A CONSPIRACY READER focuses on the more paranoid aspects of society. For subscription information visit www.paranoiamagazine.com

THE EXCLUDED MIDDLE MAGAZINE publishes three times a year on all things paranormal. For information email exclmid@primenet.com. or write P.O. Box 481077, Los Angeles, CA 90048.

FLATLAND MAGAZINE publishes a once-per-year zine that reviews the suppressed and secret evidence around us. Contact www.flatlandbooks.com or call 1 (707) 964-8326.

THE BOOK TREE provides controversial and educational products to help awaken the public to new ideas and information that would otherwise not be available. For a free catalog visit www.thebooktree.com or call 1 (800) 700-TREE.

The **INTERNATIONAL UFO CONGRESS** holds a twice-yearly, week long conference and film festival on UFOs and a variety of other subjects. People attend from around the world and it is considered the best conference of its kind. For additional information visit www.ufocongress.com or call 1 (303) 543-9443.

The **BAY AREA UFO EXPO** and Conference holds an annual conference in the fall each year. For information and a free program guide visit www.thebayareaufoexpo.com or call 1 (209) 836-4281.

CONSPIRACY CON holds it's conference on Memorial Day weekend each year. For information and a free program guide visit www.conspiracycon.com or call 1 (209) 832-0999.

Cosmic Connections conducts the **EARTH MYSTERIES CONFERENCE** in the Fall and the **CRYSTAL HEALING CONFERENCE** in the Spring of each year. For more information visit www.chetsnow.com or call 1 (928) 204-1962.

The **BAY AREA CONSCIOUSNESS NETWORK** holds its annual conference in November each year. For information visit www.bacn.org

The **NORTHWEST UFO PARANORMAL CONFERENCE** is held in the late spring each year. For more information visit www.seattlechatclub.org

Adventures Unlimited holds its **WORLD EXPLORERS CLUB ANCIENT MYSTERIES CONFERENCE** several times a year. For more information or a program guide and a free book catalog visit www.wexclub.com or call 1 (815) 253-6390.

The **ANNUAL MUFON SYMPOSIUM** is held every year in various locations. For a program guide and information on local chapters of MUFON visit www.mufon.com or call 1 (303) 932-7709.

The **BUSINESS SPIRIT JOURNAL** produces several spiritual and consciousness-related conferences each year. For information visit www.bizspirit.com or call 1 (505) 474-7604.

The **AZTEC UFO SYMPOSIUM** is held once a year in the early spring in Aztec, NM, location of a famed UFO crash. For information visit www.aztecufo.com or call 1 (505) 334-9890.

The **ALTERNATE REALITIES CONFERENCE** (ARC) hold its annual conference in the Summer each year. For more information visit www.dreaman.org or call 1 (423) 735-0848.

The **THINK ABOUT IT CONFERENCE** is held at various locations throughout the year. For more information visit www.think-aboutit.com or www.heartoftheheart.com or call 1 (319) 866-9560.

The **ROSWELL UFO ODYSSEY** commemorates a UFO crash in New Mexico for the first week in July each year. For information visit www.uforoswell.com

Problems-Solutions-Innovations sponsors the **CONTROLLED REMOTE VIEWING CONFERENCE** in the early summer each year. For more information visit www.crviewer.com

The International Remote Viewing Association holds its annual **REMOTE VIEWING CONFERENCE** in June each year. For more information visit www.rvconference.org

FREE REMOTE VIEWING TRAINING: Ongoing coursework live on the internet with Prudence Calabrese. For information visit www.aurorabomb.com or www.largeruniverse.com

LOST ARTS MEDIA produces a variety of **ANCIENT MYSTERIES CONFERENCES** and **TRAVEL PROGRAMS** throughout the year. Come travel with like-minded and kindred friends. For information visit www.lostartsmedia.com or call 1 (800) 952-LOST.

HAVE YOUR EVENT VIDEOTAPED AND/OR LISTED HERE
Call 1 (800) 952-LOST or Visit WWW.LOSTARTSMEDIA.COM

Printed in the United Kingdom
by Lightning Source UK Ltd.
106232UKS00001BA/24